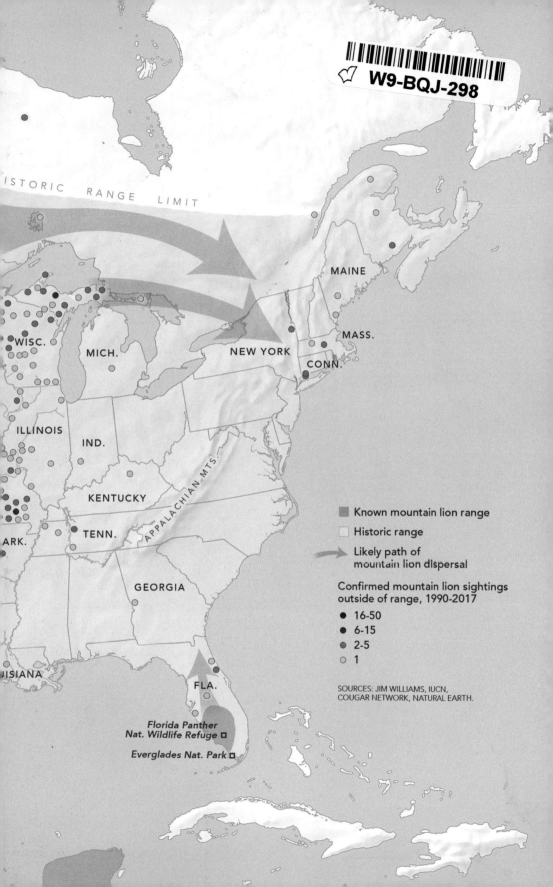

W9-BQJ-298

HISTORIC RANGE LIMIT

MAINE

WISC.

MICH.

MASS.

NEW YORK

CONN.

ILLINOIS

IND.

KENTUCKY

APPALACHIAN MTS.

ARK.

TENN.

GEORGIA

LOUISIANA

FLA.

Florida Panther
Nat. Wildlife Refuge □

Everglades Nat. Park □

■ Known mountain lion range

□ Historic range

➜ Likely path of
mountain lion dispersal

Confirmed mountain lion sightings
outside of range, 1990-2017
● 16-50
● 6-15
● 2-5
○ 1

SOURCES: JIM WILLIAMS, IUCN,
COUGAR NETWORK, NATURAL EARTH.

PATH of the PUMA

The Remarkable Resilience of the Mountain Lion

Jim Williams
with Joe Glickman
Foreword by Douglas Chadwick

patagonia®

Path of the Puma - The Remarkable Resilience of the Mountain Lion

Patagonia publishes a select list of titles on wilderness, wildlife, and outdoor sports that inspire and restore a connection to the natural world.

copyright 2018 Patagonia Works
Text © Jim Williams, Joe Glickman, Will Carless
Foreword © Douglas H. Chadwick

All photograph copyrights are held by the photographer as indicated in captions.
Cartography by Marty Schnure and Ross Donihue, Maps for Good.

First edition
Printed in Canada on 100 percent post-consumer recycled paper

Editors – Michael Jamison & John Dutton
Book Designers – Monkey C Media & Christina Speed
Photo Editors – Jennifer Ridgeway & Jane Seivert
Photo Archivist – Sus Corez
Creative Directors – Bill Boland & Christina Speed
Creative Advisor – Jennifer Ridgeway
Project Manager – Jennifer Patrick
Graphic Production – Rafael Dunn & Monique Martinez
Director of Books – Karla Olson

Cover photo: A puma in Torres del Paine National Park, Chile. Pablo Cersosimo

End sheets: Historic and current range of North American pumas, showing expansion into islands of undeveloped land.

Hardcover ISBN 978-1-938340-72-7
E-Book ISBN 978-1-938340-73-4
Library of Congress Control Number 2018945772

CONTENTS

Puma concolor, otherwise known as the mountain lion or puma, is one of Earth's most elusive creatures. Argentina. DARÍO PODESTÁ

FOREWORD

During the 1980s, wolves trotted south from Canada into neighboring Glacier National Park in Montana and became the first to survive in the US West for half a century. The little colony grew, split, and grew some more. By the early 2000s, offshoots roamed much of the northwestern corner of the state. Many folks were thrilled to have these new-old residents back, adding untamed music to the great outdoors. A lot of other Montanans wanted the packs eradicated. Some days, it seemed that about all anybody around here did any more was argue over wolves.

On one of those days, a biologist working for Montana's Department of Fish, Wildlife & Parks looked out his office window to find the street lined with outraged, placard-waving big-game hunters convinced that wolves were going to eat up all the state's elk and deer. That biologist was the regional game manager, Jim Williams. You wouldn't have wanted his job just then.

We met to talk not long afterward. It was just a casual chat, but it changed my view of the balance of wild lives in the landscapes around us when he told me, "Hardly anyone realizes that there are two or even three times as many cougars as wolves out in those woods and mountainsides. Now, the average cougar is bigger than the average wolf and consumes more wild meat than a wolf does. Cougars occasionally injure or kill humans. Wolves almost never do. Yet here we are dealing with outbreaks of near-hysteria over wolves while we don't hear much at all from the general public about cougars. Why? Mainly because the big cats are so good at not being seen."

Also known as the mountain lion or puma, the cougar is a stalk-and-ambush predator—a spring-loaded embodiment of stealth. Unlike the wolf, it seldom travels in a group, doesn't conduct nightly choruses, prefers to keep to thick vegetation or broken terrain, readily climbs to find seclusion high among the branches of trees, and often drags its kill away from a conspicuous site to dine in a hidden nook. As if those traits weren't secretive enough, this hunter is mostly active at night and in the twilight hours. Not surprisingly, another common name for the cougar is ghost cat.

I first ran into Jim Williams many years ago a dozen miles east of the Continental Divide. He was a graduate student tracking cougars across the windy slopes of the Rocky Mountain Front with the help of radio collars. Although his career as a wildlife biologist led him to work with a variety of different animals, he rarely passed up any opportunity to go off chasing ghosts. Every time we got together, I would start off wondering whether I was going to hear more cougar news, new findings about the ecology of other species, insights about the social and political forces that influence game management, or a tale from his latest backcountry trip to climb one of the area's high summits.

Invariably, given his boundless enthusiasm plus a fondness for coffee, every one of those subjects—and more—got covered before he left. The pages of this book deliver much the same Jim Williams high-octane combo of science, adventure, and conservation. But here the mix is all related to his decades-long pursuit of a special interest in cougars, with each chapter uncovering more aspects of the lives that the big cats work so hard to conceal.

Of all the large mammals in the Western Hemisphere, this feline, *Puma concolor*, is the most widespread. Its distribution extends from Canada's southern Yukon Territory all the way to Argentina and Chile. And in the second half of the book, Jim takes us to that far southern range as he joins researchers in ecosystems where the cougars' neighbors include ocelots, maned wolves, guanacos, vicuñas, and condors.

In North America, we think of cougars as being tied to the mountains and canyons out West. For the most part, they are. However, two centuries ago, their range sprawled from coast to coast. Cougars were exterminated from most of it by government-supported campaigns that relied heavily on poisoned baits. Harder to find than wolves and grizzlies, the last cats left in remote and rugged terrain escaped the continuing persecution aimed at those other large predators. Then, as the decades passed and attitudes toward meat-eating wildlife changed, cougar numbers started to rally across the western states. *Puma concolor* being the creature you don't know is there treading whisper-soft in the shadows, the resurgence of this major predator through the late twentieth century never got much attention, but it stands as one of the most remarkable wildlife comebacks in US history.

The party may just be getting started. Because adult cougars are fiercely territorial, young animals—especially males—approaching sexual maturity are forced out of fully occupied ranges. This pressure disperses cats far and wide in search of new homes with suitable cover, abundant prey, and, with luck, a mate. Some find their needs met in rural and suburban habitats where adaptable species such as white-tailed deer, raccoons, and wild turkeys provide ready meals. In recent years, cougars have appeared in various Midwest states and as far east as Missouri and even Connecticut.

These cats are like emissaries from the raw landscapes out West, probing the rest of the nation, showing us where patches of wildness remain, and bringing a fuller dimension of wildness to them. It's as if they're testing to find out just what folks have in mind when they say they want to preserve natural settings. How natural? How toothy?

Don't cougars pose a potential risk to us? Yes. But so do predator-less deer. Biologists have pointed out how restoring cougars to portions of the eastern United States could reduce overpopulated herds responsible for the spread of tick-borne diseases and for collisions with vehicles that leave many drivers injured, some permanently disabled, and more than a few dead. Here is the one formidably big, strong predator skilled enough at avoiding notice to live near surprisingly high numbers of people—if allowed to stay. We'll find out if that will happen. And judging from the way cougars keep pushing eastward from the Rockies and the Black Hills of South Dakota, I'd bet on sooner rather than later.

To be able to introduce a book about this species is a privilege, especially a book by my fellow Montanan Jim Williams. As of this writing, he's busy as ever managing wildlife here—and periodically disappearing into some nearby chain of peaks, the Pampas of Argentina's Patagonia region, or a new national park in Chile to follow big, stealthy cats.

– Douglas H. Chadwick, April 30, 2017

Underneath the steady drone of traffic an adult mountain lion navigates a wildlife tunnel below Highway 93 on the Flathead Indian Reservation. Montana. CONFEDERATED SALISH AND KOOTENAI TRIBES, MONTANA DEPARTMENT OF TRANSPORTATION, MSU–WESTERN TRANSPORTATION INSTITUTE

PROLOGUE
The Crossing

The big cat stole silent down rocky mountain slopes broken by bunch-grass, slipping unseen into the creek bottom. Behind him, the grunts of sparring bull bison faded, giving way to the morning songs of red-winged blackbirds.

The color of honey, the color of caramel, the color of dry mountain meadows, barely seen in the dim light, the mountain lion crept into the first gray of day through grasses still wet with dew, his amber eyes set on the dark of distant forests, sure to hold deer.

He was hungry. And he needed to move.

There was food behind him, deer and elk and even a few bighorn sheep and antelope. But he was young still, and knew to avoid the older and bigger male lions that patrolled those herds. And so he moved, off the Montana mountaintop, under the fence that rings the National Bison Range, down from the rocky den where he'd been born eighteen months before.

His mother had kept him moving all this time, teaching him to stalk, teaching him to kill, teaching him to avoid the old territorial males along the way. He was hardwired to roam, to eat, to find a wild empty country of his own where he could stake his territory. Deer lived in the wetland thickets and river bottoms below the mountaintop, so he followed ancient feline highways along the streambeds, moving with the deer at dawn and dusk.

The cat headed east, upriver, toward mountains backlit by sunrise, doing what mountain lions have done here for 10,000 years. But times have changed. Between his old home on the National Bison Range and the deer-filled forests of the Mission Mountains Tribal Wilderness, a minefield of danger has grown up—houses and dogs, guns and poisons. And now that strange new noise, a hiss with a hint of roar, rising and falling periodically, somewhere between here and the snow-capped peaks.

The National Bison Range is located just north of Missoula, Montana, a grassy 19,000 acres that rise in steep relief above a broad valley carved by

Pleistocene ice. It is fenced to keep the bison in, but a thriving black bear population has dug holes beneath the wire and most large carnivores move freely on and off the range. Wolves, black bears, grizzly bears, coyotes, and mountain lions all share the Bison Range, along with herds of prey.

The Bison Range also is sacred ground. The bunchgrass and forest-filled mountain complex lies within the boundaries of the Flathead Indian Reservation, home to the Salish, Kootenai, and Pend d'Oreilles people. In fact, it was a tribal member who, a century ago, herded the Range's original bison from the prairies east of Glacier National Park, over the Continental Divide, and down into the Mission Valley. The valley is framed by protected lands—to the west by the low-slung National Bison Range, and to the east by the soaring summits of the Mission Mountain Tribal Wilderness. Between lie the unprotected wetlands, river bottoms, and glacial pothole lakes so popular with deer and mountain lions and, more recently, humans.

As he worked farther out on the valley floor, the young lion slowed to a crawl. To his left, a large field stretched northward toward a barn and a few feeding deer. He was hungry, but the strange hissing and roaring sound still spooked him, so he kept moving. A lone male can go as long as two weeks between kills, if necessary, and this was not the time to take risks, here in unknown country. Mountain lions have remarkable eyes, capable of seeing clearly through the dark of dusk and dawn hunting hours, but his ears were sharp, too, and he could hear the redhead ducks, mallards, and Canada geese calling from pothole lakes as the early-spring sun rose. The territorial sign of other big cats—the scent of urine and spray, the scrapes, and scratch trees—kept him traveling quietly along the waters' edge. A big male might lay claim to 150 square miles, so this was no place to stop.

And anyway, that new noise he'd heard earlier—not exactly threatening, but curious enough to sharpen the senses—had now grown quite loud and more frequent, rising and falling steadily, a low drone of moving sound.

Somewhere on the other side of that noise a graduate student slipped on wet grass as she scrambled down a sloped highway bank. Whisper Camel-Means—a member of the Confederated Salish and Kootenai Tribes of the Flathead Indian Reservation—was here to study the effectiveness of wildlife passages tunneled beneath the rush of US Route 93. The road runs ruler-straight through the heart of the valley, a dividing line that cuts across rich habitat and separates the Bison Range from the Mission Mountain Wilderness. Her mind was on a camera trap she had set a week before, in a state-of-the-art wildlife underpass built beneath the busy north-south roadway.

For years, tribal elders and biologists had negotiated with state and federal highway officials to design a "wildlife friendly" reconstruction of Route 93.

They called it 'The Peoples' Way,' and they gave it a motto: "the road is a visitor." It would be made to serve the real residents—the elk, bears, and big cats as well as the people. Completed in 2010, it features forty-one fish and wildlife crossing structures in fifty-six miles of highway—overpasses, underpasses, culverts, and bridges, all linking streams and ancient wildlife migration paths across the valley floor, connecting habitats from mountain-top to river bottom.

Whisper's camera traps were set to capture and record wildlife crossings beneath the pulse of log trucks and minivans. This was the sound, the rising and falling hiss of tire on tarmac, the lion had been hearing. He was near the forested eastern mountains now, but these flashes of light and steel raced steadily across what appeared to be a paved ridgeline between him and the rising dark timber. He could not see the terrain on the other side, and that made him cautious. Padding closer, he sniffed a web of metal fence, then followed the fence line parallel with the highway toward a darkened tunnel. Low light and caves. He liked that. That's how he hunts. A thick layer of earth muffled the roar of traffic above, and he never heard the whirr of Whisper's remote camera.

The big cat slipped through, invisible except to the camera, and on the other side he could finally smell the sharp tang of Douglas fir and moist forest soil. He had passed unseen across one of Montana's busiest and most dangerous highways, a silent ghost hardwired to find the wild. Now he was on his own, beyond his mother's range, staking and marking his hunting grounds, slinking quickly toward a new high-country home among the deer herds of the Mission Mountains.

He was still close enough to hear the sound of the trucks behind him as Whisper slipped down the highway slope. She never worried about encountering mountain lions during the day—she'd always understood that the big cats preferred darkness. But Whisper knew to take care in bear country, so she made noise as she moved through tall vegetation and dense forest. Bears typically move on if they hear you approaching, but her mind was on that camera, not on predators.

At the tunnel, she edged along the wall to reach her camera. It was late morning now, and the sun was warming. Whisper toggled through the dig-ital images and immediately noticed a time-stamped frame that had been snapped just a moment before she arrived. A chill up the spine. A quick catch of the breath. Hair suddenly on end. A young mountain lion. *Skwtismyè* in her native language. In broad daylight. Just now. Adrenaline. And then … a smile. This was exactly how it was supposed to work.

The big cat had moved safely beneath the highway, through a cross-ing structure that she and the biologists and the engineers had designed and built. It worked beautifully. Other images, at other passages along *The Peoples' Way*, have captured bears and bobcats, deer and elk, skunks and owls, and even otters. Wild nature needs the freedom to roam—to disperse, connect, and migrate with the seasons—and the Confederated Salish and Kootenai Tribes have set the global standard for wildlife connectivity across roadways.

Most all of the big carnivores that traditionally defined our nation have been squeezed into the protected fringes, the national parks and wilderness areas that provide a last refuge. But not mountain lions. They live with us, from California to the Eastern Seaboard, even if we seldom see them. Or, perhaps, *because* we seldom see them. These big cats are evolved for stealth, to hide from their prey as well as from larger predators such as wolves and bears, and that secrecy has allowed them to live among us.

I have had the privilege to spend a career tracking and conserving mountain lions and their habitats from the National Bison Range to the Mission Mountain Wilderness, and from Montana's Crown of the Continent ecosystem to the Patagonian wilds of Argentina and Chile. Down there, we call them *pumas*, but they are the same cats, hungry for prey and for the freedom to roam. From Montana to Patagonia, the story of *Puma concolor* is a story of magical landscapes, remarkable habitats, and the fantastic people who work to protect them.

It is also an unlikely story, because it is a very lonely exception to the rule. Big, wild cats worldwide are in trouble, threatened, and endangered. Fewer than 20,000 lions persist in all of Africa. As few as 15,000 jaguars remain in the wild. And the global census of tigers has dipped below 4,000.

And yet, the mountain lions of North America and the pumas of South America are thriving, dispersing and expanding and rewilding entire continents. They are beating the odds, even at the height of the human-dominated "Anthropocene era," and their success provides a remarkable opportunity for wild nature to regain a toehold and to shape possibilities for the persistence of natural systems. They are hope for those of us who believe our future will depend, in large part, on finding the wild.

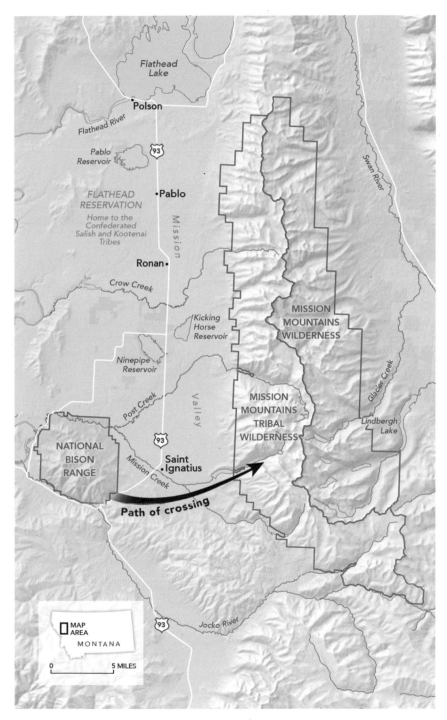

Flathead
Lake

•Polson

Flathead River

Pablo
Reservoir

93

FLATHEAD
RESERVATION
Home to the
Confederated
Salish and Kootenai
Tribes

•Pablo

Mission

Ronan•

Crow Creek

Kicking
Horse
Reservoir

MISSION
MOUNTAINS
WILDERNESS

Ninepipe
Reservoir

Post Creek

Valley

Swan River

MISSION
MOUNTAINS
TRIBAL
WILDERNESS

Glacier Creek

Lindbergh
Lake

NATIONAL
BISON
RANGE

93

Mission Creek

Saint
•Ignatius

Path of crossing

MAP
AREA
MONTANA

0   5 MILES

93

Jocko River

MISSION VALLEY Highway 93 through Montana's Mission Valley, like all roads, is a barrier to animals passing between islands of habitat. The highway is being constantly made more wildlife friendly and now includes more than thirty-five wildlife under crossings. SOURCES: USGS, MONTANA STATE LIBRARY, WILDERNESS.NET, JIM WILLIAMS

CHAPTER 1

THE CHASE

If animals could speak, the dog would be a blundering outspoken fellow; but the cat would have the rare grace of never saying a word too much.

– Mark Twain

S pooked by the clatter of the helicopter, the bighorn sheep was in full flight. I watched him run—150 pounds of compact muscle behind a set of thick, curled horns—bounding over fallen pines, dodging snow-covered boulders, and busting through scrub brush like a fullback seeking daylight. It was March of 1998, my pilot and I were an hour into our annual bighorn sheep census, conducted each spring after most of the snow disappears from the slopes and canyons in Montana's Beartooth Wildlife Management Area (WMA). The chopper was spinning, circling, and buzzing the canyon walls like an acrobatic mosquito looking for a way through a bug net.

From any vantage point it's stunning country. But seen through the clear-bubble cockpit of a Hughes 500 helicopter, it was downright sublime. To the south was the limestone labyrinth Lewis and Clark dubbed the Gates of the Mountains; to the west, the 6,792-foot profile of a reclining behemoth in the Sleeping Giant Wilderness Study Area—his feet toward the Continental Divide, his craggy face eyeing the Gates. In between, a twisting aquatic cleaver, was the mighty Missouri River.

In 1805, Meriwether Lewis, the first man with a quill pen to gaze upon this stretch of river, raved in his journal about "...the most remarkable clifts that we have yet seen. These clifts rise from the waters' edge on either side perpendicularly to the height of 1,200 feet...The tow[er]ing and projecting

Mountain lions have eyes that are adapted to seeing in low light conditions. This female rests on a ponderosa pine branch near Missoula, Montana. BOB WIESNER

rocks in many places seem ready to tumble on us." Shoddy spelling aside, the good captain's description remains spot-on two centuries later. After passing through the Gates of the Mountains, he also marveled at the "big horned animals that bound from cliff to cliff."

While I appreciated the landscape, glancing from the map to my clipboard to the ground and back again in a bucking whirlybird left my guts in turmoil. With both side panels open, the cockpit was freezing; the stench of aviation fuel overwhelming; and the din of the rotor blades nearly deafening, even with headphones on. While I get nauseous on virtually every aerial survey I do, I've learned a few tricks along the way. On my first flight as a raw twenty-five-year-old wildlife biology grad student, I chowed down a breakfast of pancakes, eggs, and bacon before takeoff and promptly deposited the meal into an air sickness bag. When our plane finally touched down—the pilot had to buzz a herd of antelope grazing on our remote landing strip—I staggered outside, stepped into a badger hole, and splattered the contents of the bag onto my Fish and Game Carhartt jacket. Luckily the jacket was old and a gift from the local biologist. But what a waste of bacon. Now I eat only a light breakfast before flying and always carry an empty coffee can by my feet. (Folgers, the coffee is OK, but the lid is fantastic—snug as a drum.)

On this flight, the bighorn ram that had been scampering up the mountainside at a right angle suddenly swerved toward a fissure in a rocky ledge, sand flying from under his hooves. *That's weird*, I thought, *why would it change direction so abruptly?* Then I saw the answer.

The hair on my arms stood up; my pulse quickened. "Whoa!" I shouted. Then a phrase I sometimes use when awe and adrenaline flood my monkey brain: "Holy crap!" Pilot Doug Getz confirmed, "Mountain lion, closing fast!"

The stealthy cat had been lying in wait, and materialized from the mountainside like a submarine surfacing, invisible one moment and in the frame all at once in the next. It was eight feet long from the tip of its nose to end of its outstretched brown tail, and hurtling toward the ram at full speed.

Mountain lions in the Beartooth prey primarily on deer and elk, although obviously they occasionally kill bighorn sheep as well. In the years that I'd been tracking, treeing, tranquilizing, and tagging lions with identifying ear tags and radio collars, I'd come upon the eviscerated bodies of many a ram, elk, and mule deer that fell victim to these perfect killing machines. But while I'd seen cats on the move from the air, never had I witnessed one in full attack mode. In fact, very few humans have.

Mountain lions hunt best at dawn and dusk—we biologists call this twilight lifestyle *crepuscular*, and cats are especially well-equipped for these low-light conditions. Their enormous eyes have lots of rods and not so many cones, meaning they can see in the dark but probably not in color. When teaching schoolchildren about wildlife, I often pass around a skull. Ask them to describe the bear skull and every one of them says the same thing: "teeth." Ask about the mountain lion skull, and they say "eyes"—those two massive holes tell the story of how these lions hunt. Solitary, stalk-ambush predators, mountain lions surprise their prey from behind, raking the flanks before crushing the throat for a swift kill. Known to some as "the ghost of the Rockies," their stealth and amazing athleticism, along with their shadowy life in the dusk and the dark, help explain why they are the only large cat on the planet not dwindling in numbers. In fact, they've been able to reclaim some of their former habitat in recent years, with lone dispersers migrating as far east as Connecticut—remarkable, though they have yet to establish viable resident populations in the East, outside of Florida.

The bighorn chase couldn't have lasted more than thirty seconds, but every detail remains etched in my mind. The sheep negotiated the steep, unstable terrain with power and precision, but the cat practically levitated, gobbling up ground at an astounding pace. Doug swung us closer to the chase and I started clicking away with my old Pentax 35mm camera. The chopper raised a cloud of dirt and we moved up again, but when the dust cleared enough for us to see, the ram was gone. Wheeling around, the sinewy cat gazed skyward. His expression was impassive, but I could almost imagine him saying: "Hey! What about some flippin' privacy!"

I was still buzzing when, just moments later, I spied a red pickup with hound boxes in the rear bed, bouncing east on the rutted road en route to Beartooth WMA headquarters. HQ is a former ranch about thirty miles north of Helena, Montana, on Cottonwood Creek, in a valley rich in grasslands that draw thousands of elk each winter. Terry Enk, a doctoral student at Montana State University, and hound handlers Scott and Gary Langford were in the pickup, riding up to the ranch to begin the season's fieldwork.

Terry was a year into a three-year study assessing, in part, the impact of mountain lion predation on bighorn sheep. Fewer of the fuzzy lambs were surviving each winter and we wanted to find out why. Putting radio-collar transmitters on as many cats as we could in the 35,000-acre wildlife management area was instrumental to the study. Capturing, collaring, and tracking wildlife is difficult, intrusive, and messy work, but it is absolutely crucial if we are to understand wild animals and to protect the habitats they need to survive. Where do they eat? Where do they travel? Where do they den? Where do they breed? Without knowing what the cats need, biologists can't help conserve the lions, and this is one way we collect that data.

I'd known that the capture team was arriving today, but the timing was uncanny. I pointed to the vehicles below. "Let's get down there now!" I shouted to my pilot. Doug set us in front of the mud-splattered pickup,

A young mountain lion unsuccessfully chases two mountain goats in the vertical world of the Gates of the Mountains Wilderness, Montana. JESSE VERNADO

the wash of the rotors raining snow from the surrounding ponderosa pines. Ducking under the blades as I exited the chopper, I pointed toward the mountain we'd just flown over and shouted that we'd just seen a big cat make a run on a ram. The team responded like an Indy 500 pit crew, cramming packs with climbing rope, the dart gun, a drug kit, food and water, space blankets, and other emergency supplies in case they had to spend the night. Out came the hounds from their boxes, baying already.

The team was ready to go. Terry looked at me and Doug. The pilot was a weathered, short, stocky man in his sixties, set to retire within the month and in no mood to follow on foot. "I'm too old to run up that hill," he smiled. "Let's fly!"

We stood by as Terry and the crew hustled over the ridge, the booming *arfarfarf* of the hounds echoing through the canyon like a canine car alarm. Soon enough, the staccato bark switched to a more plaintive *rrrrrrrr-ohohohohoh* and we knew they'd found the cat's scent.

Given how easily a mature mountain lion could dismantle a seventy-pound dog, it may seem strange that the big cat would flee. But lions have an innate fear of their natural rival *Canis lupus*. The wolf and the lion compete for prey, especially in winter. Occasionally, wolves steal lion kills—their packs have also been known to kill lions. By the same token, lone female wolves and their pups are vulnerable to ambush by a large male mountain lion. But more significantly, the wolves in a lion's territory can interfere with the cat's hunting opportunities. It's kind of like trying to keep an eye open for dangerous criminals while at the same time putting food in your basket at the grocery store.

Our tracking hounds are actually in the same family as the wolf, *Canidae*. Like a wolf, a well-trained hound has serious long-distance chops. Rick Bass wrote in *The Book of Yaak* that "hounds … run head-on straight and forever, in tune with the wild thumping drive of their hearts." Lions, on the other hand, are fast-twitch sprinters with large, retractable claws and a ninja-like ability to leap (as much as thirty feet from a standstill), and quickly seek refuge up high. Long evolutionary story made short, a team of barking Welsh Corgis and Chihuahuas could most likely cause a big cat to take flight for the nearest tree.

From the air, I could see Scott Langford's arms outstretched like a divining rod as his two frantic hounds hauled him up the mountain. A mason by trade, Scott is built like a brick chimney—but still he's able to negotiate the most rugged terrain Montana has to offer, snow or no snow, even on a slick trail with a forty-pound pack.

We landed atop the ridge just as the team was descending the steep slope toward Cottonwood Creek. By the time we'd jumped out of the chopper and scrambled down to meet them, five breathless humans and three howling hounds were clustered around a gnarled Douglas fir. Stretched out on a branch thirty feet in the air was the shadowy figure of a 150-pound male mountain lion.

Puma concolor, the second largest cat in the Americas after jaguars and the fourth largest in the world (African lions and tigers are bigger), are dedicated carnivores, able to eat up to twenty pounds of meat at a time. They also command a lot of real estate, similar to grizzly bears, wolves, and wolverines. A grown female might lay claim to eighty square miles, while a male's home range could be twice that. And they're generally solitary. Females sometimes tolerate one another on the landscape, and there's some evidence of adult females with kittens traveling together, and even of the occasional male sharing a meal with females outside the breeding season— but as a rule the big males tend to parcel up the country into individual territories. Given some territorial overlap, you can expect somewhere between two and four resident cats per hundred square kilometers (forty square miles) in good mountain habitat.

Because those territories are found from the southern reaches of the Canadian Yukon to the southern Andes in Chile and Argentina, the cats have been given many names in many languages by many people. In English alone there are dozens of names for the same animal, including mountain lion, cougar, catamount (from "cat of the mountain"), panther (the term Lewis and Clark used), mountain cat, mountain screamer, painter, ghost cat, and, the name I favor, puma—derived from the Quechua language and meaning simply "a powerful animal."

The big boy above was perched passively on a wide branch, snarling occasionally and blinking like a house cat in repose. In fact, a mountain lion is more closely related to a domesticated cat *(felis)* than it is to an African lion *(panthera)*. And this one seemed nearly as docile, except for the obvious fact that he could rearrange my face with a single swipe of his meaty paw.

Terry quickly prepped the dart, which is propelled by a .22 cartridge that delivers the syringe with an immobilizing agent (ketamine hydrochloride). Making sure to avoid the head and ribs, he fired into the lion's left flank. Hitting a stationary target is the easy part; making sure the tranquilizer has taken effect, especially when you're eye to eye with an agitated, semiconscious carnivore, requires more finesse. I put on my leather safety harness and climbing spurs, wrapped a rope around the tree trunk and eased closer to the glassy-eyed cat. His head was bobbing like a junkie's before he finally nodded off. By the time I reached him he was flat on the branch. I poked his hind leg with a stick to be sure that he was under, pleased that he hadn't

This male mountain lion was first spotted chasing bighorns from the helicopter in the Beartooth Wildlife Management Area, Montana. TERRY ENK

urinated on my head as I ascended—a nervous response that more than once has wreaked havoc with my favorite old Filson packer hat.

From a perch on a branch below him, I uncoiled my long yellow climbing rope and carefully slipped a knot around his hind legs, cinched it up securely, and then pushed him off the branch and gently lowered him to the team below. They moved quickly to secure a radio collar around his neck, while constantly monitoring his vital signs, and recorded his weight and measurements. Then, we just sat on the hill and waited until the woozy cat pulled himself to his feet, wobbled toward a clump of junipers, and disappeared downhill. Transmissions from the collar let us know he was soon back to stalking deer and elk in the Beartooth Wildlife Management Area and adjacent Gates of the Mountains Wilderness Area.

By the end of that three-year study, we'd radio-collared eight mountain lions that shared a zip code with bighorn sheep. The cats we tracked followed the seasonal migrations of elk and deer, moving between low-elevation winter ranges in the WMA and higher-elevation summer ranges. The bighorns didn't migrate seasonally throughout the Beartooth, though, and so lions were an issue only when the deer and elk overlapped with the rock-hopping sheep habitat. On average, a lion will kill a deer every week or two, but they'll also eat coyotes, marmots, grouse, raccoons, rabbits, rodents, domestic pets, and even porcupines. Our research estimated that the marked lions killed only a few bighorns per year on the WMA. And at the end of the study, our data suggested that the declines in this bighorn sheep population were not due to predation, even in an area with normal mountain lion densities.

Rather, the population problem was caused by a combination of infection and habitat. Historic disease cycles had caused the bighorns to stop migrating into higher country during the summer, which in turn led to lambs dying when the heat of summer dried out the lowland grasses. It was really a habitat and health issue, not a mountain lion problem.

That study ended, but the data that wildlife biologists (myself included) are collecting has proved critical to preserving wild nature, including big predators and their prey. I'm writing this book not only to share these amazing animals, but to offer yet another reason why we need to work together to protect wild places. These days, large carnivores such as mountain lions and bears exist on this planet for two simple reasons: 1) They have access to large, connected blocks of land (the freedom to roam), and 2) people are willing to tolerate them in the land that we share. It's as simple or complex as that. Without our tolerance of large and dangerous carnivores, they would not exist, period. We decide their fate. That's more responsibility than we probably deserve, but that's how it is.

CHAPTER 2

FINDING THE WILD

If we choose to walk into a forest where a tiger lives, we are taking a chance. If we swim in a river where crocodiles live, we are taking a chance. If we visit the desert or climb a mountain or enter a swamp where snakes have managed to survive, we are taking a chance.

– Peter Benchley, author

I was twelve years old the first time I saw Skip Frye surf. Curtis DeBreau, one of the first kids I met in San Diego, told me that Skip ruled the Point. Curtis and his crew of Pacific Beach rats spoke about him as if he walked on water because, of course, he did—several hours a day, Monday through Sunday, rain or shine. Whether riding ten-foot steely-blue bombs during winter storms, or hanging ten on a mellow summer roller, Skip was a "soul surfer"—effortless, artful, smooth as beach glass.

At the time, I couldn't have been less cool—I was a farm boy from the Midwest. My mother, my brother, and I arrived in San Diego in the summer of 1972 on a flight from Marion, Iowa, where I was born and raised, and where my parents were born and raised, too. They met in grade school, but didn't really find one another until their senior year. My mom, Joanne Fernow, was a petite, attractive, industrious farm girl. My dad, Jerry Williams, was tall and charismatic, and as he aged people said he looked a bit like Tom Selleck. I was born the day before Halloween, 1961, followed two years later by my brother Dave. My father, an Academic All-American at the University of Iowa, continued studying accounting, business law, and literature. My mother left college to take care of me.

Mom's parents owned a spread that had been in the family for three generations, and together we settled into farm country Iowa. Between the

The author in the late 1970s enjoying the saltwater breeze before a morning longboarding session in Pacific Beach, California. CURTIS DEBRAU

family farm and our house on the outskirts of town, Dave and I traveled every creek, field, and woodlot; rolled every log, stone, and stump; explored every wonder, surprise, and secret that nature kept. Think Tom Sawyer and Huck Finn, except with the chore of feeding cows at the crack of dawn.

My brother was taller, like my dad, and his world circled around sports. I took after mom, short and lean, and to make matters worse I suffered from asthma—which made it tough to be a boy in an athletic family in a town where baseball, football, and basketball ruled. My lungs were bad enough that I landed in the emergency room half a dozen times before I was ten.

My personal sanctuary was the woods and outdoors. I spent countless hours alone along Indian Creek—collecting frogs and running a trapline for muskrats, exploring the wetlands like the fictional characters that inhabited my imagination. My favorite film was *Charlie the Lonesome Cougar*, a cheesy Disney production about a big cat raised by loggers in the Pacific Northwest. (Charlie is released into the wild, meets a mate, and lives happily ever after.) And I loved *Those Calloways,* starring Brian Keith as the Vermont trapper who dreamed of building a sanctuary for migrating geese. I came for the nature, but stayed for the adventure, especially that scene when Bucky wrestles the wolverine. Disappearing into books such as *My Side of the Mountain,* by Jean Craighead George, I completely identified with Sam, the twelve-year-old who flees New York City for a solo life in the Catskill Mountains. Sam hollows out a giant tree, befriends a weasel, hunts with a hawk, and lives off the land like a woodsy Robinson Crusoe. In my version of the fantasy, though, I went west—however far I had to go to find wild nature and adventure, and animals that knock you down a link or two on the food chain.

Meanwhile, my parents were struggling. Farming expenses had soared in Iowa, and farm country was heading into recession. The family farm was one of many small, private operations that went belly-up in the early seventies. I still recall the crunch of tires rolling up my grandparents' gravel driveway as pickup trucks came in empty, then left with family possessions stacked in back. Eventually, they cleared the place out, and the next thing to go was my parents' marriage.

Which is how mom and Dave and I landed in San Diego, for a fresh start, watching Skip Frye walk on water. I was born in Iowa, but—like cutting foam for a new surfboard—I was shaped in California.

The CBS news anchor Walter Cronkite once called Marion, Iowa, the quintessential American farm community. San Diego was the quintessential California beach community, and the contrast couldn't have been greater. When we finally hit the coast and piled out of the car, it was like that scene in *The Wizard of Oz* when Dorothy's house crash-lands in Technicolor

Munchkin Land. The east-west streets in Pacific Beach were named after precious stones—Turquoise, Chalcedony, Opal, Sapphire, and Emerald. Sweet-scented orange and lemon trees grew in backyards; hibiscus, fuchsia, jasmine, and bird of paradise hung over the alleyways that crisscrossed the coastal neighborhood.

And most dazzling of all to a kid who grew up in rural Iowa, I saw and smelled the sea air for the first time. I didn't know what *infinite* meant, but when I stared out at the Pacific Ocean horizon, that was what it looked like. I took a deep breath, inhaling the pungent mixture of sea salt and kelp—and with that first scent of the ocean, I knew I wouldn't have to worry about my asthma any more. Far from the ragweed and goldenrod of Iowa, I felt for the first time in my life what it was like to be a normal, healthy kid who could breathe deeply. I will always love San Diego for that.

There was no money, of course. We lived crammed into a one-bedroom apartment, collecting aluminum cans for extra spending cash and eating a lot of popcorn for dinner. I was just twelve, but had a special work permit that allowed me to work longer hours as a minor. I logged thirty-three and a half hours per week at a lumber and hardware store, alongside an eclectic crew of ex-cons, military vets, bikers, and surfer dudes. They taught me a lot, most of it useful, but it was Fred, the garden shop manager, who gave me the best advice: "Find work you enjoy," he said, "because you sure don't want to end up working here like all of us." I'm certain he had no idea that I'd wind up chasing cats to the ends of the world.

By the time I started at Mission Bay High School, I was spending most of my time in the ocean. My buddy Curtis lived close to the beach, and his folks kept a teardrop aluminum camper in the backyard, surrounded by bright red hibiscus flowers, gardenia blossoms, and avocado trees. That was my home away from home. Some nights we crashed in the bougainvillea-covered camper in his backyard, next to our wax-covered surfboards; other nights we crashed on the beach with other surfers and girlfriends. We'd wake with the sun, pull on our shorty wetsuits, and knee-paddle into the cold, dark water at dawn. The ocean was wild in a way those Iowa wetlands could never match, an untamed escape from the day-to-day tangle of life.

I was a small-wave longboard surfer: I liked them waist-high, though I would occasionally brave the larger sets. Out beyond the breakers, relaxing on our boards talking about girls, life, and girls, we found a kind of peace in nature. Then, after biking the ten blocks to school through shoulder-high fog, I'd remember the swells while I rubbed my eyebrows and showered my

Volkswagen vans were preferred for carrying our long boards from Chalcedony Street in Pacific Beach to surf breaks up and down the San Diego coastline. California. CURTIS DEBRAU

textbooks with salt from the morning surf session. After school, after work, we'd paddle out on our boards around dusk, fishing rods clenched in our teeth, and fish for sea bass and rockfish in the kelp beds. Sometimes we'd freedive for abalone in the rocky reefs. We cooked whatever we caught over a fire on the beach. If we were still hungry, we hopped a neighbor's fence and filled our pockets with avocadoes and oranges. The next day we did it all over again. We were Tom and Huck again. I was Sam, hunting with a hawk and living off the land, Pacific style.

The ocean was our wilderness, and I explored it the way I had explored the woods back in Iowa—except now I had a band of like-minded friends to enjoy it with. If it hadn't been for surfing, I would never have put my face beneath the surface of those waves, would never have thrilled at the untamed wild and watery depths, the sharks and rays and tall kelp forests. If it hadn't been for surfing, I would never have found the cats.

At the center of our universe, remote and benevolent like the sun, was Skip Frye. Skip surfed the Point, out of our league but sometimes within view. We idolized him and were happy for whatever scraps of attention he bestowed on us. He shaped boards at the shack behind the Select Surf Shop on Mission Boulevard, and let us hang out there once in a while. We'd loiter around the alley and watch Skip work his magic—mask on, covered in white foam, moving his plane back and forth as he transformed a solid plank of foam into a work of art. When Skip finally made my board, an 8'6" nose rider emblazoned with his iconic logo—a pair of black wings stretched below his signature—I was ecstatic. I rode home on my bike with it under my arm, like a kid driving his first car.

Skip was a different breed from every grown man I'd ever known. How strange it was to see Skip, roughly the same age as my father and stoic like him, do something so beautiful and so pointless, that few people saw or cared about. His takeoff was as seamless as a cat leaping on a table. As he dropped down the face of a wave, he'd arch his back, arms outstretched, and make a wide sweeping turn to slide back up below the curl of water spraying at the top of the wave. He appeared calm, even nonchalant, as he cross-stepped along his board from the center to the nose and back again. And sometimes before the wave flattened out, he'd throw his head back in exaltation—or was it prayer?

When I donned a mask and snorkel and peeked under the waves, the ocean was a whole new magical world of wild nature, and I was immediately captivated. I'm a social guy—I'm not a lone cat—but whether it's the woods, salt water, or the mountains, I have a need to go to nature. So with all the time that I spent in, on, and under the sea, I suppose it's not surprising that when I started to think about a career, I thought about marine biology. Science is a powerful tool for understanding nature, and once you're armed with that understanding, you can be a player in the game to protect it. I wanted to be a player in that game. It's my identity. I've never really wanted to do anything except this—to understand and protect wildlife and wildlife habitat. Which is how I found myself enrolled at San Diego State University, and swimming with the sharks.

Between classes, I volunteered as a marine science interpreter at the Scripps Institution of Oceanography in La Jolla, and took a side job as a tour guide at Sea World. (If you happened to walk by the Sea World walrus pool in 1981, and heard an enthusiastic skinny blond kid talking about the mating habits of the heavily whiskered Wally and Wanda, that was probably me.) It wasn't exactly the highlight of my wildlife career, but it did wrangle me an invitation to join some Sea World marine biologists on a shark-collecting mission in the open ocean, not far from the Coronado Islands on the Mexican border.

As the new kid out to impress, I jumped into the water, ready to photograph sharks as they arrived to inspect the chum bucket floating about twenty feet away. In fact, they chose to inspect the boat instead, and after one hit the propeller with a loud *chink* I scrambled back aboard in a hurry. These were blue sharks, not the most dangerous, and we·netted an eight-foot specimen and hauled him into a tank on board. Mission accomplished— except when we tried to start the engine and found that the propeller was tangled in kelp. Over the side I went again, an abalone iron in hand, to cut the propeller free. Blue sharks continued to swim by, and I was even cocky enough to shoot a few photos with the Instamatic underwater camera hanging around my neck. When I popped my head up, the biologists hauled me out, laughing hysterically. Among the blue sharks was a mako, a close, fast-swimming cousin to the deadly great white. As long as I wasn't eaten, it was funny to them. My kind of people.

Sea World in San Diego was a special place: At that time most people around the world learned about marine mammal conservation from aquariums. I'm sure that's one of the reasons the Marine Mammal Protection Act originally passed into law—aquarium visitors were demanding protections. People have to care to before they can make change, and Sea World made people care. Who couldn't help but marvel at the power, agility, and intelligence of the orcas, enjoy a cordial relationship with the seals, and have many a soulful conversation with the octopus? Back then, we weren't really engaged in a debate about the ethics of keeping large mammals in captivity—those important conversations came much later. As far as we were concerned, aquariums were places where the public could peer into the natural ocean world and find wonder, inspiration, and connection. With such proximity would come admiration and a collective consciousness about protecting marine life around the world. Or so we hoped.

But studying animals in an aquarium setting is not the same as studying the relationships of species in complex ecosystems, the web of connections, and the interactions that make these systems whole. I wanted to explore how the pieces evolved together in nature, and how they fit together.

After three taxing years working full time and going to school, I was captive to my own frenetic schedule. I was chronically exhausted and my

My 8'6" Skip Frye noserider was perfect for ocean fishing in the kelp beds off the point near Tourmaline Surfing Park, California. CURTIS DEBRAU

grades had gone dangerously south. Just then my father made me an offer I couldn't refuse: If I joined him and Dave in Florida, and enrolled in a state college there, he would help pay my way. I could cut back on work, focus on studying, and get to know his side of my family again. So I cautiously packed my belongings, sold my car, said some tough good-byes, and flew east to the banana republic of Florida.

After a brief stint at the local community college to secure in-state residency, I enrolled at Florida State University in the fall of 1983. As I got used to this huge and prestigious school, and to a new humid Gulf of Mexico climate, I was also slowly getting reacquainted with my father, his wife Jettie, and my younger brother. It had been nearly ten years since we'd spent any time together, and we negotiated those first awkward conversations on the golf course and fishing the saltwater canals. I got to know my brother, Dave, again on those fishing excursions and through a shared love of Jimmy Buffett music. Whenever we could find the time and the funds, we went to Jimmy's shows from Key West to the Banana River to Fort Lauderdale. Buffett's barstool philosophy—nonconformity expressed through sailing, celestial navigation, fishing, eating fresh seafood, drinking tequila, and protecting the manatee—grabbed Parrotheads like my brother and me hook, line, and sinker.

Armed finally with a FSU bachelor's degree in biological sciences with a marine biology emphasis (with minors in Spanish and archaeology), I went looking for a job near my brother's home in south Florida—landing eventually at Ocean World, a 1950s-style aquarium in Fort Lauderdale that featured Davy Jones' Locker, home to "The Flying Dolphins Show." They had a dolphin training and feeding pool, California sea lions, otters, sea turtles, fish, alligators, tropical birds, monkeys, and sharks. I told the owner that I had a degree in marine biology and had previously worked for Sea World and he hired me on the spot to work with the dolphins and seals. Or so I thought.

My first morning on the dolphin and sea lion training job, he told me that I was expected to wrestle alligators twice a day. Also, there was the two o'clock show where I would wade into a waist-deep pool to hand-feed the sharks as they whirled around my private parts. Oh, and, yeah, there would be a daily rendezvous with Lucifer, the one-eyed crocodile. Once I learned where to stand in the alligator pit (just behind the gators' front limbs, away from both teeth and tail), a part of me actually enjoyed the showmanship. Lucifer was more dangerous, but the emcee had a pistol in case things got hairy. That was all good until the day the divers forgot to scrub the algae from the pool bottom. As I retreated just ahead of Lucifer, I slipped and fell next to five submerged gators. The crowd gasped in horror. I scrambled to my feet and made a break for the side of the pool, screaming, "Don't shoot! Don't shoot!"—I feared the emcee's marksmanship more than Lucifer's maw—and hurled myself over the fence, breaking cameras and drenching spectators en route. The crowd loved it, thought it was the highlight of the show! Needless to say I didn't make it a regular part of the act.

I enjoyed working with the dolphins and sea lions, but the entertainment aspect of the job felt far from the science I ultimately wanted to do. From a marine biology point of view, it was like studying to be an actor with a retired clown. This was nature of a sort, but not wild nature. It was adventure, too, but not the sort I'd been reading about since childhood.

Then one evening, roughly a year into my stint at Ocean World, I stumbled upon a Discovery Channel special featuring grizzly bears in Yellowstone National Park. I was transfixed by the rugged landscape, by the grizzlies, and by the scientists working with these powerful thousand-pound beasts. Toward the end of the show, two of the biologists tagged a big grizz, the bear still semiconscious from a tranquilizer dart. But the bear wasn't completely out, and the metal tag piercing its ear sent the big bruin into a frenzy of rage, scattering the scientists as they retreated into their car. Staggering to its feet, the bear bit through a metal tool box as if it were an apple, then rushed the red station wagon like a linebacker blindsiding a quarterback. Just as the bear mounted the front of the car, the scientist threw the wagon into reverse and sped off to safety, leaving the bear behind.

Now *that* was some cool science.

Call me restless, impressionable, or just ready for a change, but I knew right then that my days as "Bwana Jim, gator wrestler, dolphin trainer, and shark tamer" were officially over. I wanted to live in Big Sky country and study something like *Ursus arctos horribilis*—the biggest predator in "the last best place" in America. The next morning, I visited the local college library in Boca Raton and flipped through the old wooden card catalogue to see what I could learn about researchers and universities in and around Yellowstone National Park. The first grizzly bear research paper I found mentioned Dr. Harold Picton, a professor of wildlife biology from Montana State University in Bozeman, Montana.

I hustled home and dialed his university work number. "Hi," I said, heart pounding, "my name is Jim Williams. I'm interested in going to graduate school in Montana."

"What do you do now?" he asked.

Probably best not to mention Lucifer, I thought. "I'm a dolphin trainer in Florida," I said.

An awkward silence ensued. "Do you realize, Mr. Williams, that it snows in Montana?"

At least he had a sense of humor. "I grew up in Iowa, and my father has taken me to ski in Colorado, so, yeah, I've heard about snow."

He told me that I had about as much chance of getting into his graduate program as a snowball in downtown Miami unless I could get myself to Bozeman, gain some experience in the mountains, and make connections with the right professors. Even then, there were no guarantees. It was very competitive, as Montana State University was—and is—regarded as one of the finest schools for wildlife research and conservation.

Fair enough. One month later, I packed my red Jeep Scrambler, hung a shark jaw on the rear-view mirror, and drove straight through to Park City, Utah, to work at a ski resort to earn and save money for nonresident tuition. Then I headed north through Yellowstone, through the deeply incised Gallatin Canyon, and on into Bozeman and Montana State University, where I went directly to Lewis Hall, knocked on Dr. Picton's office door, and announced, "Jim Williams, sir, finally here!"

The man who would become my teacher, mentor, and a dear friend for life shook his head and smiled. "You certainly are persistent, Mr. Williams. You could do well here. We'll see."

CHAPTER 3

THE FRONT

In the process of natural selection, given a liberal allowance of time, it is the lion's claw, the lion's tooth and need, that has given the deer its beauty and speed and grace.

– Edward Abbey, *The Journey Home*

Not only did the Buckhorn Bar look like an authentic 1880s Western saloon, it often acted like one. One night during my first Christmas in town, the daughter of a well-known local rancher, home from college, was sitting at a nearby table with her friends. Also in the bar were half a dozen loggers, tough thirsty men who'd been out by Smith Creek all week cutting trees by hand. Before long, a wobbly logger began hitting on the rancher's daughter. That prompted her father's workers to lay down their pool cues and drift over. I was about to advise the logger to move on when a ranch hand tapped him on the shoulder. Three things happened, very quickly: the logger turned around; the rancher's fist sent him reeling; and the bystanders immediately joined the fray. Amid the chaos, the logger got to his feet, jumped over the bar, and sprinted out the back door of the Buckhorn Bar to the Lazy B Hotel, three doors down Main Street. The crowd followed. When the sheriff's deputy arrived, the logger was poised like a fencer in front of his second-story room, waving and revving his chainsaw every time a ranch hand advanced. Finally, the deputy herded everyone but the logger back to the Buckhorn, where we could all return to a more refined, less combustible drunkenness and frivolity.

Welcome to Augusta, Montana, "the last original cow town in the West"—at least according to the Augusta Chamber of Commerce. With

Bridger, the golden retriever, and two lion hounds accompany me as we cross the wintery boundary of the Bob Marshall Wilderness Area in search of big cats. Montana. ROCKY HECKMAN

my arrival in 1989, the population swelled to 251. My job was to track big cats and to add to mountain lion science, but most folk here were more interested in how to keep their cattle safe from the hungry carnivores.

Founded in 1844—back when Montana was still a territory—and named after the first child born there, Augusta is located fifteen miles off the Rocky Mountain Front on a vast and windy grassy plain. Look east, and you see an ocean of American prairie, where massive herds of bison thundered not so long ago. Look west, and a tremendous mountain rampart soars straight up from the grassy flats, a stretch of alpine peaks known as the Rocky Mountain Front. Those summits are some of the wildest country left in America, part of the rugged Bob Marshall Wilderness. Locals know it simply as 'The Bob,' a million pristine acres comprising the fifth-largest protected wilderness in the Lower 48, home to wolves and wolverines, bears and big cats. Its peaks crash into the prairie the same abrupt way its predators crash into the cattle herds.

Ironically, The Bob takes its name from a city slicker: Bob Marshall, born in New York City in 1901. He was a plant scientist, writer, and prodigious walker, who logged countless miles through the unmapped country around the South Fork of the Flathead River. He cofounded The Wilderness Society, and campaigned to preserve places where people could travel for weeks without crossing a road. One year after his death in 1939, just such a wilderness in Montana was created in his honor.

Augusta was where I lived: The Bob and the Front were my office. It was a dream assignment—tracking mountain lions for my graduate thesis under the direction of none other than Dr. Picton. Author of the book *Saga of the Sun* and the definitive elk migration research in The Bob, Dr. Picton was one of Montana's early wildlife biologists in this Sun River country. In fact, he was still known as Harold 'Tall-in-the-Saddle' Picton by some of the locals. Given his time in the field and depth of knowledge—and the fact that he'd trained many of the staff now working for the Montana Fish, Wildlife & Parks Department—in my world he held sway. When the time came for me to choose a master's thesis project, Dr. Picton told me that although big cats had been studied in Yellowstone National Park and some other Western states, there was little information about them in The Bob and Rocky Mountain Front. I was excited to fill in some of those gaps.

In technical terms, the Sun River drainage is inhabited by a unique species array made up of a large numbers of both resident and migratory ungulates as well as large carnivores. In laymen terms, this country is a messy and migratory cycle of eat and be eaten. The ungulates—"meat with feet" as the writer Doug Chadwick calls them—include elk, white-tailed and mule deer, moose, pronghorn, bighorn sheep, and mountain goats. The primary

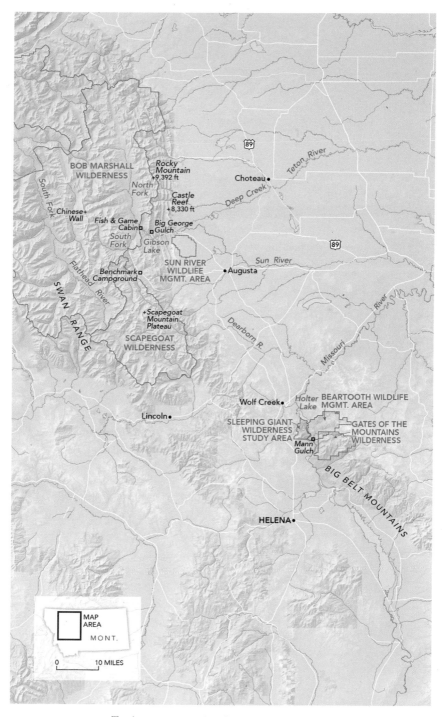

ROCKY MOUNTAIN FRONT The short grass prairie abruptly meets the ramparts of the Rockies in Montana in the greater Bob Marshall/Gates of the Mountain Wilderness complexes. SOURCES: USGS, MONTANA STATE LIBRARY, WILDERNESS.NET

carnivores are black and grizzly bears, wolves, and mountain lions; there are also lynx, coyotes, red fox, wolverines, and badgers. From a wildlife biologist's point of view, this broad "array of species" interacting across such a vast area—nearly three million acres when you include adjacent parks and wilderness areas—is unique in North America. With the exception of the extinction of wooly mammoths and the extirpation of the buffalo (which are slowly being returned to parts of the ecosystem), the rugged Rocky Mountain Front has changed very little since the Pleistocene ice retreated 10,000 years ago. This is old country, still intact, still wild.

My job here, with support from local biologists and state wildlife managers, was to spend a few years living among the mountain lions, tracking them to learn about their health, habits, and habitats. What did they eat, and when? How often did they kill? What did they kill? What kind of habitat did they prefer, during what time of year? It's big country, a geologic jumble of sawtooth ridges and deep river valleys, and to answer those questions I would travel it on foot, top to bottom, end to end. Today's wildlife biologists can gather more data more quickly, employing GIS and satellite technology to track animals remotely from the comfort of the office. But I got my schooling in the analog era, when the only way to gather information was to literally live with the lions. Less data, to be sure, but also a different sort of data. More intimate. A satellite collar can transmit a location, tell you where a cat was and when. But unless you're there, in the field, you miss the relationships that make nature work—the weather and the wind and the topography and the light that can explain *why* a cat was in a particular place at a particular time. What I lost in sample size, I gained in context.

Every time I have climbed a peak in The Bob, there were no signs of humanity in any direction. The entire area can be circled in a car—a 380-mile drive—but not a single road crosses it. This was not going to be easy. Complicating my job was the fact that Dr. Picton didn't believe in providing detailed instructions. As he told me many times over the course of the project—and as I was to learn for myself—failing repeatedly was part of the process.

And nothing prepares you for the prospect of failure like graduate-level oral exams. This process—required before I could begin fieldwork—was legendary at Montana State, and I was scared to death. Much easier to confront a mountain lion than a group of seasoned professors set on grilling your knowledge related to the biological sciences, math, and chemistry. Luckily, there was a weathered old folder that passed from grad student to grad student, containing notes from previous orals to help me prepare. Krebs cycle, carbon cycle, wildlife ecology. But still, the job of the orals is to humble young grad students. It worked.

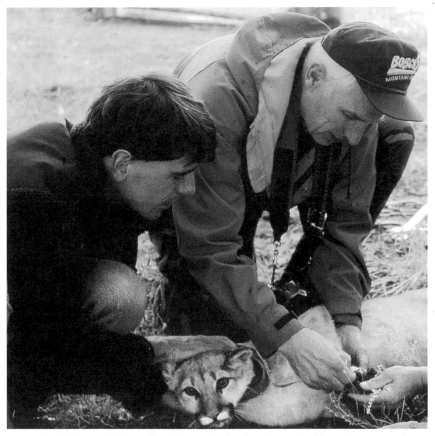

Montana State University Professor Harold Picton (right) and graduate student Thomas Baumeister collect information and measurements on a young mountain lion. Helena, Montana. JIM WILLIAMS

My experience there also defined my entire career. Augusta's bars, The Bob's rugged wilds, MSU's orals—these were the dues I paid for admission into a fantastic community of conservation biologists. And I'd gladly pay that price many times over, because it ultimately partnered me with the scientists who were literally writing the book on big cats.

Mountain lions are the most effective and efficient large predators in the Americas. Period.

They are nature's perfect stalk-and-ambush killer. What is astounding is that we, as a twenty-first century urban society, have allowed them to recover not just across the West, but also, perhaps, in the East, where individual cats—mostly young males, dispersing from home—are even now pioneering new-old territories. It's a dramatic and unlikely turnaround, against the odds, from the near-eradication of cats in this country. For decades, states paid bounties for dead mountain lions, and unrestricted hunting was encouraged in an attempt to exterminate the predator. These policies had a predictably devastating effect on lion populations; when Lewis and Clark and David Thompson traveled west, "panthers" roamed the entirety of the Lower 48, Canada, Mexico, and Central and South America all the way to Patagonia. But by the turn of the last century, the cats were virtually extinct east of the Mississippi—with the notable exception of the Florida panther, which survived only by retreating to the inhospitable swamps of the Everglades.

In the West, mountain lions found refuge in the wild, sweeping landscapes, but even there they were in trouble. My friend and mentor Maurice Hornocker, a pioneer in mountain lion and other wild cat research, estimates that by the early 1960s there were only 6,500 mountain lions left in the United States. It's a best-guess number, but we do know that between 1936 and 1961 a staggering 3,219 bounties were paid in Washington state. Another 3,582 were paid in Oregon. And in California, 12,500 lions were killed between 1907 and 1972 for bounty or for sport. So depleted were cat numbers by mid-century that from 1932 to 1950, fewer than five mountain lions were taken each year in Montana.

Hornocker, setting out to study the great cats in the early 1960s, paid hunters $50 if they could tree a lion so that he could fit it with a radio collar for tracking. He ultimately collared an impressive fourteen cats, but studying them was another matter; by winter's end, hunters had killed all but four. In 1964, Hornocker moved his research deep into the Idaho wilderness, launching a ten-year study that was the genesis of the lion science to come. It provided seminal information about all things cat—feeding habits, habitat, social structure, relationships with deer and elk, predation on livestock—and it opened eyes. Mountain lion predation, it turns out, was not having any serious effect on deer and elk herds, and neither were the cats affecting livestock in any significant manner. Hornocker's data, in many ways, cleared the way for the end of bounties and unrestricted hunting, which in turn led to modern lion management and the tremendous and unlikely comeback we are witnessing today.

Cats are now thriving in their strongholds out West. More impressive still, they are slowly but surely rewilding our continent on the backs of deer and darkness, moving across the Midwest and southern Canada, on their way to New England. They are tracking ancient river-bottom routes, following prey down the Missouri, the Milk, the Saskatchewan, the long east-west rivers that are pumping lions from the Rocky Mountain Front to the Black Hills and beyond. Anywhere there is enough human tolerance and prey, the big cats are reclaiming old ground. Minnesota's dairy country. Ohio's corn country. The farmlands of Pennsylvania, Virginia, New York. All of this is potential home range for tomorrow's cat communities. Wildlife managers have successfully built up tremendous herds of white-tailed deer across America, for the benefit of hunters, and that prey base is driving the remarkable recovery of lions. It's astonishing, really, considering that we are in the age of extinction for large predators in the Americas—and given our long history of eliminating any animal that can harm us, or, more accurately, our livestock.

So how is this happening? Why the mountain lion? And why is the mountain lion the only large cat on planet Earth that is increasing both in numbers and distribution?

It's not just the deer. It's the way we think about the wild. A radical change swept North America during the 1970s, an environmental ethos driven by the science of ecology—the science of the connections between the parts, and not simply the parts themselves. Ecology taught us the intricate relationships at play in the natural world, the "web of life" that includes everything from bacteria and photosynthetic green plants to insects to deer and elk and wolves. Most important, for mountain lions, ecology established that our native large predators also play an important role in these natural systems. Every one of the parts is needed if the ecosystem is to function naturally. Predators aren't villains. They are indispensable.

I was a young man when the Endangered Species Act passed into law in 1973, and I still remember the beautiful National Wildlife Federation posters featuring a black-footed ferret, a wolf, and, of course, a resting mountain lion. These were the very beginnings of nationwide tolerance for predators, and of a drive toward natural and intact ecological systems throughout North America. It was a time of people awakening to the role carnivores played in ecosystems.

At the same time—thanks to groundbreaking 1960s field research by Maurice Hornocker in the wilderness mountains of Idaho—we learned that the lions weren't, in fact, eating us out of business. His studies proved absolutely that mountain lions are dependent on healthy deer and elk herds. Contrary to the popular opinion at local coffee shops, the cats were not reducing the big-game hunter's prized quarry. Instead, they were part of a system evolved to keep herds strong.

It's difficult to overstate the importance of this science, as many of the cat hunters who once participated in mountain lion bounty systems began to realize that lions were more valuable alive—that they could enjoy their trained hounds while pursuing and photographing the big cats all winter long, if the carnivores were not eliminated. Those hound handlers carried heavy political clout in the rural western states. More than science and data, state wildlife commissions at the time listened to the hound handlers. Before long, hound handlers began showing up side by side with university-trained wildlife biologists, demanding that mountain lions be made protected game animals, not bountied predators—and by the early 1970s that's exactly what happened. State wildlife agencies eliminated bounties, and shifted 180 degrees to conservation and management.

The ripples spread through wild nature almost immediately. With new rules came a ban on the poison-laced baits that had been used to kill cats, but that also killed any other critters unlucky enough to sniff them out. One side effect was that wolverines, bobcats, martens, badgers, and countless other species were suddenly "protected" under the new rules for lion conservation. It was a foundation on which whole ecosystems could be rebuilt, and it helped drive the wild that would be necessary for mountain lion expansion nationwide. We made room for the lion, tolerated the lion, and wild nature did the rest, filling in the gaps with a complicated dance of predators and prey. And through it all, America barely noticed.

People died of domestic dog bites, bee stings, drownings and falls, and auto accidents. The rare encounter with a wild animal remains a statistical fluke. Humans are not part of the big cats' "prey image," and as long as we have strong deer numbers the lions mostly leave our pets and livestock alone. The cats, in essence, were invisible. We live as fairly peaceful neighbors because we cannot see them. If we knew they were there, we might have second thoughts, but mountain lions make their living in the shadows, at dawn and dusk, and often can be quite nocturnal. We see only what they leave behind—telltale tracks and deer bones, a scatter of whitetail fur, prints in fresh snow.

The big cats have evolved for secrecy, to protect themselves and their kills from other predators—from bears, and especially from wolves—and also to enable their ambush hunting style. Not only do the lions move in darkness, and in heavy cover, but they do so on softly padded paws that are covered in thick hair to soundproof their approach. Even the claws retract to quiet each step. They've evolved to be almost scentless, a protection against wolves that, in today's world, allows them to slip silently though neighborhood woodlots without triggering the alarm of barking dogs. They're largely solitary, the better to go unnoticed, and they certainly don't announce their presence by baying at the moon. In other words, they really are the ghosts of the Rockies. The adaptations that allowed them to survive and hunt in a world of wolves, deer, and elk are proving to be the key to their expansion in a world of dogs and humans.

I was sent to Augusta to study mountain lions, but over my career what I've learned about the big cats has taught me as much about *Homo sapiens* as it has about *Puma concolor*. We fear the threat we can see. Tigers and African lions are far more visible, and we've nearly wiped them out. But we don't see the mountain lion. What does that say about us, that the only big cat in the world that is expanding is the one we can't see?

During my years in Augusta, I lived in a sparsely furnished, weather-beaten faded yellow US Forest Service house on the west side of town and spent much of my free time at the Buckhorn Bar, where not much ever changed. Elk, moose, and deer antlers hung on log walls among the bleached skulls of grizzly, big horn sheep, wolf, and mountain lion. They shared space with vintage crosscut saws, rifles, and traps and framed black-and-white photographs of cowpokes in chaps and wide-brimmed hats.

I cashed my student stipend checks at the Buckhorn, dined at the Buckhorn, schmoozed and got a bit sloppy with the regulars at the Buckhorn. Sometimes I sought advice from Frankie, the owner/bartender, about how to butcher a mule deer or how to best approach the few available women in town under the age of sixty. The locals were welcoming, in their way, but I was never allowed to forget that I was just another grad student from the "Big City"—that would be Bozeman—working for pencil-pushing bureaucrats who did little except make life tougher for the locals.

There were three general schools of thought in the Buckhorn about what should be done with mountain lions: leave them alone, relocate or exterminate them, or regulate them. My project wasn't popular with any of these schools. The environmentalists—generally visiting from out East or California—reveled in the fact that these gorgeous critters were free to roam through protected habitat. These folks wanted me to just leave them alone. The folks in town who, every blue moon, spotted a mountain lion wandering through their yard at night, or worse, found that their dog, cat, chicken, or rabbit had been nabbed, wanted me to have every lion captured and relocated or exterminated. The ranchers, who saw the cats as a threat to their livestock, were also fans of killing lions. The loggers, who always wanted as little regulation as possible were of the same opinion. And then there were the cat hunters, who wanted mountain lions tightly regulated and protected so hunters could head into The Bob with their tracking hounds for wild-country sport and photography.

The branches of these dead trees tell the story of the ever present winds that buffet the Rocky Mountain Front. A bighorn ram uses the ridgeline high point to keep a look out for predators. Glacier National Park, Montana. STEVEN GNAM

Everyone had an opinion, especially with regard to how carnivores affected them. But no one seemed interested in understanding the cat in its own right, as a keystone species in a natural system. I wanted to see the lions for what they were, in the wild, rather than what they meant in relation to me, and that wasn't always so popular.

Most of the time I deflected the harassment tossed my way with evasiveness, equanimity, or an attempt at wit. One time, however, I discarded all three. It was nearing Labor Day, the end of my first summer, and I was halfway through my Buckhorn chicken dinner when a tall rancher with a worn cowboy hat slammed his whiskey glass on the bar. "Hey, College!" he shouted, "I hear the cats you're tagging are getting gangrene under the collars."

He was with several other men—ranch owners and hands, a local photographer, and a hunting guide. He took a pull on his cigarette and ambled over. "I've lived here all my life," he said. "If a mountain lion takes one of my cattle or sheep, I'm gonna shoot it! Case closed! You pencil pushers are wasting everyone's time with your study."

Wiping ketchup from my mouth, I chuckled a little though I didn't find him all that amusing. I tried to justify the study by explaining how little we knew about mountain lions in The Bob and on the east Front. "We want to understand their impact on the elk, bighorn sheep, and deer populations," I said, hoping to appeal to the hunters. "It's all about conserving species and their habitat."

Well, that didn't work. He couldn't have cared less. He'd been hunting in The Bob forever and wanted me to know that greenhorns like me were overeducated and under-informed. "We need another study like a hole in my head!" he barked. And he got an even bigger laugh when he asked, "Collected any cat poop recently?"

By that time I had examined fifty-six mountain lion kills, which represented nine prey species—most commonly white-tailed deer, mule deer, elk, and bighorn sheep. There were also two porcupine kills, two snowshoe hares, one raccoon, and one marmot. I was answering some important questions about what these cats were eating—the sort of data that can change minds and protect species. And yes, to answer his question, I had collected twenty-seven hard-won scat samples, with bits of twenty-four different prey species in that poop.

But I figured I'd keep that info to myself. "Not today," I replied, "but if you want to stop by tomorrow, I know where I can get you some."

It was about that time he grabbed me by the back of my jacket and yanked me from my chair, and he and his five liquored-up buddies hustled me outside. "Let's see what you can learn from Old Joe's yak!" he said, slamming me against a horse trailer. It took a moment for my eyes to adjust, but with my face pushed between the trailer slots, sure enough, I could see a hulking, black-haired Tibetan yak.

"Joe brought him to town to get a sperm count from the vet," one of them said, which the others found hilarious. I heard someone fumbling with the latch to the trailer. My adrenaline surged. I told myself that the first guy who tried to shove me in there would be the first guy I punched in the face or kicked in the balls. This sure was an exciting new side of wildlife science! Nothing about this on my MSU oral exams!

Then someone stepped in and said, "C'mon, let's go back inside… we don't want to upset the yak before his big day tomorrow." I felt a slap on the back and that was the end of it. A round of whiskies appeared on the bar, including one in front of me. I didn't want to reach for it, because with all the adrenaline pumping through my body my hands were shaking like a spent top.

"What's the matter, College," asked the rancher, "our booze not good enough for you?"

I tossed back the shot as best as I could and headed for the door, leaving a half-eaten chicken dinner behind. That's not something a grad student does lightly, but I'd had enough of the 1800s wild west.

Fact is, it shouldn't be surprising that studying carnivores is not too popular in ranch country. Humans have a long history of fighting and taming the wild … wolves, bears, and cats; native grasslands; forests; and even wild rivers all over the world. If we ranched worms, we'd declare war on robins. Our nature is to categorize species into "good" and "bad," based on how they affect us personally. But these animals aren't good or bad. They're just wild parts of a wilder system, playing an ecological role that keeps the tapestry from unraveling. My job, as a young grad student, was to strip out a few millennia of hardwired fear and bias, and to try and see the cat clearly for what it is—and integral part of a natural system that has been in place for a really long time and supports us all. Understanding wild nature—and better still, embracing it—is a far better approach than trying to tame it. Because ultimately, she can't be tamed. And even if she could be, I don't think even the ranchers at the Buckhorn would want to live in that world.

My primary study area was centered around the Sun River Wildlife Management Area. It was bounded on the north by Deep Creek, on the west by the Continental Divide, on the south by the Dearborn River, and on the east by US Route 287. It ranged across hundreds of square miles, from low-elevation grasslands to narrow, rolling foothills to the serrated ridges and peaks of the snow-capped Rockies—the highest of which reached into the neighborhood of 10,000 feet. There were dark conifer forests of Douglas fir, lodgepole pine, spruce, and subalpine fir, and deciduous stands of quaking aspen and cottonwood. The lower elevations held shortgrass prairies and shrublands, interspersed by buttes covered in wind-whipped limber pine savanna. The diversity made it a perfect natural laboratory in which to study mountain lion habitat preferences. Given the choice of such distinctly different terrain—and we identified several habitat types—where would the elusive cats choose to live and roam?

And what would they choose to eat, given that their menu of prey was equally diverse? Would they go for the elk and bighorn sheep, or the smaller snowshoe hares, marmots, and raccoons? We knew that some types of prey stayed year round, while others were migratory. What would that mean for seasonal movements of cats? And then there were the other predators, potential competitors at the buffet table. How did the cats interact on a landscape full of bears and wolves and wolverines, all vying for the same meal?

When it comes to eating, cats are killers. They don't, as a rule, scavenge. They like their meat fresh, and their taste preferences along Montana's Rocky Mountain Front can be pretty individualistic. Some prefer less common prey, such as bighorn sheep or moose, despite the fact that the majority favor ungulates—deer and elk. It's that way throughout the Americas: deer-sized prey are by far the norm, wherever cats range. Kittens learning to hunt will stalk smaller mammals and birds, but adults make their living off deer. Of course, a cow or a domestic sheep is about the size of a deer, and in areas where native prey have been wiped out by human development, the lions tend to turn to livestock. As the boys at the Buckhorn proved, this is a recipe for conflict.

In North America, where conservation biologists have managed to increase deer and elk numbers to historic highs—usually to appease hunters—cat predation on livestock is relatively rare. But in places like Patagonia, where the guanaco has been pushed to the brink, pumas tend toward protein straight off the ranch. In fact, natural densities of cats can and are supported almost entirely by livestock, particularly in remote Patagonia where prey species have been killed off to make room (and grass) for ranch animals.

In this competitive world—where deer and elk compete with cows for grass, and lions compete with other predators for food—I needed to answer another crucial question: How much does a cat eat? If I could answer that, then I could perhaps put to rest some of the concerns down at the Buckhorn.

Turns out, a typical cat in a typical habitat eats about a deer a week. Of course, it varies from place to place, depending on habitat, food availability, and time of year, but my study agreed with many long-term mountain lion research projects that show the kill rate generally falls between .47 and 1.31 deer-sized mammals per week. Life is tougher in the winter, when lions need more calories to stay warm, and so they kill more often during the colder months—though the meat lasts longer then, as it doesn't spoil. And females with kittens kill more often (once a week) than solo males (every couple weeks); but on the whole it's a deer a week across the ecosystem. So, given that lions have a natural density on the landscape, dictated by their strict territoriality, we've been able to prove that this level of predation alone usually has no appreciable effect on prey populations, whatsoever. In other words, in places with lots of deer, the cats are not only not eating livestock, but they're also not affecting the deer populations.

It ain't easy, staying fed. These big cats are phenomenal athletes, regularly killing prey much larger than themselves. Elk and deer are the most common meal, but lions along the Canadian Front, just north of my Montana study area, have been known to take down moose. And it's not random. During the summer, lions ambush juvenile deer and elk; in the fall, they target male deer and younger elk; in winter and spring, they go after the females. Scientists call it the "reproductive vulnerability hypothesis," but what it really means is that certain ages and genders of prey are more or less vulnerable at different times of the year, and the cats know it.

One time I sent the scat of one of the female lions we had been monitoring back to the university for analysis, to confirm what she was eating. She'd been down in the cabin area of Sun River Canyon, and when I saw the small, sharply curved claws in her scat I knew right away it was a house cat. Where lions live in close proximity to humans, it's not uncommon for them to kill cats and dogs. They frequently supplement their diet with small mammals such as marmots, hares, and porcupines—and in fact, these animals are important food sources when deer populations are scattered during summer or at low population levels. Our pets are simply an unfortunate extension of this evolutionary adaptation, another small mammal to fill the gap until the deer return. Knowing that doesn't make it any easier for Tabby's owner, but fortunately these pet predations remain relatively rare.

Of course, what a cat eats dictates where a cat lives. They choose their habitat based on how close it is to the grocery store, and that changes with the seasons. That's why they need so much freedom to roam. They're wired to disperse—to spread their DNA across the landscape and to avoid overlapping territories—but they also need to follow the migrating herds. Along the way, they must avoid the threats, including other wild predators but most importantly modern humans and their machines. Fortunately for my

Thousands of migratory elk dot the grasslands of the Sun River Wildlife Management Area near the town of Augusta, Montana. BRENT LONNER, MONTANA FISH, WILDLIFE AND PARKS

grad student fieldwork, the human impact on the Rocky Mountain Front was about as minimal as anywhere on the continent.

Our challenge would be to get enough field data so that true patterns would emerge, not just a few stories about a few individual cats. It was a job made harder by the fact that, as previously mentioned, mountain lions need a lot of room, and even in this prime wilderness they were few and far between. My success depended on getting radio collars on as many cats as possible, as fast as possible, and then being able to find those lions again on the ground. That first winter, we caught and collared about a dozen lions from January to March, when frequent snowfalls make for good tracking. The next winter, we caught another dozen.

It never got old. Every single time I held a captured mountain lion in my hands, I was in awe. Their tawny fur feels short, soft, and thick—but in fact is thin for such a northern mammal, and they struggle to stay warm in subzero conditions. It's not uncommon to see ears with signs of frostbite. And they smell, well, like nothing at all, an evolutionary strategy that enables them to both sneak up on prey and to avoid bigger predators. They are athletes, taut with powerful muscle and sinew—unlike the lumbering bears I've come to know over my career—and their paws are massive, the better to wrap around an elk's flank. Push gently on the small, black digit pads, located above the larger and leathery primary foot pad, and a deadly sharp claw immediately curves up out of the fur. I call those big front paws "deer grabbers," and they are built for the grip and kill. Meat hooks.

But even with all that power, muscle, tooth, and claw, the cats are most vulnerable during the hunt. It's tricky business, taking down prey so much larger than themselves, prey that often comes armed with some serious antlers, hooves, and horns. Being a killer is risky. Cats are finely tuned, high-caliber athletes, and making a living means avoiding injury. Some colleagues who were researching deer populations were flying over a herd one day when they spotted a big mule deer buck running hard—with a mountain lion clutched to its back. The buck slammed to a stop, tossing the lion onto a steep slope, then speared it with a rack of sharp antler. The cat limped away, bleeding, in no shape to stalk and kill and stay alive during the Montana winter.

My first six months on the job were a crash course in survival. For all of the inspiration and beauty in The Bob—sculptured buttes, colorful meadows with patches of delicate wildflowers, high alpine lakes, cold swift rivers with trout virtually begging you to toss them a line, a natural hot spring, and a Who's Who of wildlife—the place also did its best to humble me. I was always aware that I was fourth on the food chain after grizzlies, black bears, and mountain lions, but even so, most days the animals were less of a worry than the weather. There were electrical storms that brought hailstones the size of quarters and thunder claps that echoed through the canyons like an approaching army. The temperature dropped below freezing by mid-October and, by January, at higher elevations, it was often 10–20 degrees below zero and worse with the wind chill. Then there were the avalanches in the high country. And if I happened to be walking along a ledge or an exposed face when a snow squall hit like a hissing white wall, I faced the choice of staying still and freezing, or moving on and risking a dangerous misstep.

And always there was the wind, the famous Rocky Mountain Front wind, which left its mark in east-leaning trees, sparse vegetation, and narrow canyons bounded by sheer rock walls. In fact, the wind was a ruthlessly efficient cleansing agent that drove most homesteaders away during the 1910s and 1920s. Writer and naturalist Ralph Waldt, who lived and worked in this country for decades, credited the wind for keeping pesky people out. He declared the wind "the land's wild guardian…were it not for the winds, it is likely that the Front would not be nearly as pristine as it is." Or, as one longtime rancher told me, "Around here, the trees lean east away from the wind, and the people lean west into the wind. When the wind eases, it's just catching its breath so it can gain more strength." One night it hit ninety miles per hour and blew a few windows out of my old field house. Maps and paper bags of dried cat poop went airborne.

The wind is also what made flying for my research so dangerous, not to mention so rough on the guts. I had to refer constantly to a topo map to pinpoint a cat's location, and glancing from the map to the terrain and back again in a wind-tossed plane turned my stomach inside out. Science isn't always pretty, but it's generally not as messy on an empty stomach.

After a couple of flights, Jim Lowe, the almost-blind-in-one-eye ex–Air Force fighter pilot with whom I logged countless hours in the cockpit, announced that it was time for me to learn to land his Piper Super Cub.

"What about taking off?" I asked.

"If I get in the plane, I'm not worried about the takeoff," he said. "But if I pass out or have a heart attack, you'll need to know how to put it down."

So I learned how to land the plane, more or less, both of us hoping I would never have to. In fact, I landed at Great Falls International Airport several times while commercial airline pilots on the taxiway watched in wonder as I porpoised up and down until the wheels made contact.

It was also critical to learn how remain calm when I got lost in the wilderness. These were, remember, the days before GPS, and even though

I pride myself on having a homing pigeon's sense of direction, there were more than a few times early on when I had no clue which end was up. One afternoon I tracked a cat deep into a forest of lodgepole pines near Benchmark Station. Night was near and the wind in the trees sounded like crashing waves. Instead of staying put and orienting myself on the map, I started walking in what turned out to be a giant circle.

When I realized my mistake I started walking even faster. Then I ran, with a bellyful of fear, and made a larger circle still. Finally, I did the smart thing and just gave up. I built a fire, rolled my dark green Patagonia fleece jacket over a Carhartt jacket for a pillow, and fell into a less-than-sound sleep beneath a tree. It was grizzly country after all. And when the night-time howling began, it reminded me that this was wolf country, too. There's no real danger to sleeping out in grizzly and wolf country, of course, but we're wired to keep one eye open.

Despite their muscle and strength, solitary mountain lions are some-times driven from kills by wolf packs where ranges of the two species overlap. During my grad-school fieldwork we documented a gray wolf chasing an adult lion off a freshly killed elk near the South Fork of the Sun River, and biologists working across the Continental Divide, near the North Fork of the Flathead River, have recorded wolf packs killing moun-tain lions as well as driving them from prey. Tracks of a lone adult gray wolf regularly crossed my study area, and during one winter, I observed five instances of a wolf scavenging a lion kill (four cow elk, and one young bull elk). In three of the cases, the wolf worked the kills and moved on. In another, the wolf chased the lion away, returned to feed on the carcass, urinated on some of the ribs, and dragged some bones from the kill site. Typical top-dog behavior in these woods. And if you think about it, that's exactly why mountain lions run from hunting hounds, despite the fact that a lion could eat a hound for breakfast. Cats have been running from dogs for thousands of years.

Over time, as I got my mountain legs, I was able to focus less on staying alive and more on mountain lions. On the days I located a cat from the air, we'd return to the tiny landing strip in Augusta, often buzzing antelope to clear the runway first. Then I'd drive my Jeep over a tire-flattening gravel road to the trailhead near Gibson Lake, and head for the remote cabin at the confluence of the North and South Forks of the Sun River. From there, I'd shoulder a fifty-pound pack loaded with telemetry equipment, and set out on foot to the spot on the map where I'd last seen the cat from the bush plane—the starting point in my ground search for a cat I'd probably never actually see. Assuming the cat had been collared, I'd use my telemetry receiver and antenna, standing on high ground to hear the

I'm setting up a prototype camera trap in hopes of capturing rare photos of a mountain lion and her kittens in their cavernous mountain lair in Big George Gulch, Bob Marshall Wilderness, Montana. MARK WALTERS

cat's signal if it was still in the immediate vicinity. Depending on the time of the year and availability of food, resident lions often don't range much beyond their home territory. Once locked in, I'd follow the directional beep like an old man combing the beach with a metal detector. If the cat wasn't collared, or if I couldn't pick up a signal, then I'd look for telltale signs of the lion's passage. Because mountain lions dislike open spaces, I'd usually head for the closest cover, all the while studying the terrain for paw prints, scat, a tree with marked with scratches and a male cat's urine, or drag marks leading to where a lion had cached a fresh kill. It was less about seeing the cat on the ground than about building an understanding of its habits and habitats.

Lions are tidy, and they like secrets. When they've had their fill, they cover and hide their prey with vegetation, forest duff, snow, and even rocks—whatever is available. On several occasions I've discovered that a cat has dragged its kill—sometimes as far as fifty yards—into nearby brush, to eat in peace. And since hunting's tough business, they don't want anyone taking their leftovers. Once the flying scavengers—North America's ravens and vultures, or the Andean condors down south—spot the kill, they'll invite everyone in the neighborhood to dinner. So the cats dine under cover, and then tuck the leftovers away, out of sight.

Younger cats, on their own for the first time, will sometimes scavenge older meat, but for the most part mountain lions prefer their meat fresh and still warm. They'll work a carcass for about three days, keeping it hidden, before moving on and leaving behind a bit of meat, skin, organs, and bones—enough to send energy cascading down through the system, feeding everything from bears to tiny beetles along with tinier bacteria, rodents, coyotes, and scavenging birds.

Each sighting, each encounter with a lion or discovery of a lion's presence, though it might have felt like an adventure or misadventure at the time, was a precious data point. When I had gathered enough of data (though you can never have enough data) and analyzed it, I hoped to have answers to the questions that brought me to The Bob in the first place. Plot the data points on the map. Do the math, compute the route, and make the model. Then I would know where the big cats liked to live—scientists call it selection and preference. Once we had that, we could do the real work of protecting those most important wild places, once and for all.

Mountain lions are called ghost cats for a reason. Wander through lion country and they'll see you but you won't see them. One way to catch a glimpse is to think like a lion. But the fact is, they were far better at tracking me than I was at tracking them. So I tried another way: technology.

The central piece of technology for my study was the radio collar and receiver antenna. With those tools, I could fairly well pinpoint a specific lion's specific location. But the more I tracked these clandestine carnivores, the more I respected and even revered their secrecy. They were collared. I was not. And yet they knew I was there, skulking around their woods, even when I couldn't find them. They watched me hunt them on several occasions, often circling back a time or two during the day to check on me. I knew this because I had the radio collar and "watched" their every move, observing me undetected. I almost stepped on a cat once, only to find the collar signal pinging from another clump of brush a few seconds later. I never saw him, but he sure saw me.

Lions hunt and travel primarily at night, crossing rivers and mountains in all conditions. In between, and in the worst of the weather, they'll hole up under a tree or rock ledge, or find shelter in a cave. One collared female with kittens led me to a cave high on the steep slopes of Big George Gulch. The floor was littered with bones, scat, and carcasses—a mule deer, three bighorn sheep, rabbits, marmots, and even the skull of a mountain lion kitten.

It was a treasure trove for a young scientist studying food habit, and I filled my old external-frame Kelty pack with bones, and headed back to Augusta. Halfway home, the middle finger on my right hand turned red and started to throb. By the next day, a little red line had traveled up my arm, disappearing under the short sleeve of my shirt and running toward my shoulder. Turns out, the cave was home to more than just cats and bones. I'd been bitten by a black widow spider, which both impressed and distressed the nurses at the rural clinic. Antibiotics took care of the bite, but I still had to pay for an ER visit on a grad student's stipend. Again, not a bit of this was covered in my MSU oral exams.

I desperately wanted to peer into the lives of that lion family, but hanging around a spider-infested cave didn't hold much appeal. I needed a new way to see. I needed new tech. Fortunately, I knew just the man for the job. Tim Manley, a tech-savvy bear researcher, had built a remote camera housed in an army-green metal ammo box, with a motion sensor that tripped the camera. Efficient, simple to use—but very heavy—the "Manley Camera System" used a 35mm Olympus Infinity camera with a modified shutter, triggered by a signal from an infrared sensor. Powered by a car battery that lasted up to two weeks, the camera would *click* when an animal passed by the sensor, capturing it in exquisitely close detail, day or night.

It was more than clever. It was good science. The images provided a new view into nature and, most importantly, also allowed researchers to compare the ratio of marked and unmarked animals captured on film, thus providing an estimate of population size. Set up enough cameras, and you could count grizzly populations without having to handle the bears directly—good news for both the bears and the handlers. There were far too few mountain lions in my study area for that sort of population count to be practical, but the camera system was perfect for a researcher eager to photograph a family of cats in a cave.

Just one week after setting up the camera I returned to the cave: All thirty-six images had been exposed! I couldn't have been more thrilled—the camera worked better than I could have imagined, and so quickly too! I almost ran the eight miles out to the trailhead. When the film was developed I had three dozen high-quality, up-close-and-personal shots of a pack rat hustling over and around the bones. Perhaps the cats had returned as well, but I'd never know. The vain rodent had used up the entire roll of film in less than fifteen minutes. As for the cats, well, they were still invisible.

In the summer months, after a long day of following the directional beep of my telemetry receiver, I'd get as close as I could to the cat without being pushy. Then I'd down a cup of ramen noodles or a candy bar, break out my fleece jacket for a pillow, and go to sleep, ready to pick up the trail at first light. I'm at peace with myself when I am in the mountains. The worries of the world fall away out there. Everything seems enhanced, and my senses fire on all cylinders. Smells are more powerful, the light is sharper, the weather means more, and the untrammeled beauty around me is a comforting counterbalance to life's little traumas. It is sanctuary. The backcountry strips the world down to the bones, to the things that really matter. It's a perspective that can be found only in nature, and wilderness mountains have always been my cathedrals of choice. The Bob, with its ceiling of stars, never disappointed.

Lying under a tree all night, I heard every hoot owl and coyote cry, every twig snap, every distant thunderclap. And every noise was attributed, somewhere in the back of my monkey brain, to an approaching grizzly bear. I never had any real problems with *Arctos horriblis*, but the great grizzly was always on my mind as I slept under the limber pines. I figure we humans are just wired that way. Somehow, I never got quite the same chill from imagining a cat lurking in the dark. Which is odd, because while a mountain lion might be a pipsqueak compared to a grizzly, they're far more efficient killers—and until you handle a 180-pound male with a head the size of a basketball, you don't realize how big they really are. Luckily, humans just don't fit a lion's search profile as prey. We don't look like lion food. If we did, I'd have been lunch long ago.

The collared cats in our study were identified first by their gender and then by their number (for example: male 127's home range overlapped slightly with male 148's home area). But Rocky Heckman, a houndsman who knew more about the habits and behavior of these stealthy predators than anyone I'd ever met, typically named the cats we caught and collared. That's how the 120-pound lion I first called male 142 came to be known as 'Old Hoss.'

We tracked, treed, and tranquilized Hoss between Willow and Beaver Creeks, just behind the Sun River Wildlife Management Area. When I had climbed about halfway to his perch, I was greeted with a pungent stream of urine. *Fair enough*, I thought, *I shot you with a dart, you soiled my favorite hat.* It wasn't the first time a drugged mountain lion had peed on my head, and it wouldn't be the last. But it was the first time we'd captured a cat that was

We carefully lower a tranquilized mountain lion out of a tree near Elk Creek, Montana, by using a rope tied around its hind leg. JOHN MCCARTHY

missing an eye—probably the result of fight with a rival male. Hoss also had scars on his right shoulder.

Tracking Hoss over two years, we learned that the wily cat had a remarkably small home range—he was a homebody by necessity. His lack of stereoscopic vision and compromised depth perception restricted his hunting area, making him an incredibly specialized cat. Still, his ability to survive, and even thrive, was remarkable because a puma's see-in-the-dark vision is perhaps the biggest asset in its predatory arsenal.

At 120 pounds, Old Hoss was a bit smaller than an average male but he sure knew how to kill sheep. All but one of his documented kills were bighorns, two of them full-curl rams, which can weigh up to 200 pounds. Of the twenty-three mountain lions we equipped with radio collars, the adults ranged from 70 to 150 pounds. Females are considerably smaller than males, but both kill animals much larger than themselves. It's remarkable, actually. Although they sometimes leap from above onto the back of their prey, the usual method is to stalk and ambush from ground level. The stalk concludes in a lightning-fast sprint and a leap to knock the victim off balance, followed by that quick, killing bite to the windpipe. A big cat's muscular jaws and long canine teeth are evolved to cut through to bone, slicing muscle and tendon, and can crush with tremendous force—up to 350 pounds per square inch.

Of all the kills I examined, only twenty-nine were recent enough that I could determine cause of death. The vast majority—two-thirds—died via a bite to the windpipe. About a fourth of the kills were attributed to a bite to the face, evident because the prey had had its nasal-jaw region removed. And ten percent—the small mammals—were simply decapitated. Snacks, really.

Hoss, with his one good eye, was particularly specialized. Unlike most males, which patrol a far wider range, he never left his pocket of bighorn sheep country. The last time I saw him was from the air, on a monitoring flight. He was lying in wait, strategically, on a migratory route that took unsuspecting bighorn sheep through a narrow chute of rocky limestone. My money was on Hoss.

Of course, even with just one good eye Old Hoss was better at finding me than I was at finding him. Had it not been for houndsmen such as Rocky Heckman and Kelly Hirsch, and their fearless dogs, I never would have had the opportunity to spy into Hoss' wild world. During my first winter in Augusta, state biologist John McCarthy and I were driving west on Sun River Canyon Road, looking for lion tracks in new snow. Behind us were Rocky and Kelly and their dogs, Boone and Wino. As we rounded a bend, John told me to pull over. Snow was falling, adding another few inches to the foot already on the ground. The black-and-tan hounds were already baying loudly as we stepped out of the rig.

Rocky released the dogs from their leashes and they bolted into the forest. We followed, but in a matter of minutes their plaintive cries were barely audible. Hustling through a stand of pine, we slipped and slid up and down a slick and rocky trail that dropped to a steep drainage. Lions always take you to places you would never normally go. It never fails. When we finally caught up to the baying dogs, Rocky studied the cat tracks at the base of a large Douglas fir, then looked up. "Lion kittens!" he shouted. "Two of them."

Apparently, the hounds had tracked an adult female to the tree where she'd hidden her kittens. After fending off the hounds, she'd fled, attempting to draw the dogs away. I moved a few low-hanging spruce branches and discovered two black-spotted furry bundles on a soft bed of pine needles. I jotted down their genders, then aged them by examining how far their teeth had emerged from the gums. I quickly returned them to their secret hiding place—I always try to minimize animal handling, but sometimes it's necessary to collect the biological data we need to protect the species.

The dogs seemed none the worse for their adventure, so Rocky set them back on the momma cat's trail, and we hustled off down into the gulch. Soon enough we heard the sharp staccato barking that signaled: *treed cat*. There, twenty feet up a fir, was an angry female mountain lion. Of course she was angry, we had chased her with her kittens. Can't argue with that. I darted her with a rapid-acting tranquilizing drug that left her sufficient muscle control to maintain her grip on the branch. After climbing the tree with a rope—while pungent cat piss again spattered my hat—I lowered her to the ground, weighed and measured her, fitted her with a radio collar, and waited about forty-five minutes for her to recover.

It wasn't long before momma cat got to her feet and shook off the dusting of snow that had covered her. Then, with barely a glance in our direction, she made her way slowly up the hillside, back to her waiting kittens.

Hers were the first newborn kittens I'd ever come across. I've never found a litter of more than three kittens, but litters of four and five have been reported. It's hard to imagine a momma lion providing for five kittens; usually only two survive to become adults. It's a hard world, being a top predator in wild country, and these females need to be in excellent condition if they're to successfully raise kittens into adulthood. Most female lions don't even begin to breed until they've established a home range, normally at two or more years of age. In the Northern Hemisphere, breeding activity peaks in early winter, with kittens born in late winter or early spring.

I hold a tranquilized mountain lion that we darted deep in the Bob Marshall Wilderness in Montana. JIM WILLIAMS COLLECTION

The kittens we found looked good and healthy, and were a bit feisty already. They both sported dark black spots and were completely without scent, the better to hide them from predators. Their tiny claws met my hands as I reached for them, and their remarkable lion eyes were not even open yet. That would happen in another week or so. It may well have been the only time I saw a cat when it didn't see me. Still, they immediately sensed I was not mom. I knew these kittens had a steep learning curve ahead, and needed to learn how to kill prey as quickly as possible, or face starvation. For now, though, mom would keep them fed, until they moved out on their own—usually somewhere between fifteen and twenty-four months.

Mountain lion family structure is not so different from the other, relatively nonsocial, wild cats of the world. They don't live in visible extended family groups, or prides, like the African lions do. Rather, both male and female mountain lions are for the most part solitary, and hunt on their own. Females usually spend a year or two with their kittens, and that rearing-time represents the larger social unit for mountain lions. Some females will tolerate others in their home range, sharing space year-round with other female relatives, and occasionally even nonrelatives. Almost all young lions disperse from these natal areas, though, which is one reason connected and protected habitat is so critical to their survival—they need to move. It's surely an adaptation evolved to spread their DNA across large landscapes, and to prevent inbreeding.

Unlike the females, mature males rarely share a home range. When they do overlap, unrelated males often fight, sometimes to the death. Perhaps that's how Old Hoss lost his eye and earned those scars? Males have been known to share space, however, when they occupy different parts of their core home range at different times of the year. This can be especially true in areas of high prey density, such as a concentrated winter range for a large herd of elk. These big boys aren't being social cats, but are instead putting up with each other because the seasonal buffet is just so darn good.

Knowing what a cat needs to get by is the first step toward knowing how to protect it. And earning that knowledge requires that scientists team up with the folks who know this country best. Folks you might meet at the Buckhorn Bar.

Rocky Heckman, for one, saved my bacon too many times to count during those long-ago winters I spent in Augusta. Born and bred in northern Montana, Rocky was long-legged and looked every bit the western outdoorsman in his cowboy packer boots and hat, blue jeans, and studded shirt. His father was an accomplished outfitter and, years later his wife, son, and daughters would follow him into the family business. He was a skilled horseman, hunter, and hound handler, a fisherman, and a mule packer—not to mention a first-rate storyteller. He knew how to build a fire in a blizzard, and he knew his way back to the trailhead when you couldn't see five feet in front of you. Simply put, he knew how to stay alive in the wild. And he loved mountain lions. Which is why biologist John McCarthy paired me with Rocky and Kelly Hirsch that first winter.

I was still figuring out which way was north the day he took me on the trail of a huge male, who refused to be treed way back in the wilderness. "This tom," Rocky said, looking at a paw print, "is a pie-plater." I looked at the print. Yep. It did seem that, without much of a squeeze, you could fit an average-sized apple pie in that indentation in the snow. It was around three o'clock when stinging snow started blowing sideways. The sun was dropping behind the mountains and the temperature, which Rocky guessed was ten below zero, was sure to plummet still lower, but the chase was leading us deeper into the mountains. Finally, we caught up with his wet, weary dogs. Everything in me was screaming, *Let's get out of here!* But Rocky said, "The dogs, and both of us, are wet and freezing. We need to stop now."

I figured stopping was a terrible idea. I was ready to panic just at the thought of stopping. We needed to *go*. But in a matter of minutes, Rocky had gathered a dry pile of branches by reaching under the snow-covered boughs of nearby spruce and snapping the older twigs off. In a few more he had a warm fire going, the flames a comfortable sight in a whiteout. The shivering dogs stopped shivering. We even dried our wool undergarments by standing close to the flames—which made the ten mountain miles' trek to my backcountry cabin if not pleasant, then much less unpleasant than it could have been. There was no room for error, but Rocky understood exactly how to play the margins.

It's hard to say exactly what I learned during those three years on Montana's Rocky Mountain Front. Some of it certainly had to do with mountain lion habits and habitats. That's important stuff. But some of it also had to do with people, and how they relate to wild nature. And some had to do with me, and my relationship to what's wild. And that's important stuff, too. Because in a world run by humans, you can't protect nature unless you understand humans.

When I closed my notebook on the last of my fieldwork, I opened a new chapter of thesis writing. Back to Bozeman, to wrangle years of hard-won data into a narrative that those with the power to affect the lives of these big cats could use to inform their decisions. I'm still not sure what's more grueling, the Buckhorn brawls, the miles of backcountry, the winter storms, the wild wind, or the final thesis work. Hard to say, really. But I do know this: none of it—not one bit of it—was clearly captured in those oral exams.

Hours, days, weeks of sorting and analyzing the data, testing hypotheses; six months, finally, to complete the statistical analysis needed to see the

Two newborn mountain lion kittens—they haven't even opened their eyes yet—were hidden by their mother at the base of a large spruce tree. Sun River Wildlife Management Area, Montana. JIM WILLIAMS

trends clearly. What do these cats need to survive? They need freedom to roam, and diverse habitats, and "meat with feet," and tolerance from their human neighbors.

When I finally stood in front of Dr. Picton and his peers to defend my thesis, I couldn't help but be struck by how much he hadn't told me about where this journey would take me. Like I said, he never was much for detailed instruction. And for that, I will be forever grateful.

CHAPTER 4

GENE FLOW:
CATS ON THE MOVE

Scientists who play by someone else's rules don't have much chance of making discoveries.

– Jack Horner, MSU paleontologist

I n September 1988, Montana rancher Kathy Wankel and her husband were hiking around Fort Peck Reservoir when she spied a three-inch piece of bone sticking out of the ground. It turned out to be the arm of a *Tyrannosaurus rex*, and the tangle of bones unearthed over the next two years was one of the most complete T-rex skeletons ever found. Tipping the scales at seven tons, the "Wankel rex" was thirty-eight feet long and tall enough to slurp soup from a bowl set on top of the eighteen-wheel FedEx truck that recently transported it to the Smithsonian in Washington, DC. That's where it will spend the next fifty years, on loan from the Museum of the Rockies in Bozeman.

A bronze replica of the boney beast, its conical, serrated teeth as big as bananas and set like daggers in a jaw as long as a baseball bat, still stands full snarl in front of the Bozeman museum. Affectionately known as "Big Mike"—after former Montana State University president Mike Malone— the giant carnivore was eighteen years old when he met his violent end on a river bed in what is now eastern Montana. The Bozeman museum is also home to Montana's Jack Horner, noted paleontologist and technical dino- saur expert for the film *Jurassic Park.* Jack was the inspiration for the lead character in *Jurassic Park,* and worked with Steven Spielberg on all of the dinosaur films.

"Big Mike," the *Tyrannosaurus,* stands high just outside of the Museum of the Rockies on the campus of Montana State University in Bozeman, Montana. CAMERON LAWSON

To a wildlife biologist interested in evolutionary adaptation, dinosaurs are the rock stars of natural selection. They didn't just live on Earth for a long time. They dominated the planet for 135 million years. To put that figure in perspective, *Homo sapiens* have been around for only 200,000 years. and it was just 30,000 years ago that our Paleolithic ancestors painted woolly mammoths, panthers, hyenas, bears, and lions by torchlight in a cave in southeastern France.

The first dinosaurs—small, lightweight, bipedal, and carnivorous—appeared in the Triassic period, which began 252 million years ago. During the subsequent Jurassic period, the heyday of the "terrible lizard," Earth's colossal "supercontinent" split: North America and Eurasia settled up north; Africa, South America, Antarctica, Madagascar, and Australia shifted to the Southern Hemisphere. As the planet changed, so did the dinosaurs. The climate was generally warm and wet, generating lush growths of ferns and cycads and evergreen forests. Plant-eating dinosaurs grew huge and their carnivorous predators kept pace. It was a planet of plenty, and if you were a 1,500-pound *Utahraptor*, a two-ton *Gigantoraptor*, or a 100-ton *Argentinosauros*, life was a prehistoric beach. It took a giant asteroid slamming into the Yucatan Peninsula 66 million years ago to slow them down. Earth became a churning urn of uninhabitable funk: earthquakes, volcanoes, tsunamis, noxious gases, and dust that obscured the sun for a decade.

Fast-forward through 43 million years and three epochs to the Miocene, which lasted from 23 million to 5 million years ago. It was part of the Cenozoic Era, AKA the "age of mammals." Mammals exploded onto the scene, and it is during this lengthy biogeographic make-over that geneticists begin taking serious notes about the origins of the mountain lion—an old, deeply divergent lineage within the cat family *Felidae*.

Back then, India was drifting north toward Eurasia at a breakneck six inches per year, and the Tethys Ocean, which happened to be in the way, was squeezed dry. The resulting continental scrum produced the world's tallest mountain range, the Himalayas, as well as the European Alps. Further south, the Andes were born—a 4,300-mile range with fifty peaks soaring over 19,000 feet. That mountain rampart shaped the weather itself, capturing rain clouds that swept in off the Pacific and creating drier weather in southeast Patagonia. In North America, the Sierra Nevada and Cascade Mountains emerged, similarly causing more arid conditions in the center of the continent. Antarctica became isolated from the other continents, and the once-vast global ocean was slowly parceled into smaller seas separated by the newly arranged continents. That meant less mixing of warm tropical ocean water with cold polar water, causing more snow and ice to build up on Antarctica and accelerating the development of a cooler and drier planet, governed by seasons. Grasslands expanded, forests dwindled, and herbivores thrived amid this new bounty of grass. And, of course, so did the predators that ate them. Predators like pumas.

By the middle of the Miocene, say ten or fifteen million years ago, Earth looked much as it does today—but it was hardly stable. Things were still moving. Plate tectonics had driven planet-wide mountain building, which led to drier weather, which caused a drop in the sea levels around the world. That led to land bridges, which opened new routes for global mammal migrations. Around sixteen million years ago, a land bridge emerged across the Bering Strait, connecting Siberia and Alaska and allowing mammals that had evolved to meet the demands of settings such as Montana to migrate west into Eurasia and back. Five million years later (give or take a million), the volcanic Isthmus of Panama rose from the sea floor, creating a similar bridge between Central and South America.

With corridors established between Africa and Eurasia; Eurasia and North America; and North America and Central and South America, it was as if the gates of wildlife parks around the world were thrown open, allowing the residents to come and go as they pleased. And eventually, this series of intercontinental express lanes led to a game-changing exchange of flora and fauna, as rivers of DNA flowed across the planet, braiding, weaving, merging, cleaving, and flooding the world in a torrent of evolution. Toward the end of the Miocene—not so long ago, when measured against that T-Rex found up in Montana—the ancestors of today's humans split away from the ancestors of the chimpanzees, following their own evolutionary path. DNA comparisons suggest that hominoids and chimps diverged less than five million years ago, a blink of the evolutionary eye. "Life breaks free," said Michael Crichton, author of *Jurassic Park*. "Painfully, perhaps even dangerously. But life finds a way."

Though sometimes, it's more like what astronomer and *Cosmos* host Carl Sagan said: "Extinction is the rule. Survival is the exception." And certainly, more species have hit evolutionary dead ends than have persisted into our modern age. Historically, *Puma concolor* was genetically tied to a diverse cast of carnivores, including long-extinct felids such as the American lion (*Panthera leo atrox*) and the saber-toothed cat (*Smilodon fatalis*), as well as present-day species such as the cheetah (*Acinonyx trumani*) and the jaguarundi (*Herpailurus yagouaroundi*). For much of the two million years we call the "Great American Interchange," these large cats traveled freely between North and South America, spreading their genetics across the Western Hemisphere. Then, a couple million years ago, the ice arrived. Vast glaciers, creeping as far south as Philadelphia, carved a swath of extinction.

The cast of characters that vanished is a "Who's Who" of wonderfully weird mammals. North America lost the *chalicothere*, a hulking yet somehow cuddly creature that appears to be the result of a high-speed crash between a horse and tapir. Also lost were the alarmingly well-toothed bear-dog (*Tomarcus*) and the beast known as the "hell pig" (*Entelodont*)—an opportunistic omnivore with the torso of a tank and mindset of a prison bully. Down in South America, the 200-pound flightless "terror bird" disappeared, as did crocodiles as long as a stretch limo and the sixty-foot *Megalodon*, the largest prehistoric shark of all time. The *glyptodont*, an armadillo the size of a VW beetle, was wiped out, and so were mammoths, mastodons, and—perhaps our popular culture's all-time favorite Miocene mammal—the saber-toothed cat.

There's much speculation among paleontologists as to why the menacing but dashing saber-tooth vanished. Saber-shaped teeth appeared in an early mammalian lineage roughly 50 million years ago, but the great age of true saber-tooth cats didn't begin until 15 million years ago. This powerful cat, distinguished by a pair of unwieldy canines maxing out at seven inches, was represented in various genera and species over time and lived throughout both North and South America for millions of years until they died out toward the end of the last Ice Age.

When scientists from the University of California at Berkeley started digging around the La Brea tar pits in downtown Los Angeles, back in 1901, they found a treasure trove of Pleistocene vertebrates including as many as 160,000 bones and 1,775 teeth of *Smilodon fatalis*, a saber-tooth that lived 2.5 million years ago and became extinct about 11,000 years ago. Perhaps the downtown LA location explains why these big cats have featured so prominently in Hollywood. Wild cats loom large in our imagination; it's no accident that *Smilodon fatalis* was chosen as California's state fossil rather than, say, the giant armadillo.

Though the bulk of the saber tooth diet consisted of long-legged grazers, *Smilodon* surely also hunted the occasional hominid, and perhaps it's the notion of man as prey that we find so fascinating. Writing about these prehistoric meat eaters, Montana author David Quammen notes that "They were part of the psychological context in which our sense of identity as a species arose." Which is to say: humans will never get over the fact that at one point in our history, we were a source of meat. The terror that the *Smilodon* engendered in our developing brains quite likely still colors our relationship with big carnivores today. Fortunately for us, humans are simply not part of the modern mountain lion's prey image. If we were, we'd be in trouble, given their prowess as predators. But the reality is, we are a far greater threat to them than they have ever been to us.

The mysterious Brazilian highlands are the cradle of wild felid evolution in the Americas. FRANS LANTING

Down in the tar pits, right alongside those saber-tooths, were the fossil-ized remains of early versions of the modern mountain lion—the same lion still with us today, surviving, thriving, expanding even. In fact, mountain lions today cover the largest latitudinal range of any large predator—rang-ing from Patagonia to the Yukon. They are efficient, adaptable, and flex-ible enough to live in habitats with virtually nothing in common—from snow-covered mountains to steamy tropical rain forests. And when even subtle changes in climate can be enough to wipe a species off the evolution-ary map, adaptability is a highly desirable trait.

Evolution has built, in the mountain lion, a finely tuned predator. And it all started, improbably, with a shrew-sized mammalian ancestor, back in the Miocene. From that humble genetic stock grew a family tree that includes cheetahs and jaguarundi (mini mountain lions) and pumas. Perhaps that's actually not so surprising; if shrews were the size of grizzly bears, we'd all be in trouble. They are voracious like nothing else I've seen in nature.

The limb of this family tree on which the mountain lion sits is a very specialized evolutionary branch, with features honed by time, topography, and targets. A long and limber tail, the better to balance in uneven terrain. A short gut, the better to process meat proteins. Eyes with more rods than cones, the better to see in the dark of dawn and dusk. A skull that positions the eyes right up front, the better to see with stereoscopic vision, giving the cats greater depth of field. Paws with furry covering and retractable claws, the better to stalk silent along the path. Tightly coiled muscle, the better to spring straight from a standstill to a sprint, quick as lightning. Longer rear legs than front legs, the better to leap through steep and broken country. A flexible spine, the better to remain agile in rocky mountain topography.

Wolves were built with the DNA to rule the flat bottom lands, to run prey down over many miles. Cats were built to reign in the vertical fringes, to ambush prey in the uneven breaks of mountain strongholds. This separation of niche habitats—driven by and reflected in species' physiology—reduces competition between the big predators, and gives cats the space to survive.

They are the sports cars of the predator world, built to go light and fast, tuned to squeeze efficiency from every bit of energy. And like the sports car, they burn through a lot of gas. Their short hair means they cool off quickly in high mountain country, need more calories to stay warm, and so hunt more frequently. That short hair also means they steer clear of the deep snow, choosing instead the steeper open slopes. The wolf is built for fuel economy, and can run all night through deep snow on the track of prey. The lion is built like an Olympic sprinter for zero-to-sixty in a flash, and relies on silence, stalk, and stealth.

It's a tremendously successful genetic model. And like the great white shark and other highly efficient predators, it's remained relatively unchanged for millennia—the product of thousands and thousands of years of fine tuning and successful offspring survival. The mountain lion is the perfect expression of genes, in terms of how to take down living meat. Through the expression of ancient genetics, lions have evolved a hunting style that maximizes efficiency while minimizing injury. Because like a race car or an elite athlete, they can't afford any room for error. If they're injured, they don't eat.

Our best guess—and it's still a guess because lions are like ghosts—based on years of reading tracks in the snow, is that mountain lion hunting success is upward of 75 percent. Missing isn't an option. But it's dangerous business, tangling with deer, elk, and sheep, with sharp hooves and sharper antlers. The cats need to be hard-hitting to take on prey so much bigger than themselves, one on one. And so they're tough, physically robust, layered in muscle—not fragile, like a lynx that lives on bunnies. Read the DNA and the story it tells is this: stay invisible, stalk silently, ambush in an instant, go for the soft spots. Paws like meat hooks, wrapping the flanks, rake forward to the trachea, away from hooves and antlers, and crush the windpipe. Fast. Effective. Deadly. I've had to read that story as reflected on the forest floor and in the snow, and as written on countless carcasses—because in all my years of tracking cats I've never once been lucky enough to actually witness the kill.

———

When I began doing research on mountain lions at MSU, I learned there were thirty-two separate subspecies, a family of close relatives all wired for the same hunt but taxonomically distinct. Montana was home to *Felis concolor missoulensis*. Over in Colorado they had their own subspecies, *Felis concolor hippolestis*. It was pretty easy to remember where the subspecies *oregonensis* and *vancouverensis* were located; I had a harder time with *stanleyana* (Mexico) and *improcera* (Baja). These mountain lion subspecies had been set and reset by taxonomists—the folks who study evolutionary relationships—dating all the way back to Linnaeus.

Taxonomists generally fall into one of two species themselves—lumpers or splitters. Lumpers look to simplify, while splitters see separate subspecies everywhere, based on geography, skull measurements, tooth structure, and even the outward appearance of a few unusual individuals. I'm sure the splitters had their reasons for separating *missoulensis* from *hippolestis*, but all I know is that one day we learned a hunter in Colorado had shot one of the lions we had collared in Montana. Since then, Montana hunters have killed cats that had been marked in the Dakotas, Wyoming, Alberta, and Colorado. It seems the splitters hadn't taken into account how far these big cats travel, and the ability of lions to pioneer new habitats.

More recently, the science of molecular genetics (DNA) has revolutionized taxonomy. Rather than relying on appearance and fine-scale skull measurements, scientists can now trace DNA and genetic components through time to determine how closely animals are related and whether they share genetic material. Dr. Stephen O'Brien pioneered this new field, sorting out the complicated genetics of the African cheetah. On his heels came Dr. Melanie Culver, who took on the challenge of tidying up the tangle of puma lineage. Together, Culver and O'Brien formed a team that, ultimately, produced one of the most influential studies in the annals of mountain lion science.

The scope of her project was mind-boggling. Culver's team collected biological samples from 315 mountain lions across all of the thirty-two presumed subspecies—from the Canadian north to the Patagonian south. The samples came from wild lions, lions in zoos or other captive facilities, and even fifty-four museum specimens. The researchers extracted DNA from white blood cells, skin, and other tissues of the live animals; and the hide, hair, and bones of cats long since dead. The team focused on mitochondrial DNA, which evolves far more quickly than other forms of DNA and is passed on only from the mother. This genetic sampling gave her a clean "haplotype"—a linked string of mutations that, when analyzed, allowed Culver to clearly identify true subspecies.

When the dust settled, Culver's team recognized just six groups of mountain lions in all of the Americas that were genetically distinct enough to be considered true subspecies. The new groups were, not surprisingly, loosely associated with geographic barriers such as large rivers or other bodies of water, which can block the flow of DNA between local lion populations. Given enough evolutionary time, these barriers create the genetic traits of distinct subspecies.

All the mountain lions in North and Central America—as far south as Nicaragua—were assigned to the same group. South of Nicaragua lives another group, largely inhabiting the tropical rainforests of Central America. Four distinct groups prowl South America: the central group, in the Pampas grasslands between the Rio Parana and Rio Negro; the eastern group, in the Brazilian Highlands and the Amazon and Paraguay river basins; and the northern group, in the diverse high- and low-elevation habitats of Peru, Columbia, and Venezuela. The last and sixth group to be identified stalks southern South America, occupying the mountain and windy steppe habitats in the heart of wild Patagonia, stretching across both Argentina and Chile.

While reducing the number of mountain lion subspecies from thirty-two to six was a boon to sleep-deprived felid graduate students everywhere, far more important were the team's discoveries about the diversity of the continental gene pools. Generally speaking, the more diverse the gene pool of a given population, then the older, healthier, and more adaptable (think climate change and habitat fragmentation) the population is likely to be. Dr. Culver determined that the eastern South American group was the most ancestral, and that all modern mountain lions are likely descendants of this subspecies. In fact, many wild cat species originated in the vast, lush Brazilian Highlands: the cradle of modern felid evolution in the New World.

By contrast, the North American subgroup had the least genetic diversity. Remember that massive extinction event at the end of the last Ice Age, which eliminated the bear-dog, the hell pig, and 80 percent of the larger mammalian species in North America? Well, the limited genetic diversity seen in the North American group has helped confirm that mountain lions, too, were eliminated at that same time, probably due to radical changes in habitat and available prey. Competition from other big carnivores might also have been a factor. It took a while, but eventually North America was recolonized by a relatively small number of founding travelers from the Brazilian Highlands—meaning that not all of the ancestral, original mountain lion DNA combinations made it up here. This is how North American lions came to be squeezed, evolutionarily, in a "genetic bottleneck."

While the Brazilian pumas were never separated from other mountain lion groups, and so could continue to diversify, the North American lions had no option but to inbreed. This continues to this day for the isolated Florida panther population, and may also be an issue for some local populations that have become isolated due to overhunting. This suggests to wildlife scientists that our North American mountain lion might prove somewhat less adaptable than their South American counterparts when it comes to excessive predator control or environmental shifts such as climate change.

The dangers of limited genetic diversity are real, and DNA bottlenecks have played havoc with isolated populations. The most striking example, perhaps, is the Florida panther, a relict population that once was distributed from Florida and Georgia to Arkansas and Louisiana, but today is confined to Big Cypress Swamp and the Everglades. Hunting brought these panthers to near extinction, and even after they were protected under the Endangered Species Act their numbers remained low, still below fifty in 1980.

Florida panthers are quite adept at roaming under the subtropical forest canopy of south Florida near Everglades National Park. FRANS LANTING

Loss and fragmentation of panther habitat was clearly a barrier to their recovery: the cats were surrounded by water on three sides and cut off from the north by the crush of sun-loving, Disney-worshipping, snow birds who migrated to Florida each winter and urbanized every square inch of buildable land. It's not just Florida; North America's mountain lions have now been displaced from two-thirds of their historic habitat. But genetics research revealed another problem with the Florida population, common in domesticated animals but rarely observed in wildlife populations: severe inbreeding. The lack of genetic diversity has left the panther population with a high incidence of kinked tails and cowlicks (a whorl in the fur between the shoulder blades), classic signs of inbreeding. But the bigger problems, in terms of successful reproduction and a thriving population, were all the un-descended testicles, male sterility, heart defects, and compromised immune systems. A dearth of DNA diversity was literally killing the population.

And here's why science matters, and why Dr. Melanie Culver and other wildlife geneticists are so important to our field: Armed with this genetic information, those in charge of panther recovery began to introduce new genetic material into the population. To emulate the natural flow of genes between adjacent populations, eight female mountain lions from Texas were released into vacant Florida habitats in 1995. (Despite their names, mountain lions, panthers, and pumas are all the same species.) Within five years, 20 percent of the Texan genes had been integrated into the Florida population, sparking dramatic improvements in the health and size of the population—which now exceeds 100.

Today, there are so many Florida panthers that livestock conflicts are now occurring again on the expanding fringe of their range—an odd way to measure success, perhaps, but success nonetheless for the panther population. Florida's habitat problems of course, remain unsolved, and are perhaps unsolvable. These cats will need freedom to roam and a wild, connected Florida if they are to maintain the gene flow needed to survive. It's all about tolerance now—can people put up with wild nature? But despite the habitat challenges, the genetic lessons learned in Florida can be applied to other isolated populations—such as the mountain lions of Washington's Olympic Peninsula and of British Columbia's Vancouver Island—should the need arise. Science matters.

Lions are evolved to survive, to thrive, to expand, and to explore. They have proved to be one of the most adaptable large predators on the planet today. At a time when the grim trend for carnivores, especially large cats, is toward contraction and localized extinction, mountain lions are maintaining and magnifying their reach. This despite the fact that we continue to convert their habitat into farms and ranches, that they kill the occasional domestic sheep or alpaca, and that, on those most rarest of occasions, they even attack humans. These big cats are flexible, adaptable, able to find a suitable meal from the Canadian Yukon to Chilean Patagonia, and all with just six narrowly separated subspecies. They are hard wired to make it, largely through natural selection's greatest gift—secrecy—which allows them to slip through our world unnoticed, without a trace. For a wild cat in the twenty-first century, having the genetics to remain invisible to humans may be the most important survival mechanism of all.

CHAPTER 5

CONNECTIVITY BENEFITS BIGHORNS AND BIG CATS

It was a place in the Gates where the struggle between mountains and plains came face to face—below Mann Gulch belonged to the plains, upriver to the mountains and timber.

– Norman Maclean, *Young Men and Fire*

I t was already snowing when we released the hounds. We were tracking a large male mountain lion through Mann Gulch, a steep canyon in Montana's famed Gates of the Mountains Wilderness Area. Sandwiched between the Bob Marshall and Sleeping Giant wilderness areas to the north and Yellowstone to the south, the Gates is remote, pristine, and powerful. On both sides of the Missouri River, wind-worn limestone cliffs rise 1,200 feet like the walls of an abandoned fortress.

I'd been in Mann Gulch before though never in the winter tracking cats and bighorn sheep. I had also flown (bounced around, actually, pummeled by wind) over this winter range in bush planes and helicopters counting wildlife. It was January 1997, and I was working for Montana Fish, Wildlife, and Parks as a professional wildlife biologist. My area ranged from the White Cliffs of the Missouri River out east, to the Little Belt and Big Belt Mountains out west. Mann Gulch and the Gates stood sentinel over the northern end of the Big Belts.

By '97 I had also met and married my wife, Melora, back in the Flathead Valley. I'd fallen for her charms instantly, and within three months we were married. She prepared gourmet picnics for our dates, which we ate along the shores of Flathead Lake or in the high mountains of Glacier National Park, and she introduced me to fine wine and good coffees. After

You need to get up high to find some signals. Here I'm homing in on an adult male in the Gates of the Mountains Wilderness Area, Montana. TERRY ENK

all those meals at the Buckhorn, she finally taught me what good food really tastes like. Together, we'd eventually crossed the Continental Divide to Great Falls, and I began my career as a state wildlife biologist. And now, a few years in, we had a three-year-old son, Jake, and a younger daughter, Mackenzie, to fill our small but cozy Great Falls home. We were young and in love and excited to share a Montana lifetime with each other and raise a family.

Having recently survived graduate school, it was my turn now to advise a student on a research project for Dr. Picton. Terry Enk was two years into a three-year doctoral study, assessing the impact of mountain lion predation on bighorn sheep. As mentioned in chapter one there had been a major die-off of sheep in the Gates—their numbers, ravaged by disease, had fallen from 300 to just over fifty. We'd introduced thirty new sheep into the herd, but the population wasn't rebounding. Lambs weren't surviving their first year. Enk aimed to figure out why.

As luck would have it, this question overlapped with another one that was of great interest to me: the size of the range for mountain lions in and around the Beartooth Wildlife Management Area. The scientific community was also becoming increasingly focused on wildlife connectivity—the ability of animals to move between core habitats, to maintain contact with distant populations, and to keep the gene pool strong. The Gates formed a natural corridor between Yellowstone National Park and the Bob Marshall Wilderness, which in turn led to Glacier National Park and the Canadian Rockies. It was a key link in a chain of wildlife connections that folks had taken to calling Yellowstone to Yukon, or Y2Y for short. If we could collar a mountain lion here in the Gates, we could learn how far it wanted to travel—or at least how far it could.

Terry called me at my Great Falls office late one day to say he'd found the tracks of a large male lion in the snow just east of Mann Gulch. Would I like to assist with the capture? Of course I would. I was still new to the desk, but already missed trailing lion hounds into wild places. As a wildlife management biologist, my current job was to work with people—lots of people of all types—to survey and inventory wildlife, and to create policies that improve wildlife populations and habitat. Because I spent a lot of time drinking cowboy coffee, fixing fences with landowners, and solving wildlife-related problems with ranchers and farmers, there wasn't much time for pursuing the hounds that chase the cats. The idea of getting back on the trail was more than enough to override the weather warnings about an Arctic front due to blow in from the north later that day. Weather comes with the territory, so I packed my rig and headed to Mann Gulch.

Rocky Mountain bighorn sheep are safe from predators in their vertical world of rocks in western Montana.
STEVEN GNAM

If Mann Gulch sounds familiar, that's because it was the site of one of the worst wildland firefighting disasters in American history, immortalized in Norman Maclean's book *Young Men and Fire*. The summer of 1949 had been exceptionally hot and dry, and August 5 cooked at ninety-seven degrees under a stiff wind. A lightning strike had sparked a fire in Mann

Gulch, and fifteen smokejumpers from Missoula parachuted into the blaze. They landed in waist-high prairie grass—crisp and brown and crackling dry—high on the north side of the gulch. The fire had spread across just sixty acres by the time it was first spotted, and hadn't grown much when the jumpers arrived. The head of the crew, Wagner Dodge, had seen far worse.

But ninety minutes after they landed, the fire leaped the gulch. Fueled by the tall grass and winds gusting to forty miles per hour, it blazed into a colossal blowup—"two hundred feet of flame in the sky." With their path to the river blocked, the firefighters turned and headed up the nearly vertical slope. They had a 150-yard head start, maybe 200 yards at best. "This is a story," Maclean wrote, "in which cartography and plot are much the same thing."

Were it not for Maclean, an Iowa native who taught English at the University of Chicago for forty-three years, the events of that tragic day would be long forgotten. Author of the classic *A River Runs Through It*, Maclean spent fourteen years writing *Young Men and Fire* and died before the manuscript was complete. Published posthumously in 1992, it won the National Book Award and changed the way wildfires are fought in North America. And for readers like me, who savored every page, it turned a remote and grassy hillside littered with crosses into hallowed ground.

The January sun was just rising when I met Terry at the Willow Creek campground, just north of Mann Gulch. It was two degrees Fahrenheit, far colder with wind chill, and fire was the last thing on my mind. The sky was gray as wet slate, and whitecaps raced across Holter Lake. We were joined by hound handler Gary Langford and a wildlife biologist, Craig Jourdonnais, known for the outdoor footage he supplied local TV stations. *Let's find this big tom cat quick*, I thought, *and get the heck out of here before we get caught in the cold and end up as wool-clad popsicles.*

Much to my dismay, the baying dogs sprinted straight up Mann Gulch, toward a high ridge now barely visible in the falling snow. Before long, the hounds' plaintive cry was swallowed by wind. Roughly halfway up Mann Gulch, the gentle slope turns into a pitch that's as steep as a thatched roof. Head down, sweating hard even in the icy wind, I followed the dog-on-lion tracks that led us from one ridge to another. The cold scorched my lungs and my quads burned as I trudged higher. "If it keeps snowing this hard," Gary said, "we're going to lose the tracks." We nodded, too breathless to reply. Craig shifted the big movie camera on his shoulder, looking a bit like a Himalayan Sherpa, and kept pushing up the slope, into the advancing storm.

―――――――

Where the smokejumpers landed on the north side of Mann Gulch, the tall grass was dry as dust. The fire was below them, on the south side, and above was a rim of rock, a natural fire break that resembled the armored plates of a stegosaurus. At 5:35 p.m., Wagner Dodge watched the blaze leap across the gulch, cutting off access to the river. The men—most between the ages of seventeen and twenty-three—had been heading down toward the fire; now the blaze was climbing swiftly toward them. Dodge began leading his crew back up the tortuous incline. At 5:53 p.m., with the fire 500 feet behind, Dodge ordered the men to drop their heavy packs and tools—and to run. "It roared from behind, below, and across," Maclean wrote, "and the crew, inside it, was shut out from all but a small piece of the outside world."

Walter Rumsey, one of the two men who made it over the rocky ridge, said of his frantic dash: "I kept thinking the ridge—if I can make it … I could not definitely see the ridge from where we were. We kept running up since it had to be there somewhere. Might be a mile and a half or a hundred feet—I had no idea."

My first time in Mann Gulch—hiking through the charred trees during a hot, dry summer—I stopped to read the names on the thirteen concrete crosses anchored to a steep slope of swaying prairie bunchgrass. It was about this spot where Dodge, realizing he couldn't reach the ridge in time, had the sudden inspiration to light an "escape fire"—essentially torching a small patch of ground to starve the main fire of fuel, so that it would pass around his scorched parcel. He shouted to his men to join him, but either they couldn't decipher his instructions or chose to ignore him, and they raced ever upward. Pressing his face to the freshly blackened ground, Dodge found a precious inch of oxygen as the inferno passed around him and managed to survive. Rumsey and seventeen-year-old Robert Sallee made it to the ridge, and then to a barren rockslide that stopped the flames. The others succumbed on the hillside.

―――――――

Visited during the summer, Mann Gulch has the somber, contemplative feel of a cemetery. But in winter, in a howling wind with the snow blowing sideways, it's more like a battlefield. I barely noticed when we passed the last of the crosses, the sticky snow rounding its hard edges. Once on top, I stood below the immense limestone ridge—the remains of a prehistoric ocean reef—and paused to catch my breath. The lion's prints tracked on, over the limestone rampart and into the deeply incised Meriwether Canyon. Heading down, into the wind now, my hands and feet were growing numb. We'd been pushing hard for more than four hours, barely pausing to eat or drink. While it was a relief to be on the forgiving side of gravity, my old duct-taped storm jacket and wool pants were caked in snow, my long underwear drenched in sweat. We were in a remote canyon in the middle of a storm late in the day, and I was well aware that our margin for error had grown very thin. Now, actions would have consequences.

We had perhaps two hours of daylight remaining, and as we slipped and stumbled down the rocky reef to the river, I longed for my skis to speed the descent. Finally, the ribbon of the Missouri appeared and we could hear the familiar baying of the lion hounds over the wind ripping down the river. "I think they're going to tree the cat inside Meriwether Canyon," Terry said, and we turned back into the wind.

Following the tracks along the river's edge, we scrambled over rocks slick as soap. It was three o'clock and snowing sideways. Days are short here in the northern winter. When we finally reached Meriwether campground—little more than a port-o-potty and a picnic table—I was shaking hard, uncontrollably. Back in those days, we still didn't know how to layer our winter clothing properly. Gary studied the tracks around a large fir tree. "The dogs treed the cat," he said, "but it must have jumped and boogied further up into the canyon."

Kudos to the cat, I thought. We'd left at daybreak and had been on the move for almost nine hours, and continuing on in this storm had disaster written all over it. We needed to turn around, it would take at least another three hours to get back to the rigs—and cold and wet as I was, I thought there was a decent chance I wouldn't make it and would need to hunker down for the night and weather the Arctic storm. I can't remember who suggested we burn the campground picnic table, but I know I jumped at the idea and helped to pull the rickety benches apart with stiff hands. Once the fire was blazing, we stripped off our wool coats and sweaters and huddled around the fire to dry our undergarments in the swirling snow.

Did the picnic table—a fire in Mann Gulch—save our lives? All I know is, we were lucky. We'd get home that night, late but alive. "Probably most catastrophes end this way, without an ending," Maclean wrote.

"Let's get out of here," Gary said. He stepped away from the blaze and fired three rapid pistol shots to call the dogs. We waited a little longer until finally he shook his head. The cat was leading those hounds deeper into the Gates, and there was nothing we could do about it. When we finally made it back to the road, our vehicles were buried in a foot of new snow. Gary left his wool jacket inside the hound box, hoping the dogs would follow our tracks back. Sure thing, next morning he found them asleep inside their nearly buried shelter. The lion was long gone, most likely curled snug in a den, somewhere in Meriwether Canyon.

Two weeks later, the same male tomcat was back in the Beartooth region. The weather was better, and this time Terry got a radio collar on him. We tracked his movements for months—clearly this 150-pound lion was the resident male in the Beartooth. We learned he was traveling from the Beartooth to the Big Belts and across Holter Lake to the Sleeping Giant, a tremendous range of wild country. This taught us two very important things: first, a mountain lion would want to travel that distance; and second, he was able to make his way between the two wilderness areas unimpeded.

The key word here is unimpeded. For many animals living in cold climates, migration is as important an adaptation as is a thick coat of winter fur. Mule deer in northeastern Montana travel an average of sixty-four miles from their winter range west of Glasgow to their summer fawn-rearing sites up north, in Saskatchewan. Canadian pronghorn migrate south for a hundred miles or more to reach their winter range in Montana's Missouri Breaks. Elk that summer in Yellowstone National Park travel some 125 miles north, to winter at Dome Mountain Wildlife Management Area in the Paradise Valley.

Even animals considered the stay-at-home types must move in order to escape bad weather, to locate better food, or to find a mate. Every summer, Glacier National Park's mountain goats negotiate steep cliffs to reach salt licks several miles away. Moose in the Cabinet Mountains Wilderness travel a dozen miles in deep December snow, downhill from high alpine lake basins to the Fisher River Basin near Libby. Grizzlies make sweeping seasonal "food migrations" to find high-protein bear-friendly fare like cutworm moths, huckleberries, and white bark pine cone seeds. Nature is a nomad, and she needs to move.

These migratory patterns are as old as the barnacles on Noah's ark. What's new is the residential sprawl in western Montana, and the oil and gas fields in the state's eastern reaches, that come with miles of fences and roads. These obstacles often disrupt "connectivity"—the degree to which animals can move through the landscape from one place to another. One 2012 study revealed that a radio-collared pronghorn, fleeing frigid winter conditions south of Glasgow, traveled more than 350 miles, alongside other migrating pronghorns. But during an aerial survey that same winter, researchers spotted 400 pronghorn, trying to migrate south across east-central Montana, blocked by a barbed-wire fence. With nowhere to go, they lay down in the crippling cold (forty degrees below zero) to conserve energy. Eventually, they found a gap in the wire and continued their journey. But that was just one of the many fences they would face, and there wouldn't always be a gap. Fences, farms, and freeways; subdivisions; dogs, guns, and poisons: It's one hell of a commute, even when the weather is cooperating.

Up in Mann Gulch country, in the Gates of the Wilderness, wild bighorn sheep have long migrated along historic routes from summer habitat in the mountains to winter grazing in the foothills. Come spring, they reverse course and follow the new growth uphill from low-elevation winter range to alpine summer range. Some sheep in the Bob Marshall Wilderness migrate just a few miles, while others travel forty miles each way. Because bighorn sheep don't deviate from established seasonal ranges, biologists speculate that most Rocky Mountain bighorns follow migration routes that were established 12,000 years ago, at the tail end of the last Ice Age.

But by 1935, due to overhunting and disease, the native bighorns that had been migrating between the Gates and the Beartooth Wilderness Areas were nearly gone. Between 1971 and 1975, the state relocated 113 sheep from the Sun River to the Beartooth Wildlife Management Area, and by 1983 the population had swelled to 300 and had once again established some seasonal migration paths. But these newcomers didn't know the old routes, and never did complete the full historic migration.

Then another wave of disease swept through, decimating the herd and leaving just fifty-one survivors in its wake. Again the state biologists intervened, transplanting more sheep to the area. By 1995—the year Terry Enk embarked on his three-year bighorn study—there were seventy sheep in the Gates, but the herd was in trouble. Not only were these bighorns *not* migrating at all, but the lambs, which appeared robust in the late summer, were dying off by late fall. Why was the herd failing? Why had they stopped migrating? What were the disease vectors? Why was lamb survival so dismal? And how did predation from big cats fit into the mix, if at all?

Terry's research eventually showed that many of the wild bighorns had rubbed noses with domesticated sheep on private land, and contracted lung worm pneumonia. Because the resulting die-off claimed many of the older ewes—the leaders that initiate and guide the herd migration of the herd—the Beartooth WMA bighorns had literally lost their way. The herd had "forgotten" the old routes. This was devastating to the lambs, who in the hot and dry of late August must switch from mother's milk to an all-veggie diet. Had the herd moseyed higher up on the Beartooth, or into the Gates, the lambs could have dined on green, nitrogen-rich bunchgrass and forbs. But by staying put in the lowlands, where summer sun had parched the green to brown, the lambs were forced a diet of dry, nutrient-deficient forage, leaving them undernourished and more susceptible to pneumonia and predation.

Terry's study answered the key question: living year-round on the winter range was not a successful strategy. Turns out, mountain lion predation was not preventing the recovery of the bighorn population. It was a chain of events, and the first link was people—or, more specifically, the proximity of domesticated sheep. The lions might add some small degree of insult to the injury, but the damage had been done long before the predator arrived. That means we can't blame the carnivore, though often we do. It also means that restoring this historic herd will require time measured in generations. To this day, we are still dealing with poor lamb survival in the Gates, though there have been several more wildfires on the Beartooth WMA and the native bunchgrass is in great shape. All we need now are some sheep that will migrate when the going gets hot.

———————

While Terry was gathering data on sheep, we were gathering data on mountain lions and feeding it to Dr. Lance Craighead, executive director of the Craighead Institute. The institute is a conservation and wildlife research group, founded in 1964 by his father, the renowned grizzly researcher Dr. Frank Craighead and Frank's brother John. An expert in habitat connectivity, genetics, and conservation planning, Lance had been mapping the range of large carnivores that travel through wildlife corridors between Glacier and Yellowstone. His focus was bears and wolves, but when we approached him with the idea of including mountain lions in the study, he jumped at the chance. Most critically, he supplied us with several expensive, high-tech radio collars.

Until the early 1960s, biologists tracked big game on horseback or on foot, relying heavily on luck, dogs, and guesswork. Then Frank Craighead and his identical twin, John, invented the radio collar—a tool, it turned out, that was instrumental in saving the Yellowstone grizzly from extinction. In a career filled with milestones, it was perhaps the Craighead brothers' greatest achievement.

The brothers Craighead were already acclaimed and world-class wildlife biologists when, in 1959, officials at Yellowstone National Park invited them to study grizzly bears. Two friends—an amateur radio operator and an electronics engineer—helped them develop their prototype radio tracking system. It was a game changer that shed a bright new light on the mightiest predator in North America. For the first time in history, researchers could track grizzers to their dens and, if you were named Craighead, burrow in with them. Daring, yes, but as Frank's wife, Shirley, recalled: "They were hoping the bears weren't awake." Former collegiate wrestlers, the Craigheads did pull-ups and other calisthenics in case they had to climb a tree to elude a grizzly.

For the next twelve years Frank and John trapped and tracked and examined dozens of Yellowstone bears. Remember the documentary that inspired my move West, the footage of researchers scrambling into their rig as the tranquilized grizzly comes to and attacks their station wagon? It's a classic in adventure filmmaking, and the chiseled, ruggedly handsome Craigheads play their part to perfection. "When releasing grizzlies," Frank sagely advised afterward, "point them away from you."

The Craigheads were the first to hypothesize that snowfall plays a role in the onset of hibernation; the first to thoroughly document the bear's home range and diet in Yellowstone National Park, the first to provide reliable population estimates, the first to understand how very slowly grizzly bears reproduce, the first to establish that grizzlies need even more room than Yellowstone's 2.2 million acres can provide, and the first to determine that the grizzly's chief cause of death was *Homo sapiens*. When they started in 1959, grizzlies were considered a threat and a nuisance; the Craigheads' research proved that the bears were vital to Yellowstone's ecosystem. Or, as Frank wrote in his 1979 book *Track of the Grizzly*, "These magnificent creatures are in many ways the epitome of evolutionary adaptation, but in order to survive in today's world, they need our understanding. Without it they are doomed."

Their work, made possible by the invention of the radio collar, was instrumental in securing the grizzly bears protection under the Endangered Species Act in 1975. And now Frank's son, Lance, was offering us the latest tech for our mountain lion research. It was the key to the animal kingdom, a way to follow these mysterious cats remotely and unlock their secrets.

I'd first met Lance at his office on Bozeman's MSU campus, a room littered with books and research papers, and dominated by a curious mobile made of whale, walrus, and grizzly bones. I remember thinking, *Wow, I'm speaking to a Craighead. This is wildlife biology's royal family.* Fortunately, he was also just a downright nice guy and fellow graduate student.

Now, as the director of the Craighead Institute, Lance was working on understanding the links in the migration chain: to ensure the survival of large mammals like bears and lions, he knew we needed to limit habitat fragmentation and improve wildlife connectivity. Easier said than done.

For much of the twentieth century, conservationists focused on protecting core habitats—safeguarding islands of sanctuary such as wildlife

John and Frank Craighead take measurements from a tranquilized bear during their pioneering grizzly bear study in Yellowstone National Park, Wyoming. CRAIGHEAD INSTITUTE

management areas, national wildlife refuges, and national parks. Save the best habitat, the thinking went, and wildlife will survive. But, as we've seen over the last thirty years, critters don't fare well on islands. Wild nature needs to move between and among core habitats, migrating with the seasons, adjusting to changes in habitats caused by plant diseases, insect outbreaks, wildfires, droughts, longer-term climatic cycles and trends, and other phenomena—the always-shifting conditions of natural environments. You need the habitats, but you also need the corridors between the habitats. You need to protect, but you also need to connect. A decade of studying grizzly bear genetics in Alaska had convinced Lance that disconnected populations can lose the genetic diversity and resiliency they need to ward off disease and to survive natural disasters.

If we manage lands for the survival of our large predators—the so-called "umbrella species"—then we also guarantee the survival of many other species in the ecosystem. Because the big carnivores require large undisturbed habitats, linked by wild corridors, solving the territorial requirements of these species forces us to define both large core protected areas, and smaller protected connectors, in a networked regional ecosystem.

Sometimes, this means putting protective lines on a map and creating new land designations such as wildlife management areas or newly designated

Mountain lions softly walk unseen and unheard as they prowl through the wild. Humboldt, California.
MICHAEL K. NICHOLS

wilderness. Other times, it means teaching hunters to distinguish between black and grizzly bears, so grizzlies can pass from place to place undisturbed. Still other times, it means restricting certain uses, such as motorized recreation in the backcountry, to reduce disturbance in a seasonal breeding or rearing range. Or perhaps making seasonal changes, such as asking ranchers in key migration routes to alter some fences or open some gates at certain times of the year.

For any of that to happen, biologists, planners, landowners, and decision makers must know which routes wildlife use and what obstructs or disrupts that movement. That's where our research and the Craigheads' collars come in. Lance and his team wanted evidence that the Big Belt Mountains in central Montana were still functioning as a corridor between larger blocks of less-developed land to the north and south. We wanted to understand how lions were impacting sheep populations. Our work overlapped with a cat we called M4—male number 4. He'd been captured up in Beartooth country with his sister, F4, not long after they'd left their mother but while they were still traveling together. Unfortunately, F4 drowned a month after she was collared, attempting to swim across the Missouri. M4 promptly disappeared, and after many searches we assumed he had left the Beartooth. But that fall, a cat was legally taken during the winter hunting season in the Little Belt Mountains, far to the east of our study area. It turned out he was the missing M4, who had negotiated the open grassy foothills of the Big

Belts and the steep Smith River canyon to look for a new home range in the Little Belts.

To Lance and Terry Enk, this meant the east-west travel route between the mountain ranges was still functional, thanks mostly to large, undeveloped agricultural operations such as the Dana Ranch and Sieben Livestock Company. Landowners—especially the big ranches of the West—can play a vital role in conserving corridors by tolerating the wildlife that moves across their property. In fact, private ranch and farm lands in Montana like Sieben Livestock Company host more seasonal migrations—mainly elk, pronghorn, and mule deer—than many public land holdings. That's why the Montana Land Reliance, a statewide land trust, offers a bumper sticker that proclaims: "Cows, Not Condos." Of all the dangers to wildlife that modern life presents, permanent residential development impact is absolutely the most deadly.

And despite the fate of F4, other cats such as M2 and M3 confirmed that mountain lions could link to lands in the north by swimming across the Missouri and padding on into the Sleeping Giant Wilderness area, which in turn links to The Bob. And M1, the first cat we caught, finally answered the question of whether lions could travel south, toward the Yellowstone ecosystem. Terry followed M1 as far south as Elk Ridge, just beyond the Beartooth in the Big Belt Mountains, before the cat disappeared—establishing, I hope, a new home range in parts unknown.

Over the course of a decade, Lance and his Craighead Institute created a series of maps illustrating the travel corridors still connected for lions, grizzly bears, caribou, wolverine, and other species in the northern Rocky Mountains. These have been used by land managers in Montana and several other western states, who recognize the economic logic of maintaining connectivity through science-based land-use planning. Simply put, it's a whole lot cheaper to protect wildlife corridors *before* the freeway, subdivision, or fence is built.

That midwinter afternoon up Mann Gulch, it was clear how little can stand between life and death. Another inch or two of snow. An hour of light. A shift in the wind, or a well-placed picnic table. For animals that depend on seasonal migrations, it can be as simple as a hole in the fence or, more crucially, a decision to build a wildlife-friendly fences. But first, we need to know where the animals are, where they're going, how they'll get there, and what they'll need when they arrive. And so we chase the hounds that chase the cats that find the wild.

CHAPTER 6

THE CROWN OF THE CONTINENT

Wherever you travel, from the deepest valley to the highest summits, you are never alone. Countless eyes will be upon you, and dozens of noses will test the air as you approach.

– J. Gordon Edwards, *A Climbers Guide to Glacier National Park*

U p here in Montana, governors have been known to wear cowboy hats and bolo ties, and folks joke that a tuxedo is a new pair of blue jeans and a denim jacket. The state takes its name from the Spanish word for mountain and is best known for its big sky, wild bears, high peaks, broad prairies, trout fishing, boom-and-bust mining towns, dinosaur bones, and the Unabomber. The state is bisected by the rugged north-south spine of the Continental Divide. East of that Divide the Great Plains unfold to endless horizons. That's where you'll find Circle, the town farthest from a Starbucks in the all of the Lower 48, population 617. West of the Divide are most of Montana's 100-plus mountain ranges, a ragged and sawtoothed jumble of snow-capped summits and plunging wilderness valleys.

It's our nation's fourth largest state, but ranks just forty-fourth in population and forty-eighth in population density—about seven people per square mile, compared to about 10,000 people per square mile in Washington, D.C. Montana is home to about 1 million people and 2.5 million cows and, as most Montanans are proud to report, only Alaska has more grizzlies. In fact, all of the alpha predators that roamed North America when Europeans first arrived two centuries ago are still here— which is why so many of the wildlife biologists who study bears, wolves, lynx, wolverines, and mountain lions come to Montana. And more often

Lofty Mount Gould and the Grinnell Glacier nestled below are visible from the steep couloir approach to Mount Grinnell. Montana. BRET BOUDA

than not, they head to the most remote and rugged part of our state: Glacier National Park.

Glacier is my park. It's a wild mountain park, and it has a hold on me that will never loosen. I live thirty-three miles from the main entrance on the west side, and although I've driven through that gate countless times, I still feel the thrill that first-time visitors experience. The park is so rugged and wild that I will never see or climb all of it, and so alive that even the parts I know well are constantly changing. An avalanche can roar across a favorite trail, reworking it with downed trees and boulders. Spring floods change the course of familiar streams, transforming entire valley bottoms.

For hundreds of millions of years, the spectacular alpine terrain that is the 1.2 million-acre park was a flat limestone seabed, covered by a shallow ocean. Roughly 50 million years ago, during a tectonic collision, a mass of rock three miles thick and 160 miles long lifted skyward, shifting 50 miles to the east. A mere million years ago, glaciers advancing and retreating through the high mountains tore at the sedimentary stone like a geological sculptor wielding a chisel made of time itself. By the time the first Native Americans arrived, roughly 14,000 years ago, Glacier had been carved into its current rugged physique.

Yellowstone has Old Faithful. Yosemite has Half Dome. Glacier's geologic centerpiece is Triple Divide Peak, a rare mountain summit that serves as the water tower of the continent. Icy streams run off the summit to three oceans—the Atlantic, the Pacific, and Hudson Bay, which in turn leads to the Arctic. George Bird Grinnell—famed conservationist, writer, and the father of Glacier National Park—realized the unique nature of the triple divide, and in a 1901 article wrote that "far away in northwestern Montana, hidden from view by clustering mountain peaks, lies an unmapped corner." He dubbed it the Crown of the Continent, in honor of the triple divide. Grinnell marked it "a land of striking scenery.... Here are canyons deeper and narrower than those of the Yellowstone, mountains higher than those of the Yosemite. Some are rounded and some square-topped, some are slender pinnacles, and others knife-edged and with jagged crests, each one a true sierra. Many are patched with snow, and the highest wear their white covering from year's end to year's end."

Grinnell's description—the Crown of the Continent—today defines a vast ecosystem, 18 million acres sprawling across the U.S.-Canadian border, with Glacier National Park at their wild heart. This is the confluence of soaring Rocky Mountain ranges, their icy caps vanishing into hundreds of streams and waterfalls that tumble beneath green canopies of ancient forest. It's impossible, really, to appreciate how many mountain peaks pierce the Crown until you climb a summit and the sky becomes a vast blue sea, whipped by wind into an endless reach of frothy whitecaps. My family and I spend summers clambering high in the company of these white-haired elders, standing on the shoulders of Chief, Siyeh, Bearhat, Red Crow, Sinopah, Oberlin, Medicine Owl, Going-to-the-Sun, and Rising Wolf.

Many of the mountain names are borrowed from the Crown's first stewards, the Native American people who still call this place home. Blackfeet and Kootenai, Salish and Pend d'Oreille. These are modern cultures, alive and thriving today and with roots driven deep into the wild Crown. To the Blackfeet, these mountains are a spiritual retreat, a place they know as the "Backbone of the World." They still hold ceremonies here, still seek vision and power among the peaks. To Blackfeet, mountain lion is *naatíyo*, "two teeth," most admired of the cats, whose hide is valued above that of any other animal. To Salish, the lion is *skwtismyè*, literally "large predator." To others, the lion could impart its powers of stealth and prowess, making a great hunter, and many wore quivers of lion hide to capture a bit of the predator spirit. To still others, the cat translates as "long tail," the animal most nervous around his two-legged human brothers, a shy and secretive neighbor known for a silent nature.

Just as the land shaped the physiology of the mountain lion, so did the mountains of Glacier Park and the Crown of the Continent shape their human inhabitants—the people and the place have evolved together for thousands of years.

For centuries on centuries, Native Americans have sought solitude and vision and guidance atop the vertical flanks of Chief Mountain, a 9,080-foot peak that resembles a warrior's headdress. My son, Jake, and I climbed the summit late in the summer before he left for college, and we could feel the power of the place. The view from the Chief proves the incredible changing nature of nature—the upheaval of peaks behind, the long stretch of prairie before—and I understood in my bones that my boy had become a man, and that he was ready to start a new life.

One way to know Glacier National Park is by the numbers: 762 lakes, 200 waterfalls, 23 named glaciers (melting fast, and down from 150 glaciers in 1850), and roughly 1,500 square miles of cedar, hemlock, larch, fir, and pine forest. With a topography that ranges from 3,000 to 10,000 feet, Glacier is one of the most intact temperate ecosystems on Earth, supporting five different life zones, 75 species of mammals, 275 species of birds, and an astounding 1,100 species of vascular plants. But a better way, perhaps, to know Glacier is to live it directly. It's one thing to understand how wet maritime air from the Pacific collides here with colder, drier continental air to create tremendous downdrafts. It's another to be very nearly swept from the summit of Pollock Mountain while climbing it with your daughter. My entire family literally crawled from the great cleft in the mountain's south-ern face to gain the summit, as winds hammered us from all sides.

Of course, among those seventy-five mammal species are the predators—the meat-eaters among the park's "charismatic megafauna"—the grizzly and black bears, the wolves, wolverines, lynx, bobcats, red fox, pine marten, bad-gers. And also the mountains lions. The land we now know as Glacier Park has always had lions, though they weren't always welcome here. Even in national parks, the concept of wildlife protection originally applied only to game animals—deer, elk, moose, bighorn sheep. In fact, back in 1918 a full eight years after Glacier had been named America's tenth national park—an early park naturalist wrote a book on the wild animals of Glacier in which he proposed eliminating mountain lions in places. His rationale? Fewer lions would mean more big game—and since lions were so rarely seen, they were of no use anyway.

What he didn't understand, but our science has since proved, is that you don't need to kill lions to control their populations. The cats, thanks to their fierce territoriality, limit their own numbers naturally. By staking, marking, and defending clearly defined home ranges, mountain lions very rarely ex-ceed more than about two to four adult resident cats per hundred square kilometers (forty square miles). The hunting and killing of mountain lions does, however, disrupt the felid social order—which in turn may lead to more human-cat conflicts in the long-run. But no one knew that in 1918. Neither did they know that, by selecting to protect deer and elk and other big-game animals, they were in effect selecting to protect mountain lion food. In other words, they were providing the prey base that all but guaran-teed a robust and growing lion population.

Eventually, as wildlife sciences matured and the field of ecology emerged, Glacier's brass began to manage for a more natural system inhabited by all native species, predators included. This still creates controversy in some circles, because large carnivores are wide-ranging and many wander beyond Glacier's boundaries. And yes, even within the park, predator attacks on humans occasionally occur—though they are few and far between. Other risks, such as drowning in Glacier's cold, fast water or falling from a cliff face, are a much greater threat to park visitors. But fatalities from these ac-cidents don't trigger the ancient fear centers of the human brain in the way a bear or lion attack does. It's not rational, but it's real. It's how we're wired.

In Glacier, most every human fatality due to wildlife is the result of a surprise encounter with a mother grizzly and her cubs or a photographer pressing too close on a trail. The bears are minding their own berry business, grazing huckleberries and rolling logs for grubs, and a hiker ambles through, much to the alarm of everyone involved. Mama bear responds by doing her

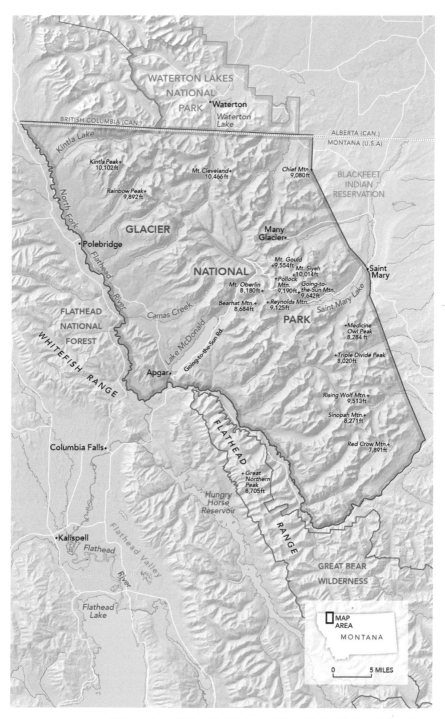

GLACIER NATIONAL PARK Waterton Lakes National Park in Alberta, Glacier National Park in the United States, the Great Bear Wilderness, and the North Fork of the Flathead River in British Columbia and Montana are all part of the wild heart of the Crown of the Continent landscape. SOURCES: NPS, USGS, PROTECTED PLANET, WILDERNESS.NET, MONTANA STATE LIBRARY, NATURAL EARTH

The wolverine is the largest land-dwelling member of the weasel family. This one has been feeding on a winter killed elk carcass, Glacier National Park, Montana. STEVEN GNAM

job—she eliminates the threat, then hustles the cubs over the hill. Usually, the hiker gets away with some bites and cuts and one hell of a story. Rarely, the hiker doesn't get away.

Though mountain lion attacks are exceedingly rare, the big cats and people do cross paths. Glacier has somewhere in the neighborhood of 2 million two-legged visitors per year, mostly packed into the three summer months of mid-June to mid-September. That's more than 4 million eyes available to spot a mountain lion. And yet, almost no one spots a lion. John Waller, lead carnivore biologist for Glacier National Park, is a widely recognized bear expert—but he also manages mountain lions. (Actually, as any carnivore manager will tell you, it's less about managing bears or lions and more about managing people.)

John maintains an extensive cat sighting and incident database, a comprehensive record of encounters between visitors and lions in Glacier Park. Between 2000 and 2013, Glacier Park played host to about 27.3 million visitors. During that same time, those visitors reported just 668 mountain lion encounters. So for every 42,000 people who visited the park, one had a moment with a lion. That's just .002 percent of all visitors. A full three-quarters of those moments—about 500 encounters—were sightings of a big cat in the wild. Another sixty or so visitors reported seeing some kind of lion sign: a track, a kill-site carcass, the sound of a lion scream. Those folks never even saw a live lion. A very fortunate twenty people saw a mountain lion actually making a kill in the wild. A less lucky half dozen visitors reported they believed that they, themselves were stalked. Just two people, of the 27.3 million who visited—.000007 percent—were attacked by a cat. And the number of fatal attacks in Glacier National Park was exactly zero.

Glacier National Park is vast, rugged, remote, and almost entirely road-less, with many hundreds of thousands of acres where few people ever explore. Once you're off the scant network of trails, you're in real wilderness, a backcountry alive with predators and prey where seeing another human is a very, very rare sight indeed. Deeply forested, riddled with the thick green of glacier-fed river bottoms, the park was a sanctuary for prey and the lions that eat them back when both had been hunted into retreat, and it remains a sanctuary for predator and prey today. Here, especially around deeply forested and popular Lake McDonald, you can be sure that for every person who sees a mountain lion, the big cat, watching silent from the forest, has already seen a hundred visitors.

It's lucky for us humans that we don't register as a prey species—but it's even luckier for the mountain lions, because people have guns and that ends poorly for the cats. On my first trip to Glacier, to advise park staff on mountain lion management, I was greeted by several well-armed rangers. My first thought was that something really bad was going down, and my moment in the spotlight was going to be postponed.

"What's with all the guns?" I asked.

"Park Service protocol," Charlie answered. "Any time we deal with dangerous animals we want to be prepared."

Having treed many an adult mountain lion just by yelling and clapping my hands, the guns looked excessive to me.

If Glacier National Park is the wildest part of Montana, then the North Fork—named for a branch of the wild and scenic Flathead River that flows down from British Columbia and marks the western boundary of the park—is the wildest corner of Glacier. How wild is it? Put it this way: A human hiking in the North Fork ranks about fifth on the food chain.

Framed by the low-slung and heavily timbered Whitefish Range to the west, and the soaring spires of the Livingston Range to the east, the sixty-two-mile long North Fork Flathead River Valley is a predator's paradise. It is the only place in the United States where mountain lions, lynx, wolves, and grizzly bears share habitat in abundant numbers—along with black bears, coyotes, wolverines, fox, marten, otter, ermine, and more. They're there, of course, for the moose, elk, deer, marmot, squirrel, and porcupine. That means the North Fork is one of the few places on Earth to watch alpha predators interact. It's a predator party.

During a radio-tracking helicopter flight on October 25, 1993, a US Fish & Wildlife researcher was shocked to see a wolf pack attacking a grizzly sow and her cub in the North Fork. The pack, seventeen strong, separated mother and cub, alternating its pursuit until the bears hustled up trees. That's just not the sort of thing that happens in other places. The North Fork is uniquely wild. The researchers later looked for signs that the grizzlies had been killed, but found none.

"No other ecologic complex exists like it," says Dr. Maurice Hornocker, celebrated wildlife biologist and patron saint of puma research. More often, he said, grizzlies benefit from sharing the land with wolves—as well as with lions—because bears can snatch kills from lions and can feed off carcasses left by both lions and wolves. But in the North Fork, the wild is wilder.

I first explored the North Fork in the fall of 1993, driving north on the only road in—a kidney-buster that eats tires the way a cheese grater eats knuckle skin. The rocky route passes through a distinctly boreal landscape: tracts of meadow grass and wetland interspersed with thick forests of lodgepole and ponderosa pine, spruce, birch, larch, cedar, and Douglas fir. About fifteen miles short of the Canadian border, I stopped at civilization's last outpost: The Polebridge Mercantile. The Merc is the heart of Polebridge, a tiny town whose residents live without pavement, powerlines, or phones. The lack of amenities, combined with that damnable road, keeps the riff-raff in, they like to say. They only downtown business besides the Merc is the Northern Lights Saloon, and the only change the locals like is the turn of the seasons.

Inside the Merc, old rawhide snowshoes hang above the counter alongside crosscut saws, guns, and bear traps. Nailed to the building's hand-hewn log walls are racks of antlers and glassy-eyed mounts of elk, deer, moose, and bear. A faded wolverine pelt shares space with dusty black-and-white photos of grizzlies sauntering through town, snow piled high enough to swallow the building, and wildfires sending greasy plumes 30,000 feet into the sky. There's a pot-belly stove, and a warm pot of coffee, and an outhouse in the back. But best of all, there's the smell of baking. Cinnamon rolls, sticky buns, apple turnovers, chocolate cookies, huckleberry bearclaws. If a better bearclaw can be found, either side of the Mississippi, I sure don't know about it.

Dr. Maurice Hornocker, the world's preeminent mountain lion researcher, holds a tranquilized mountain lion in New Mexico. KEN LOGAN/LINDA SWEANOR

There are lots of reasons the North Fork remains so wild and thick with predators—topography and terrain and climate and park protections—but mostly it comes to this: there are damn few people.

Much of what we know about the big cats in the North Fork comes from the study led by Toni Ruth and her mentor, the previously mentioned Dr. Maurice Hornocker. Hornocker is widely regarded as a pioneer in global mountain lion research—he studied pumas, lynx, bobcat, and ocelot in North America; leopards in Africa and Asia; jaguars in Central and South America; and Siberian tigers at the eastern end of Russia and Manchuria. Along the way, Hornocker also conducted extensive research on bears, wolverines, river otters, and badgers, published more than a hundred scientific papers, made several documentaries, and wrote and photographed for *National Geographic*. In my circles, he's as close to a celebrity as you get.

Toni Ruth joined the Hornocker Wildlife Institute at the University of Idaho in 1987, and it wasn't long before this lean, indefatigable biologist became project leader in one of the first experiments with mountain lion translocation, down in New Mexico. A few years later, in 1992, she took the lead on another Hornocker initiative, this time in the wilds of the North Fork of the Flathead. Her work—which involved coordinating four concurrent research studies on coyotes and wolves—would take five years to tackle the question: There are predators and there are prey; but what happens when alpha predators such as lions, wolves, and bears compete for the same prey in a harsh winter environment?

Wolves had recently recolonized the North Fork after years of near-eradication by hunters, and researchers were keen to learn how this new player would affect the predation game. No one knew, for instance, what wolves would mean for mountain lion survival. The first wolf pack to recolonize the Lower 48 was actually discovered by University of Montana professor and good friend Dr. Bob Ream and his field crew, Diane Boyd and Mike Fairchild. It became known in Montana and around the United States, quite appropriately, as the 'Magic Pack.'

The first wolf appeared in 1979 in a North Fork meadow on Glacier Park's western fringe, and the pups—the first born here in half a century—arrived in 1985. These were the first wolves to take up residence in the western United States since the 1930s. Incredibly. there are now more than sixty wild wolf packs in northwest Montana alone.

The question was, how would those two carnivores, lions and wolves, sort out the landscape they now shared? Could they once again coexist, or would the lions yield their ground? Only in rare places such as the North Fork, with uniquely intricate networks of predators and prey, could you ask such a question. Toni's arduous, multi-layered study—the first ever done on wolf-lion interaction—revealed an exciting and unexpected natural world that frankly thrilled the scientific community.

Tracking mountain lions in the extremes of the North Fork is serious business. Winters are long and painfully cold, and the snow is extremely deep. It's also terrifically isolated, and if anything goes wrong, there is just one long, slow, horrible road out.

The terrain makes following the hounds difficult and dangerous. Toni and her hound handlers and mountain guides would follow the dogs across the sometimes-frozen, sometimes-not-frozen North Fork Flathead River in subzero temperatures—when getting even a little wet can be life-threatening. Navigating the dark, twisted tangles of dense conifer forests, with blown-down trees stacked like barricades, made for long and exhausting days in the field. If the hounds happened to cross paths with a pack of wolves, they were in danger of being torn to pieces. And one alarming discovery made by the team was that not all big grizzly bears stay holed up in their dens for the whole winter. Some, it turns out, wake up and wander around, lured by carcasses left by the predator party of wolves and lions. It's definitely harder to keep up with your hounds when your head keeps swiveling at the sound of twigs snapping behind you.

But Toni, a pretty hard-core predator herself, persevered. As she said in an *Outside* magazine article: "My favorite thing is simply being out in lion country, tracking a cat, thinking that around the bend I could find a kill or knowing that a cat may be watching me. I find great comfort in this." Eventually, Toni and her team collared an impressive forty cats in the North Fork.

The first order of business was to determine the overlap between the resident mountain lion home ranges and the established wolf pack territories. If the cats and dogs eschewed each other's company entirely, that would be interesting—and it would make for a mighty short study. It was the potential overlap that would prove truly fascinating. Wolves prefer more open territory suited to chasing down prey, mountain lions prefer the mountain slopes that offer thick, concealing coverage.

Turns out, North Fork wolves and lions overlapped to a large extent, especially in winter when deer and elk concentrated at lower elevations where the snow wasn't as deep. But to keep some distance, the lions primarily prowled "core use" areas within their home ranges, and these prime hunting grounds were always located outside of the areas most frequently patrolled by wolves. Cats, Toni learned, did not feel safe in wolf territory. While there have been instances of a cat defending its kill against a lone wolf—or even

Three bighorn sheep rams surveying the winter wild beneath the high peaks of Glacier National Park, Montana. STEVEN GNAM

killing a solitary wolf—that's the exception to the rule. Dogs chase cats, not the other way around, even when the cat is 180 pounds of pure lion muscle.

Toni's work revealed that wolves, operating in packs, are serious trouble for lions. She documented the battles as wolves drove lions away from kills, or scavenged kills that lions had cached. It's a tough life, being a wild lion, but it's especially hard when you're forced to make additional kills because the wolves keep stealing your food.

As Toni tells it:

> I remember finding a fresh kill in the middle of frozen Kintla
> Lake in Glacier National Park during winter. I went out to inves-
> tigate, and while I was crouched over the kill I looked up and saw a

pack of wolves barreling down on me from fairly far away. I stood up and they kept coming. I think they thought I was a bear or some other critter on their kill. I finally waved my hands and yelled and they eventually veered off, continuing up the lake, while looking at me over their shoulders. Sure had my adrenaline pumping and made me think about how a mountain lion must feel when feeding on a kill in this North Fork country... they need to keep looking around at all times.

And the wolves weren't always content with simply pilfering a free meal. Not infrequently they would also chase and tree the cat. Adult mountain lions knew to seek refuge in mature Douglas fir trees, with broad, sturdy branches to rest on as they waited out the wolves lurking below. But younger cats were at risk, and kittens and yearling lions were far more likely to panic and climb the nearest tree, even if it was a slender lodgepole or nearly branchless larch. With no place to rest, the young lions would eventually tire of clinging to the trunk and jump to the ground to flee, only to be chased down, killed, and eaten by the pack.

Add the hungry grizzlies marauding for carcasses and plundering the spoils, and it was clear that the predator party posed problems for more than just prey. In the summer months, the big bears would follow scavenger birds, ravens and magpies, to lion kills, and the lion would invariably give way. Again, this meant more work for the cat, but at least—unlike the wolves—the bear would focus on the kill and leave the big cat to slink off alone.

And in winter, some bears—one of Toni's most startling discoveries—would follow mountain lion or wolf tracks in the snow, to locate and raid their kills. If a grizzly could scare up enough calories this way, it would not need to den. No one had ever seen this behavior—but then few researchers had access to such a rich world of predator interactions.

Coming across a carcass in the North Fork, especially at midwinter, is like flipping open the morning paper; all the latest news is written right there in bold print. A lone set of bear tracks criss-crosses a snarl of wolf prints, overlying a cat track. Three wolves, at least, maybe four, with two youngsters tagging along. Deer hair is frozen to the ground, snow stained red. A lone coyote came through; looks like he stole a meal quick and ran, one of the wolves hot on his tail. A wolverine arrived later, after the rest had left, his tracks mixed up with marten and ermine. And around the carcass, in the deeper snow, the stick-figure tracks of a raven and a magpie, and the brush strokes of wing on snow. An eagle was here, as was a crow.

Follow the story back, toward the edge of the meadow, and the narrative unfolds—it was a solo cat, not too big, probably a female. The deer was with a small herd—they bedded on that open shelf, above the meadow—and when the cat flashed out of the rocky outcrop they scattered into the willow and dogwood at the river's edge. But the snow was deep—see the spot here, where the deer bellied out as her legs postholed through the drifts? That slowed her down, and the cat flanked her from the right. They tangled here, and the deer wallowed a moment in the snow before she bolted another fifteen yards, to the kill site, where the cat finally found the jugular. Follow the drag marks to the deep cover, where the carcass is stashed under a dark spruce.

The cat had time to feed here—you can see how she neatly plucked back hair and hide—but the wolves weren't far behind. She went west when they arrived from the north. The grizzly bear came later, to scavenge the scraps, and left a pile of scat that was later picked over by a crow. Someone got a meal here. Someone left hungry. There were consequences. This is the wild, as complete as it gets, and it feeds us too, nourishing our understanding of how nature really works, the connections and competitions that weave the web.

Toni's observations of lions in the North Fork provide powerful support for the theory that the lion's secretive and mysterious behaviors—such as selecting remote and protected denning areas, resting and bedding in rugged or brushy landscapes, concealing their freshly killed prey with vegetation or other available materials, and climbing trees with speed and ease—probably evolved in the company of bears and wolves. These animals shaped one another, just as they were shaped by the landscape and by the speed of their prey. In this way, at least, competition is a singular sort of cooperation.

If you're a mountain lion in the North Fork, she learned, staying alive through the winter is not a given. The combination of deep snow and bitter cold temperatures takes a toll on white-tailed deer, which are the lions' primary source of calories. And when prey is scarce—and you're also feeding any number of wolves and the occasional bear—sometimes it's just too much. Of the forty collared mountain lions in the North Fork, six starved to death during the study period—a number unheard of in any previous lion study. This startling finding suggested that sharing habitat with a newly recovered wolf population proved a limiting factor for the resident mountain lion population. It was surprising, ground-breaking science, and an ominous glimpse at what the big cats face in the far Canadian north.

Toni likes to call mountain lions the Clark Kent of the carnivore world. Meek and mild-mannered, they lead a quiet life, trying hard to go unnoticed. When they need to feed themselves, however, off go the glasses and on goes the cape—they are capable of killing armed and dangerous prey up to seven times their weight (moose). But even Superman has his kryptonite. As landscapes become more developed by humans, and quality hunting

Although wolves are native to the Rockies, their recovery has been a concern—livestock conflicts, big game impacts, and predation on lion hounds—in many rural Montana communities. STEVEN GNAM

grounds become smaller in size and more fragmented, competition between lions and other large carnivores will undoubtedly increase. In many places, the lions' adaptability will help it survive despite this human footprint, because the competitors—wolves especially—are simply not tolerated by people. But in places where the full family of predators persists, habitat loss may well prove dire; subordinate to both wolves and bears, mountain lions will wind up on the losing end. And that would be a shame.

As Toni Ruth says, "They give us this sense of wildness. Even those of us who study them rarely get to see them. So there's still a mystery about them." All the more reason to protect wild country, to give them freedom to roam, to ease the predator pressure by safeguarding big tracts of wild habitat— places such as Glacier National Park and the Crown of the Continent.

CHAPTER 7

FOLLOWING FRAGMENTATION

*Man is the most insane species. He worships an invisible
God and destroys a visible Nature. Unaware that this
Nature that he has been destroying is this invisible God he's
worshiping.*

– Hubert Reeves, Canadian astrophysicist

Caribou click like castanets when they walk, the result of tendons that roll around a bone in their feet. One writer compared the racket of a migrating herd to the ticking of a thousand metronomes. It's thought the sound may serve to keep the herd together in case of a white-out. Caribou also grunt like a full-bellied relative pushing away from the dinner table at Thanksgiving. At least that's what came to mind as I sat on an all-night watch outside a 130-foot corrugated trailer containing nineteen caribou, on a remote hillside in British Columbia.

It was March 2, 2012, a cold and starry night with a crescent moon that kept ducking in and out of silver clouds. Montana wildlife biologist Tim Thier and I were on a snowy knoll outside of Kimberley, BC, a tiny town once home to the world's largest lead-zinc mine and now a faux German ski resort with the largest freestanding cuckoo clock in Canada. Our job was to make sure that mountain lions, wolves, dogs, and wayward humans did not threaten the precious caribou cargo that had been captured near the Tuya Mountains and driven more than 1,000 miles south to our staging area.

While sitting in a pickup truck for eight hours alongside two tons of gruntin'-n-clickin' caribou might not sound like the most exciting night out, Tim and I, the lone Yanks in the otherwise all-Canadian crew, were thrilled to be part of the Mountain Caribou Recovery Implementation

Bull caribou's complex antlers are shed every winter and regrown again during the spring and summer.
Spatzizi Wilderness Provincial Park, British Columbia, Canada. JOE RIIS

Project—a long-winded title for what happened to be one of the most ambitious wildlife conservation projects undertaken in North America.

Caribou are curious critters, painstakingly built by natural selection for a life lived in the high north. *Rangifer tarandus* have kinked underfur that traps warm air against their body, and hollow outer guard hairs that give them buoyancy for swimming. They are one of the few ungulates able to metabolize lichen, their main source of food in the winter. They are also the only ungulate species in which both the males and the females typically grow antlers. The comically large racks on the males, which they shed each spring, seem to have been assembled from two giant boomerangs and a couple of coat racks with three sets of twisted pegs. Caribou take their name from the Mi'kmaq—in their language, xalibu means "pawer" or "shoveler." Their hooves look like concave dinner plates split down the middle, and are roughly the same size as those of the moose—yet the xalibu weigh only half as much. Down in Montana's Glacier National Park, the Kootenai name for Logan Pass translates as the place where "Bigfeet was killed"—which more likely refers to caribou than to sasquatch.

Like Swiss Army knives, their hooves are multipurpose: they act like shovels for scooping snow to uncover vegetation; like snowshoes for navigating deep drifts; and like swim fins for crossing swollen rivers.

Known as reindeer in Scandinavia, Siberia, and Alaska, these beasts are so well insulated that even their noses are covered in fur. Historically, caribou roamed the roof of North America from Alaska to Quebec, Newfoundland, and Labrador, and until the early part of the twentieth century, as far south as New England, Idaho, Montana, and Washington. The Gwich'in people—the "People of the Caribou Place"—still rely on caribou for food, tools, and clothing and have followed the Porcupine herd in Alaska and the Yukon for millennia. Migratory caribou herds are named after their birthing grounds—in this case, the Porcupine River. Though numbers fluctuate, that herd comprises approximately 169,000 animals (based on a July 2010 census), migrating more than 1,500 miles each year between their winter range and calving grounds on the Beaufort Sea. I've said it before: Nature is a nomad.

While all caribou look much alike, the three main subspecies in North America are distinguished by their zip code and migratory patterns. The barren-ground or boreal caribou—most often seen on the National Geographic Channel dodging wolves, crossing swollen rivers, and prancing in massive numbers across the tundra—travel as much as 2,500 miles a year, a record for any land animal on the planet. While these peripatetic beasts have seen their numbers dwindle over the past half century, there are still as many as a million caribou in Alaska and Canada's Yukon Territory. Then there are the large herds known as northern caribou, living in west central and northern British Columbia. Also known for their marathon migrations, they calve in high alpine terrain during the summer before heading south to winter in lower elevation pine forests or wind-swept ridges, where the snow is shallow and their precious lichen easier to dig out. Their population is unknown but scientific consensus suggests the remaining herd is declining.

And finally, there are the woodland caribou, the endangered ungulates that brought Tim and me to British Columbia. Woodland caribou are different from other caribou because they live year-round in the dense, high-elevation old-growth forests that few other animals call home. When winter arrives and most animals—including predators like wolves and mountain lions— move to lower elevations, mountain caribou migrate uphill, where they tread on top of the snowpack and devour the hanging arboreal lichen known as 'old man's beard.'

Masters of concealment, mountain caribou once inhabited large blocks of old-growth forests in the northern United States from Washington to Maine. Their shy and secluded lifestyle combined with their inclination to stand and keep predators under close watch rather than to flee instantly has, quite frankly, left them vulnerable to people who can shoot from a distance. As a result, by 1930 they were shot out of Montana, making them the only big-game animal that most Big Sky residents never knew they lost. These days, in the United States, they have dwindled to one small herd in the Selkirk Mountains of northern Idaho and northeastern Washington. Known as the international Selkirk population, there are fewer than forty caribou left in this herd. Farther north of the border, fewer than 1,500 persist in British Columbia, but their numbers are falling fast—down from roughly 1,900 in 2007.

During the 1990s, the number of woodland caribou in the southern Purcell Mountains of British Columbia began dropping like the temperature in Kamloops in January. Forest fires, hydroelectric dams, oil and gas development, timber roads, global warming, human settlements, highways, railways, hunters, reservoirs, and the logging of old-growth forests meant the already sparse caribou suddenly had far less habitat—and far less lichen. The gas prospecting routes, logging roads, and timber cuts all opened the high-elevation habitat, carving corridors for newcomers and making what had been exclusive caribou country attractive to the deer and elk that thrive in younger and more disturbed habitats. Those ungulates, in turn, attracted the mountain lions that are now moving north, to the end of the world, traveling as always on the backs of the deer and elk that follow the roads of man and the warming world of changing climates. The reclusive caribou, unfamiliar with these new predators, made for an easy meal.

What had long been a moose-caribou-wolf system (with low population densities beneath heavy forest canopy) transformed almost overnight into a deer-elk-lion system (with high population densities amid open country), and caribou paid a heavy price. Folks tend to blame the cats and the wolves for eating the caribou, but really it's us. It's the roads and clearings we've cut into that dark and ancient green that have transformed the entire ecosystem. By the year 2000, biologists in British Columbia feared that without new stock, mountain caribou in the southern Purcells would soon be gone. Which is how I came to be babysitting all those caribou, on a January night not far from the Montana border, high in the Canadian Rockies.

In 2001, Canadian biologists began devising a plan to save this region's mountain-dwelling woodland caribou, which along with beavers, hockey, and the Canadian Mounties remain one of their country's most cherished national symbols. After a few stops and starts, all the elements finally came together in 2012—by which time the herd in this region had dwindled to just fourteen caribou. The donor herd came from up north, in the traditional territory of the Tahltan First Nation, and was shipped 1,000 miles south, to the territory of the Ktunaxa First Nation. Working with these indigenous nations, for whom the caribou carries a profoundly cultural as well as a natural significance, project leader Leo DeGroot's multiagency team aimed to move twenty caribou south in 2012 and another twenty the following year. The goal: restore the population to pre-1995 levels by 2017—roughly 2,500 animals province-wide. It was an extreme and drastic strategy, for an extreme and drastic situation.

Logistically complicated and startlingly expensive, the plan kicked off with twenty caribou net-gunned via helicopter. The biologists placed each caribou, blindfolded and hobbled, in an animal-transport bag and flew them to the staging site. There they were evaluated by a veterinarian, fitted with GPS collars, and finally transported the 1,110 miles from the Level-Kawdy herd near Dease Lake to our staging area outside of Kimberly. Bundles of arboreal lichen were flown in for the caribou during transport, quite likely the largest lichen air lift in history. The transport truck, manned by two drivers and a vet, left on February 29 and drove nonstop, except for refueling, arriving at the release site on March 2.

By first light, Tim and I had left the caribou and returned to town for a quick snooze. When we returned at 8 a.m., the staging area was bustling like a movie set. Two dozen biologists, veterinarians, and volunteers soon gathered around a tribal elder from the Ktunaxa Nation Council. Accompanied by a drummer, he offered a prayer in his native Kootenay language, his words becoming more fervent with each strike of the drum. A translation followed: "Our people have known and respected the caribou for thousands of years. Now they are disappearing. It isn't the wolves' fault or the fault of the mountain lions. It's man who has changed the habitat for our brothers the caribou." His words hung in the air, mingling with the rush of wind and the grunting of caribou. Then the moment shattered into the January cold, as two AStar helicopters appeared like monstrous hummingbirds, their twin engines drowning even the wind.

Because I'd handled wild elk and bighorn sheep in Montana, I was enlisted to usher the caribou out of their tractor-trailer stalls and into the handling pen. There were only three males in the mix, as we wanted as many breeding females as possible. Field biologist Dave Lewis handed me a three-by-five-foot sheet of plywood with handles and a peek-hole cut up top. "Watch their hind legs, eh?" he instructed. "They kick like jack hammers."

I jumped into the trailer nervously, opened the first aluminum door and squeezed between two females. Both went airborne like dueling jack-in-the-boxes, their eyes popped wide and wild. The animal on my left immediately slammed me against the aluminum partition; I stepped from behind my plywood shield like an aging matador coming out from behind his cape, whacked the animal on the hindquarters, and off it bolted out of the truck, through the chute, and into the corral. The males, which weigh as much as 300 pounds, hit me with even beefier blows. Thankfully, their antlers had been pruned back when they were captured up north. The boys in British Columbia actually gave me a treasured thank-you plaque with an antler from one of those caribou.

One by one, body-slam after snot-knocking body-slam, we hustled them out into the pen where field biologists wrestled the animals to the ground, immobilized and tranquilized them, adjusted their radio collars, and loaded them onto a sled attached to a snowmobile. Tim Thier drove the snow machine to the choppers, where they were loaded like evacuees rescued from a shipwreck. In Montana Outdoors, Daniel Person called the helicopters "whirling Noah's arks" that "whisked the animals, two at a time, to higher ground and deeper snowpack."

By 4 p.m., we were done. It had been a complex, well-choreographed operation, and Tim and I felt privileged to participate. But what followed was, in retrospect, nearly as predictable as it was tragic.

Past attempts to transplant caribou have come up short, and mountain lions have been a factor. Back in the 1990s, a transplant of 103 caribou into the Selkirk Mountains of northern Idaho, to augment a remnant herd of thirty resulted in a net gain of just eighteen animals. A mountain lion that biologists dubbed "Mr. Nasty" took three for sure, and probably many more.

High in the Purcell Mountains of British Columbia a female caribou awakens in the deep powder after being tranquilized and transported by helicopter to her new alpine home. TARA SZKORUPA

Caribou didn't evolve with cats, and cats have made good use of that as they've pioneered territory newly opened by roads and clear-cuts—and by warmer winters, which have sent cats north as far as the Yukon, where they had not been previously recorded.

But we had a plan. Here in the southern Purcells, our newly introduced caribou would be released at an elevation well above the lion's range. Biologists had even collared a few wolf packs and a handful of lions, studying their range before the caribou were released into the relative safety of the snowy Purcells. We'd done our homework, weighted the odds toward success, and watched with hope as our caribou wandered into the wild. Daniel Person, again writing for Montana Outdoors, captured the day: "Off the helicopters and out from under sedation, the caribou ambled away, trudging through fresh powder into a stand of trees. Video of the release shows snow matted onto the caribou's coats, making them look like the ghosts they have become across much of their American range."

It's a romantic image, fitting an animal often referred to as "ghost of the forest." What scientists didn't anticipate was how the transfer might affect the existing local herd. Biologists had expected the transplants to follow the tracks of locals up into the snowy high country of the Purcells, above lion and wolf territory. Instead, frightened by the racket of the helicopters, the locals bolted. As my friend Leo DeGroot told Montana Outdoors: "I think they woke up from sedation and said to themselves, 'That was awful; we're getting out of here.'" And seeing no other caribou around, the next day they were ten miles away. The same fright-flight instinct kicked in when the second group arrived. "Instinctively," said DeGroot, "some headed to lower elevations, where they eventually ran into mountain lions or wolves."

Simultaneously managing both predators and prey is never easy, especially with endangered species. Science and biology take you only so far before nature herself intervenes, and before personal values come into play. In this case, the Tahltan Nation was worried about the caribou from their donor herds, and wanted the receiving parties to kill wolves and mountain lions in order to protect their caribou. The Ktunaxa First Nation, on the other hand, whose homeland overlapped the release site, wanted no part of predator control. Mountain lions and wolves are an important part of Ktunaxa culture, and tribal members didn't see why these predators should be punished simply because we'd chosen to introduce some easy pickings into their range.

In the end, a nervous compromise was struck: only radioed-collared lions or wolves that had actually been implicated in a documented caribou mortality event would be killed, on the assumption that having been successful once, they would try again. Not fair and not ideal, but neither was the destruction of the woodland caribou habitat that led to this problem in the first place. The industrialization of wild land, not the predators, had boxed the species into a corner.

Down in the Gates of the Mountains, the real problem for bighorn sheep was disease, brought by domestic sheep, brought by people. Here in the transboundary Rockies, the real problem was old-growth clearing, brought by roads, again brought by people. In both cases, the predators added a certain insult to injury—but they were not the injury itself. For that, we need to look quite a bit closer to home. We inherited an emergency. We took a risk. And it's worth trying, because although animal transplants fail—and it's common to fail—they also occasionally succeed; and when they do it's inspiring to watch the rewilding of mountain country.

Five of the caribou transplants headed south, across the border into Montana. For most, the visits were fatal: A pregnant cow, just days from giving birth, broke her leg and was killed by a lion. Two were taken by wolf packs. Another was presumed dead when its radio collar went into "death mode." And it was roughly four months after the initial release when Leo DeGroot called to warn me of yet another probable caribou death. Based on the lack of movement from her satellite tracking unit, he reported, a female caribou located just south of the Canadian line in Montana was most likely in a pile of predator scat. Leo, a rangy backcountry skier who seems to smile even when he's grinding uphill, happens to know more about caribou and their habits than anyone I know.

So a team of biologists and I loaded the snowmobiles and headed out, intent on collecting organ samples as per the request of the BC provincial veterinarian. While the team gathered tools for the field dissection, I post-holed through spring snow toward the GPS location, following a slide-track downhill that had classic mountain lion drag-mark written all over it. But when I glanced up, I was shocked to see the panicked, wide-eyed gaze of a caribou. "She's alive!" I shouted.

It was seven miles back to the truck, and for the next several hours we lifted, slid, and carried this tick-ridden, paralyzed caribou off the mountain. Back in town, the vet removed the ticks, administered an IV and meds, and—voila!—she responded immediately. It turned out to be a simple, but without our help, deadly, case of tick paralysis. Remove the ticks, remove the paralysis. After many phone calls and a visit to Homeland Security on both sides of the border, I climbed into a darkened trailer with the caribou, cradling her head to help her breathe. We delivered her back to Canada, where biologists monitored her until she was healthy enough to be flown back to the high Purcells.

North of the border, the caribou didn't fare much better. By June, just four months after the release, ten of the nineteen had died—six from predation (four by lions, two by wolves); two from injuries; and two from unknown causes. The majority of the deaths took place when caribou wandered into mountain lion territory below 4,500 feet in elevation. One year later, only one caribou, a bull that remained up high, had survived.

The biologists in British Columbia knew it was risky. They knew that the source herd up north could consist of animals conditioned to roam far and wide. And, yes, Leo DeGroot and his team were hoping for a higher survival rate. Under natural conditions, native predators in native habitats do not eat their way through native food supplies. If they did, they would have starved out long ago.

It's only when the system itself becomes compromised that the traditional interplay threatens survival. At those times, even the best efforts guided by the best science can come up short. But despite the bleak results of our caribou convoy, a helicopter survey in spring of 2013 showed a healthy bump in calves surviving their first winter—suggesting that our surviving bull or one of the locals had been busy. That's significant. But the precipitous decline of the mountain caribou is indicative of a more comprehensive and complex conservation problem—namely, loss, fragmentation, and conversion of wild habitat, compounded by a warming climate. When it comes to old-growth forests, the caribou is like a canary in a coal mine. Or, as Marco Musiani, an evolutionary biologist at the University of Calgary, said, "The caribou is a sentinel or indicator of climate change that can be read, studied, and learned from. [They are] telling us a story that we are impacting the environment."

Though Musiani is generally pessimistic about the future of the caribou in British Columbia, he also says that rather than seeing the situation as doomed, we can learn from this experience and adjust future efforts accordingly. Which is just what DeGroot and his fellow scientists are doing. What we need, finally, are strategies for making sure that future transplants stay put in their preferred high-country habitat, under what's left of the old-growth canopy and away from the lion and wolf range.

There's room for them to roam in southern British Columbia, and in the roadless reaches west of Glacier National Park in Montana, places where these cold-adapted northerners can still find the snow they need to survive—the snow that's just too deep for predators such as mountain lions. One option is transplanting fewer animals from healthy high mountain subpopulations, and temporarily keeping females and calves in "maternity pens" for protection before releasing them into a resident population. To increase the likelihood that transplanted caribou will bond with residents, a similar "soft release" is also being considered in which transplanted animals will be penned for a short time with resident caribou prior to release. Even captive rearing in a zoo is a viable option. All we need, really, is a small DNA injection into a healthy population, to jump-start recovery.

There are a host of other initiatives under consideration, such as liberalizing the hunting and trapping of wolves and moose. And many scientists have called for a ban on logging in old-growth forests, as well as restrictions on snowmobiling and heli-skiing—both activities that cause caribou to disperse. Sadly, those initiatives seem less likely to occur, as humans are notoriously hesitant to place restrictions on themselves and their activities, whether for work or for play. After all, it's a whole lot easier to blame the predator.

Perhaps conservationist John Bergenske, the fierce and persistent protector of Canadian wildlands who helped create the Purcell Wilderness Conservancy, summed up the situation best: "Artificial means may be necessary to assist the caribou until their situation improves," he said, "but it's a desperate situation."

Whether you use highfalutin' terms such as "anthropogenic footprint" or "human modification of habitat," or you simply call it the mess we've made, it appears climate change already has had a significant impact on Canada's wildlife. In the vast northern reaches, the indicator of uncommon change is the mountain lion. Unlike the long-haired, broad-pawed Canada lynx—the only wild cat able to survive in the Arctic—mountain lions are not built for extreme cold and deep snow: They have short hair, relatively little body fat, and small paws given their considerable weight. That's why the majority of the 4,000 to 6,000 mountain lions in British Columba live in southern British Columbia. Over the past twenty-five years, however, wildlife biologists have noted that a few adventurous male lions have ventured up into central British Columbia, where their favorite white-tailed and mule deer reside in relative abundance. They're following the new human roads, and the new warming winter trend. And as they move north, they're running into the caribou that are clueless because they have never met a lion. Of course, at some point, roughly around the fifty-fifth parallel—imagine a line from the bottom of Alaska running east across the province—frigid temperatures and deep snow stop interlopers.

Or at least they used to. Now it seems that the firm line marking the "northern end of the world" for the mountain lion has moved farther north—all the way to the British Columbia/Yukon border and beyond. Where that upper boundary line is now—if it even still exists—is a subject for debate and discussion.

In the boreal north of central British Columba, the wildlife community transitions from a deer and elk habitat to a moose, bear, wolf, and caribou system. The former is idyllic for lions; the latter, problematic. Some scientists think this northern expansion is partly a case of the lions reclaiming territory they once called home. As was the case in the western states, mountain lions were "managed" here as a bountied predator until the mid-twentieth century—so much so that they were exterminated from eastern Canada. It wasn't until 1966 in British Columbia, and 1971 in Alberta, that the mountain lion achieved the protected status of a big-game animal. But here again, the footprint of man has affected change: Expansion of farm lands and the construction of gas and oil lines through northern forests have provided new forage grasses for white-tailed deer. And, as sparks precede fire, where *Odocoileus virginianus* goes, *Puma concolor* will follow.

Mountain lions typically hunt at lower elevations during winter where their prey is deer and elk. Woodland caribou thrive at higher elevations in the deep snow pack. Glacier National Park, Montana. SUMIO HARADA/ MINDEN PICTURES

Though there had been many reported sightings of mountain lions in the Yukon Territory for years, there was no physical evidence to substantiate the claims—no scat, no hair, no tracks, no photographs, no actual lion. Until the year 2000. A couple hiking northeast of Watson Lake in the Yukon—that's 60.06 degrees north—found a dead and emaciated mountain lion curled up in the back of a burnt-out car. Apparently the lion was using the car as a shelter, and died shortly before being discovered (he wasn't fully frozen despite temperatures of seventeen degrees Fahrenheit). Tracks found outside the car suggest he was traveling with a companion, a brother or sister, perhaps. The dead lion, an adult male approximately three years old, showed no evidence of disease but he weighed just eighty-three pounds—roughly thirty pounds below his fighting weight—and his stomach was empty. Clearly, he couldn't find enough calories on the hoof to endure the severe cold.

To date, this appears to be the upper edge of the mountain lion's northern range. Ramona Maraj, a carnivore biologist based in Whitehorse, thinks the evidence points to a sparse smattering of dispersing young toms, or sibling pairs, as she has seen scant evidence of a self-sustained, breeding population in the Yukon. A dispersing male can travel as many as 500 miles in a single season, whereas females will travel only a quarter of that distance.

What Maraj does know is that elk and deer are venturing from northern British Columbia to the Yukon in significant numbers. "We have regular vehicle collisions with deer in Whitehorse," she said. "And deer are now seen as high as the Arctic Circle in the Northwest Territories. Increasing climate change will only exacerbate this trend." The cats can't be far behind.

A similar scene is playing out in neighboring Alberta, where mountain lion populations have been expanding since the 1970s. Again, not only are mountain lions turning up far north of what scientists thought was their previously established range, but they're also moving east, like settlers in reverse. Climate change has warmed the way, and logging and oil and gas line construction have cleared grassy paths for the deer to migrate north. Not only that, but the lions in Alberta seem to be particularly resourceful; they've been known to eat deer, moose, elk, bighorn sheep, mountain goats, feral horses, other pumas, the rare lone wolf, coyotes, red foxes, lynx, black bears, marten, beaver, porcupine, snowshoe hares, red squirrels, hoary marmots, grouse, ducks, geese, and ravens—which means they're incredibly adaptable and opportunistic. This spells disaster for the woodland caribou in central Alberta. As Nathan Webb, a former carnivore biologist for the department of Alberta Sustainable Resource Development, says, "The arrival of the most effective large carnivore in the Americas to the boreal north ecosystem will only make the caribou problem worse."

Over the past decade, breeding populations of mountain lions also have become established outside their previously well-defined eastern boundary, along the foothills of the Rocky Mountains in Alberta. In 2005, biologist Kyle Knopff and his wife, Aliah, began tracking lions in Alberta's Rocky Mountain foothills, a multiprey ecosystem with eight wild ungulates— white-tailed deer, mule deer, elk, moose, feral horses, mountain goats, bighorn sheep, and caribou. Between December 2005 and fall 2009, they collared and monitored forty-four mountain lions. They found that while the overall mountain lion population subsisted mostly on deer, individual diets were diverse. Some cats consumed primarily deer, others bighorn sheep, while still others favored feral horses (which are more common in west-central Alberta). Larger males tended to kill larger prey—elk, moose, horses—while females selected smaller deer.

It was a fascinating study, but what struck me most was how far these lions had traveled east. In a second study begun in 2007, along the Alberta-Saskatchewan border, researchers captured high-quality photographs of an entire lion family group—strong evidence that a breeding population exists in the region, likely in the protected reserve of Cypress Hills Interprovincial Park. In 2008, wildlife biologists captured and collared their first lions in the Cypress Hills, a mature male and an adult female, who soon gave birth to four healthy kittens. This is the easternmost breeding lion population known in Canada to date, but post-persecution populations have rebounded so well that breeding populations likely already exist in Saskatchewan and may also have spread to Manitoba, Ontario, Quebec, and the Maritime Provinces, crossing the continent along the Boreal Shield.

Here's what we do know for sure. Mountain lions in Alberta are doing what lions always do: faithfully following their favored deer. What we are now witnessing appears to be the beginning of a slow but significant push east, with cats traveling in the wake of increasing white-tailed deer populations. Perhaps it's a recolonization of former lion habitat in the central Canadian provinces. Perhaps it's altogether new territory. Either way, it's clear that human encroachment and changing climate has thrown entire natural systems into flux. And as the world changes, some will win and some will lose. For now, it appears this period of upheaval may prove good for the mountain lions up north, but it's surely more bad news for the beleaguered and endangered woodland caribou. Unless we protect the high and isolated old-growth forests of caribou range, unless we show some small amount of restraint—unless we cool the warming temperatures, restrict old-growth logging, limit road building, eliminate poaching, and curtail disease transmission from deer to caribou—then we can hardly blame the lions for doing what cats do.

FREEDOM TO ROAM: CORES, CORRIDORS, AND CONNECTIVITY

– Rick Ridgeway

For many wild animals, "to survive" means "to roam." Seasonal migration between habitats is a pattern passed from generation to generation of hawks, waterfowl, pronghorn, and thousands of other species. For species that do not seasonally migrate—such as pumas—the ability to find new mates in new places protects genetic health and diversity. And freedom to roam often determines whether or not wild creatures can adapt to change. Wildlife corridors provide that connectivity in today's human-dominated world.

People are isolating habitats with cities and highways, and fragmenting them with fences and fields, and reducing their size. Since the 1960s, conservation biologists have been able to measure with increasing accuracy the minimum sizes of protected areas needed to ensure the long-term survival of all the species in a given eco-zone. No surprise: big animals like pumas need big spaces.

That's the first problem. The second is that, in addition to habitat fragmentation from human development, habitats are also shifting because of human-caused climate change.

One key solution is protection of wildlife corridors that connect protected core areas, so that large mammals like pumas can move betweeen protected areas, effectively giving them the large landscapes they need for long-term survival. And when large mammals thrive, so does what biologists call the trophic cascade—the impact of apex predators that creates a balanced, connected, and healthy habitat.

For the last two decades many governments, environmental NGOs, scientists, and citizens have increasingly advocated for wildlife corridor identification and protection. Patagonia launched the Freedom to Roam campaign to increase awareness of this "corridors and cores" strategy. At the same time, increasingly sophisticated tracking devices have given wildlife biologists insights into the most effective corridors to designate for migrating species and to keep core habitats connected. All this has helped inspire increasing protection of wildlife corridors and construction of highway wildlife crossings.

Yet much work remains, and many threats are increasing: despite the promise of wind energy to decrease greenhouse gas emissions, wind turbines also increase mortality of migrating birds; increasing oil and gas development boosts attendant roads that intensify habitat fragmentation; and if the Trump administration advances its effort to build a border wall with Mexico, this too will restrict wildlife's freedom to roam.

There is also reason for hope. The Half Earth (half-earthproject.org) and Nature Needs Half (natureneedshalf.org) movements that advocate setting aside half of the planet as protected core and corridor areas—each gaining momentum—would not only give wildlife the freedom to roam it needs to thrive, but at the same time increase forests and grasslands that are vital carbon sinks providing partial solutions to climate change. A double-win against a double-edged challenge.

Rick Ridgeway is the vice-president of public engagement for Patagonia and a long-time environmental activist.

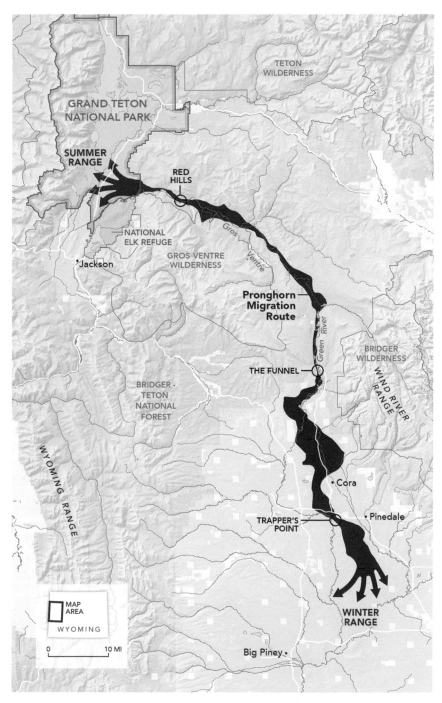

WILDLIFE CONNECTIVITY Dr. Joel Berger with the Wildlife Conservation Society discovered the path of the pronghorn migration route in northwest Wyoming near Grand Teton National Park. By following radio-collared antelope Dr. Berger and his colleagues identified the exact migration route and potential threats and barriers to these historic migration routes. SOURCES: USGS, WYOMING GEOSPACIAL HUB; MODIFIED FROM DR. JOEL BERGER AND STEVE CAIN, 2014 – WILDLIFE CONSERVATION SOCIETY AND NPS

CHAPTER 8

LOCALS ONLY

Public sentiment is everything. With public sentiment nothing can fail. Without it, nothing can succeed.

– Abraham Lincoln

I t wasn't yet eight thirty on a Saturday morning, but already four dozen hardcore hunters and hound handlers milled outside the conference room in Kalispell, Montana. It was January 7, 2006, and my staff was getting ready to present our new hunting regulation proposals at the town hall–style meeting held every two years in my district. Flying year-round in wildlife monitoring helicopters, often very low and over remote terrain, we had recorded how many fawns, calves, kids, and lambs made it through their first winter. Armed with these stats, we knew how many big-game animals could be taken without harming the overall popula-tion. While we planned to review hunting regulations for white-tailed and mule deer, elk, mountain goat, bighorn sheep, and moose, the real reason folks were queued up like Black Friday shoppers was our new proposal on mountain lions.

From the first Native Americas who paid homage to their spiritual guardians in cave carvings, to the bounty hunters who nearly eradicated lions from US soil at the dawn of the twentieth century, to the hound handlers now packed into our conference room, humans have long been fascinated by mountain lions—usually a one-sided affair that rarely worked out well for the cats. Except for the endangered Florida panther that survived deep in the Everglades, lions were eradicated east of the Mississippi by 1900. The

The purchase of a hunting license to take this deer contributes to America's largest and most successful wildlife conservation program. Gallatin National Forest, Montana. DUSAN SMETANA

last mountain lion seen in Massachusetts was in 1858; in Vermont, 1881. Out West, where hunters were paid by the pelt, lions survived, but barely. In 1911, a dead lion in Oregon was worth $10; by 1939 it was $50. Were it not for America's vast public lands, particularly the rugged backcountry and other roadless areas out West, combined with the cats' solitary nature and near invisibility, the only lions left today would be in the zoo.

Nearly 1,900 lions were killed in Montana between 1869 and 1962, when the bounty system finally ended. The animals could still be killed without limit until 1971, when Montana reclassified lions from predators to game animals and instituted a regulated hunting season. Two years later, Congress passed the federal Endangered Species Act. Finally, in 1986, Montana adopted the quota hunting system, which called for a stop to cat hunting as soon as a set number of lions were reported killed. But while that system did afford better protection for lions, it still left too many females to be killed in some areas—a serious threat to the overall lion population in northwest Montana. So, after years of deliberation and work, we had come to this conference room with a new proposal, based on sound and hard-won science. We were here to do what was best for the cats.

In the northwest corner of Montana where I worked as a wildlife manager, *new* means *change*, and change makes the natives very restless. Roughly 30 percent of all Montanans are licensed hunters, but in our wild, game-rich region just below the Canadian border, it seems as if almost everyone hunts. Which is why, by 11 a.m., the conference space was packed so tight we had to open a partition to double the size of the room. And every time I glanced out the window, another jacked-up pickup with a dog box and a gun rack rumbled into the parking lot. It was going to be a long day.

Our quota system had been in place for twenty years. It was a simple first-come, first shoot system, and once the quota was reached, the hunting season closed. But the reality was that we had a supply and demand problem: too few cats and too many hunters. We simply could not keep up with the pace of the hunt, and inevitably the quota was exceeded before we could shut it down. In several areas, the professional hunting guides were driving the pace, racing to take cats as quickly as possible before the quota was met so they could send their out-of-state clients home happy.

By our estimates, somewhere between 40 and 50 percent of the northwest Montana mountain lions taken in 2005 were killed by out-of-state hunters led by in-state guides. In one area, more than 90 percent of the cats were taken by nonresidents. The mad scramble to beat the quota was creating a free-for-all, and it wasn't good for mountain lions or for the hound handlers. But hunting is more than sport, and it's more than meat in the freezer. It's a way of life, a worldview, and as such, it can get pretty

Hound handlers represent the mountain lion's strongest voice for conservation in most rural western states. Eureka, Montana. JIM WILLIAMS

emotional. I already had witnessed just how heated it could be, six years before in another northwest Montana town.

It was December 2000, and Jerry Brown, a wildlife biologist with thirty years of experience, had invited me up to Libby, Montana, the day before mountain lion season opened. He wanted me to see firsthand the chaos of our quota-driven hunt. Jerry has logged so many hours climbing in the Cabinet Mountains Wilderness that folks refer to the young goats there as 'Jerry's Kids.' He's an old-school mountaineering biologist, a firm believer that wildlife managers need to understand their areas from the top to bottom—meaning they should "climb every peak and take notes in the parking lot." So here I was, notebook in hand, ready to count lion hunters.

An old timber and mining town swallowed by the surrounding 2.2 million-acre Kootenai National Forest, Libby today is still home to loggers and miners—and though the region is struggling economically, its people remain wise in the ways of the woods. The pickup trucks in the parking lot had hounds in the back and bumper stickers proclaiming that "Gun Control Is Being Able to Hit Your Target!" Many of the rigs had Montana plates, but there were also trucks from Wisconsin, Michigan, Kentucky, Pennsylvania, Illinois, New York, Washington, and Idaho—115 trucks in all. But in this region, the seasonal quota was just twelve cats. I didn't need advanced calculus to recognize that we had way too many hunters with way too many revved-up hounds about to hit the hills in pursuit of way, way too few mountain lions. The hunt would start at dawn. "Come morning," Jerry observed, "we could be in deep trouble."

At dawn the phone in Jerry's office was on full boil with hunters and outfitters calling in to report yet another lion killed in another location. Just thirty minutes later, Jerry had me call the boss, who in this case was my local Fish and Wildlife Commissioner, appointed by the governor himself. "We need to shut it down," I told him. The Commissioner didn't hesitate. "With all these dead cats on the ground so fast, and good tracking snow, we have no other choice," he gruffly replied.

But the damage had been done: twenty-four mountain lions—twice the quota, and the majority of them female—had been killed by hunters, outfitters, guides, and clients in just sixty minutes. It's awfully difficult to reconcile this crazy madness with the solitary spirit of a fair-chase hunt. Referring to the outfitters who charged out-of-state hunters between $3,000 and 5,000 per hunt, *Outdoor Life* famously called it "The Montana December Dash for Cash!"

As the longest-tenured wildlife biologist in the region, Jerry was convinced that we needed a new kind of quota, a system that randomly selects a small number of hunters from a large pool of applicants. Would-be hunters could apply for a license in hopes of winning a computerized draw. Under this new lottery-style system, hunters would have a four-month window to take a lion, meaning much more time to enjoy the snowy north woods and their dogs. Each successful applicant would be eligible to hunt in just one district, allowing wildlife biologists to more precisely manage cat populations. More importantly, biologists could adjust the number of licenses granted in any region based on the latest mountain lion science.

These were big changes, especially for folk who didn't much like change. But the most controversial proposal was still to come—limiting out-of-state applicants to just 10 percent of available hunting permits. Locals liked it, since they were feeling overrun by out-of-towners, but it was a direct hit to the outfitters who made their living on clients from out of state. The moment Jerry and I proposed the new rules, a whole bunch of outfitters called for our heads and demanded we be fired. The writer Ivan Doig calls these working-class hunters and loggers "the lariat proletariat"—men with hands like hams, a cowboy's work ethic, and a live-free-or-die attitude. In short, they were hard men you didn't want to cross—and also the sort of people you didn't want to confront armed only with a stack of papers and some science. But that's exactly what we were doing, six years after that December day in Libby, here in the Kalispell conference room.

━━━━━━━━

Glancing at Jerry during our presentation, I kept thinking about the years of research and planning that had gone into our proposal. Months on months on months of careful and diligent work, year after year, often conducted amid yet another call for our heads. Yet no matter how much we were vilified, we kept our focus on the lions and not on those who felt most aggrieved.

By 2 p.m., the mood in Kalispell was as feverish as a revival meeting when a busload of atheists pulls up. There were 400 people in the room, and 399 were champing at the bit to have a turn at the mic. Given the length of the meeting, and the fact that it was Saturday and happy hour was fast approaching, a tidy number in the wool-and-flannel crowd would step out every now and again to visit the hotel bar—and return in a still feistier mood. One outfitter in a leather cowboy hat, a bushy brown beard, and a mighty chest that gave his suspenders a ride, stepped to the mic. He started by praising the existing quota system, and finished by saying: "If it ain't broke, don't fix it!" More than half the crowd, it seemed, erupted with applause.

But of course, it was broke.

Sitting at the skirted table on stage next to me, the current state Wildlife Commissioner, stared him down. A big man with a booming voice, he was an expert backcountry horseman, born and raised in rural northwest Montana. "I've been out in the field and talking to enough hound handlers to know there are problems we have to correct," he said. "I don't care what anyone thinks, we want to do the right thing for cats!"

Those who had not applauded the outfitter now shouted and nodded their approval for the commissioner.

A wiry hunter who seemed more mustache than man focused his fiery eyes my way: "You don't know what you're talking about! We don't need any more government regulation. There's more cats out there than you think!"

Then a local hunter launched into a diatribe about all the shady tactics used by commercial guides to get their clients a cat. "We're in a race with lion hunters who run the roads starting at one in the morning," he complained. "There are no quality hunts anymore. The season's too short, and they're killing too many yearling cats. Permit-by-lottery will force successful hunters to wait a few years to get another cat, and that's only fair. The old quota system might have worked in the 1980s, but there's just way too many hunters up here in northwest Montana now from too many states."

Referring to that "sissified" left coast state (where hunting mountain lions has long been banned), another local hunter shouted, "We're becoming California!" That set off another wave of catcalls, and somewhere between "Screw the lottery!" and "That's bullshit!" a fight broke out in the hallway of the hotel. And through it all, that thick stack of facts, the best cat science on the planet, sat untouched in front of me, useless in the face of entrenched beliefs.

So it goes when it comes to keeping the peace between those who want to protect predators and those who want to shoot them at will. Hunting in general is a pretty hot topic, but when it comes to hunting alpha predators—bears, wolves, lions—profoundly divergent personal values and emotions, rooted deep in generations, boil immediately to the surface. Big-game outfitters, gun clubs, nonhunting wildlife advocates, ranchers, timber companies, and developers all have their own agendas.

Some people, even ones who will never step on the trail, celebrate the fact that mountain lions still stalk wild places out West. Others view predators as vermin, little more than a threat to livestock, pets, and their fellow man. And even among hunters, the chance to track North America's stealthiest cat is, for some, a right and a thrill; while others vehemently object to killing lions for any reason. In between, biologists like me focus on protecting habitat first and managing wildlife populations second. It's a tricky balance, and we never get it exactly right, but as any wildlife biologist will tell you: managing wildlife is easy work compared to managing the people who care about that wildlife in a bewildering variety of ways.

Me, I hunt and fish. It's part of the annual cycle up here. Winter is for skiing. Spring and summer are for hiking, climbing, rafting, and fly fishing. Late summer brings huckleberry-picking season and the last crisp, clear days for exploring the high country of Glacier National Park. And when the days grow short and the nights ever cooler, when bull elk begin to bugle as they fight for mates and deer antlers harden as they rub away the summer velvet, that's the time when Montanans dust off their hunting rifles, maps, and aerial photos. It's time to fill the freezer with local, grass-fed meat.

Growing up in San Diego and Florida, I didn't hunt until I arrived in Montana as a graduate student. The lure of all that free meat back when I lived on cheese, crackers, and peanuts did hold a certain appeal, but it wasn't the hook-and-bullet crowd that pressured me. Rather, it was a new friend and fellow grad student, Thomas Baumeister, who lived to hunt and did it both ethically and safely. Thomas was my big-game hunting "professor." He patiently showed me

Specially trained hounds and their handlers are partners with wild cat researchers to locate and tree the mountain lions for safe capture and immobilization. Missoula, Montana. BOB WIESNER

how to make an ethical shot, how to properly field dress a deer, and, when we got back to our basement apartment, how to prepare the meat for the freezer. I really wanted to try and earn my meat from the land, from wild habitats, and not from a neatly wrapped and stacked display at the grocery store.

I took my first solo hunt on the Rocky Mountain Front, when I was still a graduate student in Augusta. Some hunters like to set up shop in one place, pull out a thermos of coffee, and wait. Not me. I'm useless at sitting still. Instead, I launched into stalk mode, setting off down a trail near the Sun River Wildlife Management Area, one of Montana's many conservation acquisitions that have been funded either totally or in part by hunters, and exclusively for wintering wildlife to call home after a long migration.

About an hour down the trail, I spotted a small herd of mule deer in a high basin roughly three miles away. As Montana author Rick Bass wrote in *Sierra* magazine, "... to disappear in their pursuit—to get lost following their snowy tracks up one mountain and down the next. One sets out after one's quarry with senses fully engaged, wildly alert: entranced, nearly hypnotized." Speaking rhetorically, he equates the hunt to a type of pilgrimage: What else is the hunt but a stirring of the imagination, the quarry or goal just around the corner, or over the next rise?

A hunter's imagination has no choice but to become deeply engaged—it is never the hunter who is in control, but always the hunted. The prey have forever directed the predator's movement. In today's world, many hunt the wild with binoculars or with cameras, which can be just as thrilling. They capture images and videos along with memories of days in the field and the satisfaction of being hot on the track. We're all working from the same set of glands and the same wiring, our shared ancestors having evolved with big animals. How we hunt is up to us, but the hunt is in us all.

Late that afternoon, I drew within 100 yards of the herd. Hiding behind a ledge, I peered through the rocks for twenty long minutes. Growing colder as clouds rolled in, I was aware of my heartbeat and the smell of bunchgrass, wet limber pine, and Douglas fir. My entire world existed on that ridgeline, focused in that moment. Then I caught movement through the forest above my right shoulder. It was a young buck, a yearling mule deer with six-inch antlers. He was with several does, feeding on a clump of snowberry.

Slowly, very slowly, I raised my Winchester and peered down the barrel. Taking a calming long breath to stop shaking, I aimed for his heart and squeezed the trigger.

As I climbed through tall bunchgrass toward the buck, my breathing was erratic, my hands shaking, my heart racing. While I don't feel much of anything when I buy meat at the store, I was drowning in waves of emotion and adrenaline now. I'd ended a life, and that fact seemed so huge, so overwhelming. But I'd also tapped into something hardwired into my DNA, something ancient and profoundly human. "The hunted shapes the hunter," Bass wrote. "The pursuit and evasion of predator and prey are but shadows of the same desire."

An increasing number of people, in Montana and elsewhere, enjoy the same chase but without the rifle—the exhilaration of wildlife observation and the split-second that captures the image via camera, the excitement and wonder of simply being in the presence of wild animals. I'm one of those people, too, and have spent many satisfying days watching wildlife roam free while hiking and climbing these hills.

My kids are literally made of wild meat DNA, of animal flesh built from recycled grass, pine needles, and wildflowers. No feedlot, no slaughterhouse, no fossil fuels, no big pharma, no GMOs, no cross-country shipping, no Styrofoam and plastic packaging. Just like local wild salmon on the coast, you absolutely cannot get healthier meat any other way—it's organic and free-range. It's an old, old way of life.

Of course, hunting predators such as mountain lions is something else entirely. It's not for me. I'm simply too close to them, and it's not my kind of meat. In that way, I'm not unlike the Salish and Kootenai and other first peoples who hold the mountain lion sacred and respect ancient traditions against hunting a fellow predator. I have had the unfortunate job of killing lions in the line of work, when a cat prowls into town and creates a danger to human neighbors, but it is always regrettable. And ultimately, we do not need to hunt lions. They self-regulate their population numbers through their extreme territoriality.

Lion densities are the same everywhere—from the Flathead Indian Reservation, where they do not hunt cats at all, to the timbered hills around Libby, where houndsmen have been hunting lions for generations. They are "behaviorally limited," to put it in the terms of science, from Montana's northern heights to the mountain reaches of South America.

And there is some evidence—though not enough yet to be sure—that hunting mountain lions can actually result in more predator problems. Scientists call it the juvenile delinquent hypothesis. Big, mature male cats have certain behavioral traits: they kill other males that range inside their territory, they sometimes kill kittens and yearlings, and they keep other lions scattered away from their home range. Shoot that dominant male, however, and the field is suddenly wide open. As many as a half-dozen transient juveniles—teenagers, really—can move in and move through the old cat's range. And with all those juvenile delinquents running loose in the neighborhood, you can expect trouble—cats in the deer herd, cats in the henhouse, cats stalking livestock. At one level, it's counterintuitive, that killing a predator could make predator problems more acute. But at another level, it makes a whole lot of sense, because of the ways lions behave. We don't have all the science to prove it, let alone to understand it fully yet, but it the juvenile delinquent theory seems to fit what we see on the ground.

That's why mountain lion hunting seasons and quotas must be so carefully refined. We must take into account the entire landscape, the ecosystem, it's smaller bioregions, cat populations, gender, age classes, social dynamics. Because lions are so connected and fluid when they disperse from their family groups, we need to manage the hunt to maintain those mature males—because they are the ones that maintain the social structure.

But hunting isn't always about the science. Sometimes, it's about social license—about having the people's support for wild nature, including her predators. By allowing a certain amount of hunting, we guarantee a constituency who will speak for wild cats. What's best for the cat, ultimately, may be to hunt a few—in order to secure public support for the rest. That's not science. That's people and politics. And it's real. It was the houndsmen, after all, who came to the aid of the lion in the fight against commercial interests and bounties, and they still hold wildlife agencies accountable today. But we need to balance the system; hunters often want to take the biggest, strongest, most handsome male they can find—the mature trophy cat.

From a population perspective, lions can withstand that kind of selective hunt, to a point. But from a felid social-structure perspective, killing those males can be a problem. The desire for a big cat focuses the goal on the territorial males that, in terms of population stability, should be the least-often removed. It's a difficult balance between the social, the political, and the scientific.

As a hunter myself, I don't condemn lion hunters, I support them. They are often the most effective advocates for lion conservation, particularly in conservative western states. But as a scientist and conservationist, I will always be prepared to protect mountain lions as a natural component of a wild and healthy ecosystem, and I will work to ensure they are around long after I am gone. Part of that work is staying cool in the public meeting rooms of northwest Montana—and part of it is compiling the facts in that stack of paper—because in the long haul, science matters.

The lottery system we proposed was based on hard science that was years in the making. In the mid-1990s—a full decade before that Kalispell meeting—the state of Montana approved funds for a long-term analysis, studying the impact of hunting on mountain lions. It was a monumental effort led by Rich DeSimone, a veteran research biologist and passionate advocate for sound mountain lion management. A long-distance runner who competed in hundred-mile endurance races, Rich had the right temperament for this project—careful, methodical, persistent, patient.

At the outset, he and I sat down with a bunch of maps and selected a study area: the Garnet Mountains. Situated between Missoula and Lincoln, the Garnets sit at the intersection of central and western Montana habitats, with diverse prey ranging from white-tailed and mule deer to large herds of elk. The mountains there also are a patchwork of differing levels of human impact—roadless blocks of core habitat adjacent to road-filled corporate timberlands. And Rich knew the hound handlers and other hunters there were concerned about lion numbers and overhunting. That last element was critical, because we knew he would need their cooperation.

To determine how many cats can be taken by hunters without jeopardizing the health of the lion population, wildlife managers need to know how many animals inhabit a hunting area—or at least whether numbers are rising, falling, or stable. A rising population can withstand more hunting, whereas a falling population may not withstand any hunting at all. We also need to know how removing different ages and genders will affect the overall population—for example, a loss of females usually lowers a population far more significantly than a loss of males, because one male can impregnate many females.

At the time, a lack of good cat population data was causing conflict and confusion with hound handlers, and it also left the state vulnerable to challenges by urban folks with antihunting values. Animal-rights groups successfully blocked a proposed mountain lion hunting season in California, when the state was unable to prove that its annual harvest—the number of lions that could legally be shot—would not harm local populations. In Washington and Oregon, similar laws were passed against using dogs for hunting lions. Without strong scientific evidence showing that our carefully regulated hunting seasons were compatible with healthy lion populations, Montana was similarly vulnerable. We had more than enough anecdotes and opinions and beliefs, but we needed actual data.

Rich's job was to document what a hunted population looked like—density, composition, productivity, mortality, recruitment, dispersal, and home range size—and to learn about the ability of a heavily hunted population to recover. So we allowed aggressive hunting to continue in the Garnet Mountains for three years; and then, with the support of the local community of hunters and ranchers, we closed the hunt entirely for

Clad in buckskin attire, native Montanan Steve Hawkins was a wilderness outfitter, conservationist, and hound handler that fought for big cats in western Montana. COURTESY OF THE HAWKINS FAMILY

three years, allowing the population to rebound naturally so that Rich and his team could measure the changes. The "rate of recovery" results would prove relevant to other regions and continents, all the way south to Patagonia, and would mark a new understanding of lion behavior, biology, and protection.

Rich and his team captured and marked 121 cats over the long course of the study. Some collars contained GPS units, recording a lion's location every five hours. And each week, the field team used special airplanes to safely follow the lions' movements and home ranges. Along the way, they documented and analyzed sixty-three mortalities, primarily from hunting.

Fast-forward ten years, during which endless hours of fieldwork had provided a powerful new lens into lion life. The data—surprising no one, but providing the needed evidence—proved that cat populations are indeed affected by hunting. In fact, at aggressive levels, hunting reduced survival for all age classes and disrupted the dispersal of juveniles. The Garnet Mountains work established that hunting alone reduced the region's lion population by 35 percent in just three years. Importantly, the study also provided evidence that an adult female mortality rate of more than 10 to 15 percent per year will likely trigger a population decline—invaluable information for a wildlife population manager. It was a gold mine of data, which would change the way hunting regulations were crafted.

Long distance mountain runner and mountain lion researcher Rich DeSimone finishes up recording data on a young cat as part of his Garnet Mountain research project in west central Montana. JIM WILLIAMS

And even more startling were the insights into what happened after the hunting came to a halt. The population completely rebounded in just three to five years. While hunting reduced the population size, it didn't seem to alter the natural lion biology. Cats could come back, and they could do so with remarkable speed. Reproductive traits such as annual litter size, birth interval, maternity, age at dispersal, and breeding age remained unchanged, despite the fairly drastic decrease in population. This is encouraging for future cat recovery and rewilding efforts not just in Montana, but across the globe. Turns out, it's all about female survival and human tolerance. The cats will do the rest on their own.

Rich Desimone and his team also proved that, in a large landscape, significantly restricting hunting, or creating a small refuge from hunting, in as little as 12 percent of the mountain lion habitat can ensure a stable regional population. Lions are quite resilient if we allow them to be. If the objective in a given area is to reduce cat populations through hunting, you definitely can. Easily. Almost too easily. We need to be careful.

But if the objective is to increase lion populations to a more natural density, simply back off the hunting and the population will respond. It's not complicated, and it means we can set different population objectives for different places, and adjust the management. In areas where we have more public land and fewer livestock, such as northwestern Montana, we can have more lions and can manage populations at or close to their biological potential. In eastern Montana, where lions come into conflict with livestock, we can manage for fewer lions while trying to increase landowner tolerance.

Of course, it's never that simple. Society intervenes—and not just human society, but also cat social structure. We now suspect that hunting disrupts the local feline social order. As I mentioned before, taking a resident male mountain lion opens the door for several younger males to claim the now-vacant habitat. For a brief period, the density of cats is higher than when the large resident male policed and guarded the neighborhood—and these teenagers can be prone to getting into trouble. Kill a cat to mitigate conflicts with livestock, and you just might increase conflicts with livestock.

But many hunters want to chase the older, mature, bigger cats—and this poses a conundrum for wildlife managers trying to set hunting regulations. Because just as those bighorn sheep down in the Gates of the Wilderness "forgot" how to migrate after the elders died off, it's possible that lions could "forget" the social norms of territoriality and self-limiting population if the adult males are mined out. These are behavioral norms maintained since the last Ice Age, and we cannot afford to lose them.

Mountain lion conservation, it seems, is always about more than the numbers—it's also about making sure that lions are still being lions, still sustaining their social and territorial structures, still having full impact on their prey species and on entire ecosystems. And to do that, again, we need ever more data.

———

Desimone's research ultimately shaped our proposal for Montana's lottery-style permit system. The old quota system, in practice, was not nearly precise enough to achieve the results the science told us we needed. So one month after that raucous 2006 meeting in Kalispell, we returned to Helena, the state capital, for our final public meeting and vote. In order to change from the quota system to the lottery-style permit system, we needed at least three votes from the five-member Fish, Wildlife & Parks Commission. A decade of research, a big chunk of my career, and not a small amount of my professional credibility was on the line, not to mention the future of wild cats—and emotions had not cooled. At 7:45 a.m., the wildlife chief called me on my cell phone. If his voice hadn't been so grave and frantic, I might have thought he was setting up a bad joke: "An outfitter, a hound handler, and a lawyer are in the bathroom, and they're about to come to blows."

I hustled to the men's room. The meeting wouldn't start for another half hour but the three men—one now pinned against the bathroom wall—were already engaged in vigorous debate, Western style, on the finer points of hunting reform. The outfitter hadn't even made it back to his hotel from the bar the previous night, and had instead headed straight to the Commission meeting to talk about his favorite subject: mountain lions and dogs. The fracas, unfortunately, set the tone for the entire meeting that followed. But amid the passion, and between the dissention and the debate, it became clear to all sides over the course of the next few hours that a fundamental paradigm shift had taken place.

Whether it was the influence of our multiyear campaign, the weight of the science, their own direct experience, the lobby of the local hound handlers, or a little of each, the big- game outfitters—the men who might suffer the largest financial hit, should we change to the permit system—had come to the conclusion that change was unavoidable.

The testimony of three men in particular played a pivotal role in saving the cats. These men weren't geeky scientists, or binocular-wielding bird-watchers, or the type the hardcore hunting crowd might dismiss as tree-hugging kooks. Nope, these were good old boys with Montana written into their DNA: a retired teacher and hunting advocate, a Kalispell hound handler, and a respected big-game outfitter. These three guys, who knew more about the intricacies of mountain lion life than most wildlife biologists, saw clearly that the free-for-all hunts were killing too many cats, creating a problem the old quota system could no longer solve. In other words, cats were on their way out and that, in the long run, wasn't good for anybody.

Listening to their testimony, which carried big political sway with the Commission, I thought again about a little conservation secret that a lot of people don't know: As a group, hunters and anglers may provide as much or more *practical* support for habitat and wildlife than all of the dedicated conservation groups combined. They tend to punch above their weight, in terms of conservative Western politics, and they're increasingly savvy about the need for protected habitats and intact ecosystems. More and more houndsmen are advocating for land protections, and are treeing cats only to "shoot" them with cameras and video recorders—a kind of "catch-and-release" lion hunting that has become extremely popular among those who love the chase but want to conserve the species.

In addition, the annual license fees of hunters and fishermen cover a healthy share of the cost of Montana's conservation programs. Montana isn't the only state to use license fees to fund conservation—it's a nationwide program known as the North American Model of Wildlife Conservation—but we in Montana probably cover a greater percentage of our conservation budget this way than any other state. Nonhunting groups have repeatedly sought a seat at this conservation table, promoting citizen taxes to benefit wildlife—and hunters, unfortunately, have sometimes defended their turf by opposing those measures—but for now, hunters continue to carry the cost. It is a proven model and has been critical to keeping Montana as wild as it is.

Hunters have economic and political clout as well. Research shows that hunters and anglers spent $1.26 billion across the state in 2014, giving them a preeminent role in Montana's economy. Hound handlers, who tend to be politically conservative, have the ear of their state representatives and senators. They know the land like they know members of their own family, like they know their dogs, and they stand watch, monitoring every rancher, outfitter, or government agency they think might compromise mountain lions or their habitat. They're committed—as one hound handler testified at the public meeting, "I've been through three wives, but still have the same hounds. That's how important they are to me."

Of course, that political clout can be a double-edged sword—hunters aren't always expert in the ways of wildlife and they can just as easily use their outsize voice to push for damaging kill quotas as they can for conservation. There are areas where we've hurt lion populations, because some deer and elk hunters think killing cats will result in more big game. They're usually wrong, of course, and game managers need to be careful. They don't hunt cats in California (the state with more mountain lions than any other), and they don't hunt cats on Montana's Flathead Indian Reservation, either. Yet both places are chock-full of deer, and lion encounters remain rare.

Setting hunt quotas is not a once-and-done sort of job, and we never get it exactly right. It's an iterative process, a constant learning curve, and it requires vigilant monitoring and cat counts, year after year after year. Just in the past decade, the reality on the ground has changed in Montana: in 2006, hunters killed 282 lions in my state; by 2015, that number had climbed to 468. Of course, cat numbers have rebounded during that same decade, so it's all relative. The point is, management requires constant caution, because the wild world is always changing. Today, we have new technology for counting cats, including DNA analysis, and that's helping us manage quotas—but setting hunt limits is about more than science and math. Sometimes it requires enlisting the help of hunters, and sometimes it requires pushing back against hunters' misguided predator-prey notions, in favor of healthy natural systems.

Just as hunters need scientists and scientists need hunters, both increasingly need nonhunters, even if they don't always like it. In today's changing times, as populations shift to an urban lifestyle, we almost certainly need to bring more nonhunters to the table, involving them in both the decision making and the funding of conservation programs that protect wild nature. At the same time, it's important for urban conservationists to recognize that the passion that most hunters feel for their pastime is not just about guns and trophies, or even about the meat that it puts on the table.

It's about participating in nature in a deeply profound way. There's a broad area, I've found, where the interests of the most ardent hunter and the most gun-adverse environmentalist overlap, and in that space lies the hope for nature's future, both predator and prey.

There's a mythic quality to the fair-chase hunt—with camera, rifle, or binocular—that can't be denied and is part of its powerful allure. Hunting connects us to our ancestral past, when we needed to stalk and kill in order to survive, and when our lives were inseparable from those of our prey—and our predators. Today, hunting may not be about physical survival, but it still feels essential, like art or music. And like art and music, not everyone may choose to participate, but we all can still respect the craft, the art, the imagination, and the dedication and the passion.

And to ensure that this ancient experience isn't lost to humans forever, we need to protect ourselves from ourselves. Sometimes, that means making room for something you might never experience yourself. Sometimes, that means accepting more regulations in the woods than you might wish. But that's the reality in the twenty-first century. The crowd in the Helena meeting room, diverse as they were, got the message. The houndsmen and the outfitters got the message. Even the board of commissioners—beholden as they are to stakeholders—got the message. Though just barely. Their vote came back three to two: out with the open quota, and in with the new lottery-style permit system.

CHAPTER 9

SUBURBAN LIONS

*It's hard to care deeply for something that might turn on you
and eat you.*

– Peter Benchley, author

The frantic call came in at about 10 am. A bunch of guys with guns had a house in the middle of Montana's scenic Flathead Valley, near the mountain resort town of Whitefish, surrounded. Apparently, they'd trapped a mountain lion under a barbecue deck.

"It's probably that habituated cat we've been trying to remove for the last several weeks," replied the front-desk staffer who took the call. Habituated predators—animals that have become accustomed to living large in the presence of people—are an especially tricky management challenge. On the one hand, people don't want to see, up close and personal, the death of a wild animal. On the other hand, people want to feel safe in their neighborhoods and subdivisions. And of course, there's tremendous risk: habituated animals tend to return, again and again, to human haunts; if you choose to relocate or otherwise haze the animal, and it comes back and hurts somebody, you can imagine the headlines. We are, as a rule, extremely tolerant of predators when they stick to the wild, but we are understandably far less so when they amble into town and den up beneath the back porch.

Realizing that time was of the essence, I grabbed the nearest coworker, borrowed the wolf biologist's shotgun, pocketed a handful of shells from the ammo locker, and jumped into the truck. As soon as I was on the road, I called Erik Wenum.

Hollywood's iconic logo shines brightly behind a large male mountain lion that is prowling in what is left of wild Los Angeles. California. STEVEN WINTER

I hired Erik a long time ago from a highly competitive field of wildlife-conflict biologists. He has since proven that he's not only good with bears and lions, but he's fantastic with people—the people who leave horse feed out and then call when a bear breaks down the barn door, the people with unsecured trash bins, the people with sweet-nectared bird feeders, the people who haven't strung electric fencing around the chicken coop. Erik's first priority, of course, is protecting those folks from predators. But a close second on his priority list is protecting the predators from those humans and their enticing snacks. It's remarkable work, and it's possible in large part because Erik is unflappable in a crisis. He knows how to talk to people who are panicked, scared, or angry, and he's good with everyone—young, old, city slickers, or country folk.

It's never fun to put an animal down, especially for simply being in the proximity of people. Sadly, though, there are times it must be done. It's actually surprising we don't have more wildlife-human conflict, given the names of the new subdivisions that fragment our wild valley bottom: Lion Mountain, Cougar Ridge, Whitetail Estates. We seem to name our neighborhoods for the animals we displace when we build our homes. Still, conflicts are relatively rare, despite the fact that the human footprint is constantly treading farther into wildlife habitat. Mountain lions, in particular, can become extremely habituated to living among people—especially the younger lions that are striking out to claim a territory of their own. They're inexperienced, and looking for an easy meal in a place not already occupied by an older, savvier cat. Too often, a subdivision fits that bill, but this coexistence of carnivores and humans can present a significant safety problem, especially for children and pets. Often, the habituated mountain lions will take up residence in a barn, or an abandoned building, or in the "wild" spaces between suburban homes. And when you start seeing a lion in a backyard in the middle of the day appearing entirely comfortable with the presence of people, then it's time to start worrying.

The people who choose to live in this corner of Montana are, in large part, accustomed to sharing year-round space with predators—grizzly bears, black bears, wolves, coyotes, wolverines, lynx, bobcats, mountain lions. In the late 1980s and early 1990s, cat conflicts were at their peak; bounties had been lifted in the 1960s and lions were protected as game animals in the early 1970s, so cat populations were finally rebounding. But people had yet to learn how to live with their new neighbors. About that time, biologist Shawn Riley came up with a plan for "zone management." Essentially, it meant aggressively managing lions close to town, and letting them run wild farther from town.

Riley understood that maintaining truly wild lion populations would mean protecting large areas of remote mountain habitat, and he worried about the sprawl of subdivisions and development that was spilling into these wild places. A building boom was pushing homes higher into the hills, and Shawn knew that some segment of the cat population would inevitably get a bit too curious, and choose to live among the people. The building boom of the 1990s and early 2000s coincided with a boom in wildlife conflicts—a record number of lion-human clashes in western Montana. The cats were coming to town in increasing numbers, so many that we coined a new name for them: 'mild-wild' cats, as opposed to their 'wild-wild' cousins. Neighbors just called them town cats.

Needless to say, the presence of a few sizable felines among the backyards, schoolyards, and baseball diamonds of the valley freaked a few people out. The situation ultimately came down to a simple, if unsatisfying, trade-off: the lives of a few individual lions, in order to secure the reputation and the future of the entire regional population. Because these big cats need more than habitat. They also need social license, the support and tolerance of people. If these mild-wild lions got a bad reputation for eating Fido and Kitty, for breaking into the coop, for leaving tracks at the bus stop, then inevitably our wild-wild cats would be tainted by the bad rap and people's tolerance for lions would decline. At the time, regional mountain lion populations remained healthy and robust. So under Shawn's zone-management scheme, all lions that became habituated—that were seen regularly during the middle of the day, that made kills on homeowners' lawns, that took up permanent residence in subdivisions—would be killed. Cats passing through would be given more latitude. Cats sticking to the shadows of the wild would be left to do what cats do.

In Montana, it's worked like a charm. For the most part. Of course, people still don't like to see wild animals killed, and it can be hard for some folks to stay focused on the big picture. I get it: It's easy to relate to an individual animal and its fate, but much harder to relate to healthy habitats and overall populations. It's our job as biologists to concentrate on the large-scale population impacts, rather than the harm to an individual animal. I feel the same sympathy as the next guy when it comes to killing a work of nature, but my capacity for sympathy also takes in the sweeping landscape, the healthy wildlands, the habitats and their inhabitants, and entire lion populations across generations past and future. And when it comes to mountain lions, especially, I believe that our energy should be directed toward protecting big and connected habitats, and toward increasing human acceptance and tolerance.

Which is exactly what I was doing, shotgun at my side, as I pulled into the suburban driveway of the house with the lion under the barbecue deck. Four men, all armed with long rifles, surrounded the tidy and well-kept home. Locked and loaded, waving their guns around, full of adrenaline in the middle of the neighborhood, they were pretty much my nightmare scenario. I was more worried about the armed posse than I was about the wild cat.

"Whoa, whoa!" I shouted, climbing out of the truck. "Everyone put your rifles down and empty the chambers—everything's going to be OK."

There's nothing like a mountain lion in a dark corner to make our ancient monkey brains go into high alert. We're hardwired to think of a confrontation with a big cat as an intrinsically bad situation. As humans, without fangs or claws or much in the way of defenses, we're naturally vulnerable to large, flesh-eating animals. We react, often, with unfortunately predictable results.

"We've got him trapped under the deck!" the men yelled as I approached. One of the crowd pointed his rifle at a dark opening underneath the deck.

I pulled on a headlamp and squeezed into the tight, dark hole—hoping not to get stuck, Winnie the Pooh-style. I've been on enough of these calls to know that the posse has usually cornered a house cat or a big yellow dog. Sliding through the hole on a slick of damp clay, I started scanning the crawl space with the beam of light from my headlamp. Nothing. I scooted a few more feet in. Still nothing. I was getting claustrophobic.

Then I heard something that went straight to the terror part of my psyche: a low, rumbling growl right behind me, and to my left. I craned my head around and saw two huge eyes glowing in the beam of my headlamp no more than three feet from my nose.

"Pull me out! Pull me out fast!" I yelled, and my coworker yanked me out by my feet.

"Give me the shotgun," I stammered. "It's our lion!"

Mountain lions are spectacular and beautiful animals—my favorite creature in the animal kingdom. And I had to shoot this one. It was a bad day for us both, and when they pulled me out, lion in hand, it didn't really matter that I knew I'd done what needed to be done. Knowing that you're protecting the big wild cats, and protecting people, and protecting wild nature. Knowing that mountain lions should not be allowed to live in suburban neighborhoods. None of that makes it any easier, at least not in the moment. But throughout the past twenty years, this is part of how we've maintained close to natural mountain lion densities in northwest Montana, albeit with some level of hunting. The forests and mountains that surround our homes and ranches have survived intact as prime lion habitat, thanks to broad public support—or, at the very least, tolerance.

The Flathead Valley, just west of Glacier National Park in northwest Montana, is home to mountain lions, grizzly bears, black bears, moose, deer, elk, the occasional wolf, and of course people. BRET BOUDA

The model was put to the test, in a big way, back in 1996, when northwest Montana was hammered by an unbelievable winter. It started snowing before Halloween, and the ground was still white on Mother's Day. Snowplows ran nonstop, buildings collapsed under the weight of winter, and chiropractor offices filled with old men after wielding their snow shovels. The record snows also cut the local deer herds in half, and left entire lion families short of food. The big cats, not surprisingly, started showing up everywhere, looking for a meal. Erik Wenum— always cool, always collected, always mustachioed under his trademark Filson skimmer hat—moved from crisis to crisis. Lions in basements. Lions crouching under exercise bicycles. Lions in living rooms. Garages. Dog kennels. Downtown alleys. Golf courses. Lions everywhere they might find a meal, and not necessarily a wild meal. The weather drove human-lion conflicts into overdrive, and it seemed a day didn't go by that the local newspaper didn't run a picture of a big cat holed up in a barn, or a house, or a garden shed.

Myself and wildlife biologist John McCarthy release an orphaned mountain lion that was raised in captivity near Augusta, Montana. JIM WILLIAMS COLLECTION

The food shortage couldn't have come at a worse time. Deer populations had been strong, and had increased during a lush summer. Those high deer numbers, in turn, had led to high cat numbers. When the crash came, there were a whole lot of lion mouths to feed, but no deer to feed them. We had been on the edge of local community acceptance for these normally secretive big cats, and now the secret was out. People were scared. But Wenum just gritted his teeth and set to work, taking call after call and facing cat after desperate cat. It wasn't fun, and it wasn't pretty, but throughout the following spring and summer he removed almost all of those starving and habituated mountain lions from the valley. Some went to zoos, though many others had to be killed. Since then, by design, Erik has maintained an extremely low density of cats on the valley floor, especially in and around homes and neighborhoods.

Still, not every town cat is removed. If a lion is just moving through, Wenum works with homeowners to develop safety plans for pets and children. And if a cat sticks to the fringes and stays out of trouble, Erik's not likely to hunt it down. But when a cat takes up residence, and loses its fear of people, it has to go. Shawn Riley's original zone-management plan for problem lions still works well to this day, and many other regions have since adopted similar strategies. It's a far different approach than we take with other predators. Troublesome bears, for instance, often can be relocated into the wild hills, far from town. In fact, when Erik is not busy chasing cats he often can be found trapping and moving problem grizzly and black bears. Out of the chicken coop, back into the remote mountains. He then removes the food source, strings electric fence around the coop, removes the bird feeders. That's what it takes to live in western Montana.

Unfortunately, relocation usually doesn't work with mountain lions. Way back in my grad school days, I experimented with releasing some lions that had been orphaned as kittens. We'd heard lion relocation had worked in a large wilderness area in Idaho. And it did work. For a while. We released a young female that had been raised as an orphan by the Fish, Wildlife & Parks Wildlife Center in Helena, placing her in the limber pine forests of the Sun River Wildlife Management Area. But rather than using the WMA, as anticipated, she instead moved east onto the short grass prairie, following Barr Creek down to Willow Creek.

It took only about a month before I started getting calls from the elementary school in the town of Augusta, about kids seeing a mountain lion near the playground. I immediately jumped in a plane, locating the radio-collared cat in a large cottonwood forest near town. Back on the ground, I drove straight to the school and started interviewing the kids. "It's real friendly," one little girl told me. "It follows you, and looks at you friendly-like in the bushes as you walk by."

All I could think was *Oh shit*. A young boy had been killed by a habituated mountain lion a few years prior, just north of Missoula, Montana. And this cat, raised by humans, was clearly habituated. We'd moved it into the wild, but it had returned to town. She had to go.

We learned from this and other cats that habituated lions rarely act like truly wild lions again. Unlike bears, relocation of lions after they've come into conflict with humans just doesn't work; they simply return to the spot they've become accustomed to—sometimes covering incredibly long distances to do so. There is some hope, however: new research from British Columbia and California, where they give the big cats a pass if they don't return after being relocated. But this requires expensive satellite radio collars and a trusting local community, both of which can be hard to come by. I hope it succeeds; there's nothing I'd like better than to put Erik Wenum out of a job, and stop killing habituated lions.

By responding quickly to incidents such as mauled livestock, game wardens and biologists can target the specific mountain lion that did the killing. Remove the perpetrator of the crime, and wild mountain lion populations will remain healthy while human populations remain happy. It's far from perfect, considering people are ultimately responsible for building in lion country, but it sure beats the bad old days when our response was to put a bounty on predators and kill them on sight, no questions asked.

Fortunately, most wild lions stalk only wild places and kill only wild prey. That will change, inevitably, as we encroach farther into the wild, developing natural habitats and carving home sites from high-mountain country. I'd like to think that the pioneering work we've done here in Montana's Flathead Valley might offer some lessons for living with cats long in the future, not just in the Crown of the Continent but throughout their range, from the Yukon on through the Americas to the far southern expanses of Chile and Argentina.

A female cougar traverses a ridgeline in the Snowy Range foothills of Wyoming. Shortly after this image was captured, her two grown cubs walked into view. JONNY ARMSTRONG

PREVIOUS SPREAD: A mountain lion returns to a kill it had cached under the snow in the foothills of the Snowy Range, Wyoming. JONNY ARMSTRONG

THIS SPREAD: Banff National Park in Alberta pioneered wildlife crossing structure design and research in North America. Canada. FLORIAN SCHULZ

TOP: A mule deer doe surviving winter's grasp. Snowy Range, Wyoming. JONNY ARMSTRONG

BOTTOM: Migrating pronghorn antelope face many barriers including crossing cold and fast rivers. Here they are crossing the Green River towards Grand Teton National Park, Wyoming. JOE RIIS

RIGHT: An elusive Canada lynx pads through snow chutes near Seeley Lake, Montana. STEVEN GNAM

PREVIOUS SPREAD: The grizzly bear "sees" the wild through their nose. Swan Valley, Montana. STEVEN GNAM

THIS SPREAD: Glacier National Park's iconic Heavens Peak shines brightly behind a mature mule deer buck in an alpine meadow filled with yellow glacier lilies. Montana. STEVEN GNAM

TOP: A bighorn sheep ewe peers down from her protective rocky ledge. Western Montana. STEVEN GNAM

BOTTOM: In some locations, porcupines are a favorite food of mountain lions. Glacier National Park, Montana. STEVEN GNAM

RIGHT: Telltale tracks of the largest cat in the Rockies have been left on this crossing log. Western Montana. STEVEN GNAM

THIS SPREAD: A red fox inspects the picked over remains of a mule deer that was killed by a female mountain lion and her two offspring. Snowy Range foothills, Wyoming. JONNY ARMSTRONG

NEXT SPREAD: A family group of mountain lions relax in a cave entrance near Jackson Hole, Wyoming. Subadult lions do not leave their mother until one and a half years of age. THOMAS MANGELSEN/MINDEN PICTURES

DOWN SOUTH, WAY DOWN SOUTH

In South America, "south" is more than a direction, more than a description, more than a mere adjective. The South, the far south, the still farther, and even farther south is a mystique, a magnet, and a mystery, a shorthand expression for the inexpressible, a hint, a suggestion, at times a purely imaginary place, at times a beckoning idea, at times only a hazy and romantic notion.

–Lito Tejada-Flores, author

"Jim, we need you to fly down south. Way down south." Those fateful words opened a new chapter in my life that turned out to be even more sweeping and vast than the Montana wilderness. They slipped out, between sips of beer, from my good friend and fellow biologist Rick Douglass. Rick teaches at Montana Tech, and helped found the Montana Chapter of the Partners of the Americas, an organization that pairs different regions of the Americas in people-to-people partnerships to solve some of the hemisphere's toughest challenges. So I suspected that when he said, "Way down south," he didn't mean Wyoming.

"Go down south for what?" I asked suspiciously.

"Pumas and people, Jim," he replied. "Do you like to travel?"

Rick and I were celebrating an award for a PBS documentary I'd helped produce with my old graduate advisor Dr. Picton about the history of Montana wildlife conservation, *Back from the Brink*—and we were on a roll. What better time to hatch plans about conserving far-flung places still *on* the brink?

Turns out, Partners of the Americas had paired Montana with the Patagonia region of Argentina. Both landscapes are big, wild, and remote, with mountains and windswept prairie, cowboys, predators, and prey. And though they call them pumas and we call them mountain lions, the same

Southern beech forests are native to Argentina and Patagonia. Fall colors show brightly below the iconic Mount Fitz Roy near the town of El Chaltén, Argentina. CHOONGOK SUNWOO big cats live at both ends of the world. Rick wanted me to join a project in Patagonia to translate what we'd learned up north about building tolerance for meat eaters in ranch country.

At the time, Patagonia was a mysterious land I'd only read about and could only vaguely find on a map. I was unconvinced. We sipped more local microbrews. Rick kept explaining. Seemed he'd played host, here in Montana, to some Patagonian biologists who told him their biggest problem with cat conservation was the conflict between pumas, people, and livestock. That much I could relate to. And neither the South American biologists nor the Partners group had much in the way of funding. Again, I could relate. What they needed were passionate people at both ends of the Americas with the energy to push projects ahead. That also sounded familiar.

"You'll love it!" Rick said. "You'll land right smack-dab in the middle of Patagonia and you'll never forget it. It will haunt you forever."

He bought another pint of Moose Drool beer. I relented. "What the hell!" I said, grasping Rick's hand and giving it a firm shake. Then I headed back to my hotel, to call my wife and to Google where exactly Patagonia is.

Two months later, I was on the first of what would prove to be many planes south. Just getting to Patagonia from Montana is a two-day journey.

The first flight, into the megacity of São Paulo, Brazil, was filled with bumpy thunderstorm clouds high above the Amazon River basin. The second, into isolated Asunción, Paraguay, was when I knew my adventure 180 degrees south had begun.

"Prepare for landing," the pilot announced in Spanish. I looked out the window and saw huge stands of palm trees rooted in soil the color of red brick. The runway was bordered by the same red earth, rising quickly to meet us. Then, just as we swung low in final approach, the engines roared and I was pressed back into my seat as we again powered into the sky. Passengers screamed, and the pilot rattled in Spanish so fast I couldn't keep up. He was flying the airliner like a Montana bush plane. Soon we had leveled off at altitude once again. The Paraguayan woman in the seat next to me translated: evidently, a tapir or a capybara had bolted onto the runway just as we were about to touch down. The pilot had pulled up and put the nose skyward to avoid smearing tapir on his plane.

Asunción is a lovely tropical city, and my first real stop as a Partners volunteer. They were holding a conference there, with representatives from all South American countries, and I was to represent the United States as a goodwill science ambassador. Between meetings, I explored faded but

ARGENTINA & CHILE From northern Argentina to southern Chile, there are numerous protected national parks and conservation areas that rival any others on Earth. SOURCES: CONSERVACIÓN PATAGÓNICA, NATURAL EARTH, PROTECTED PLANET, DIVA-GIS

Healthy grasslands and the brilliant yellow flowers of the nineo plant conceal a prowling Patagonia puma. Torres del Paine National Park, Chile. BENJAMIN OLSON

colorful colonial architecture and the historic presidential palace. It's a city surrounded by jungle and the remote Chaco forest, the wild pressing hard and insistent against town—anacondas and piranhas patrolled the river, jaguars prowled the banks, and tropical pumas padded silent.

Later, at a reception on a warm and humid tenth-floor balcony, lightning was dancing over the Paraguay River when a stately older gent approached.

"You're from Montana?" he said with a nod to my name tag. "I know somebody from Montana."

I smiled. "Montana's a pretty big state," I said, "and we have almost a million people now."

"Well, maybe you know him," he said. "His name is Eddie Stubblefield."

I choked a bit on my drink. "Who?"

"Eddie Stubblefield," he repeated.

"Well," I said, "you're not going to believe this, but I married his daughter." Now it was his turn to sputter. He even fell back into a chair, looking incredulously at me.

"That is remarkable," he said. "I held your wife in my hands, right after she was born. She had the most beautiful blue eyes."

This retired American professor was a good friend of my father-in-law. And in that moment, the vast distance between the Americas was bridged. I was home here, among family friends and pumas both.

I've always dreamed in landscapes. Turns out, I've been dreaming of Patagonia.

My first brush with the region happened a world away, however, along Montana's Rocky Mountain Front. That's where I met Martín Funes, an Argentinian wildlife biologist traveling North America on the track of big cats. His wife, Graciela, had woven stories about the beauty of Junín de los Andes and their neighborhood volcano, and I'd been dreaming those images ever since. Now, finally, I'd come to see for myself.

"Welcome to Patagonia," Martín said, greeting me at Argentina's San Martín airport. It was like coming home. It looked just like Bozeman. We loaded the bags into a Wildlife Conservation Society truck and headed north, onto the eastern front of the Andes, toward the riverside community of Junín de los Andes. Rounding a small hill, the stories Graciela had told me back in Montana came to life—a jumbled range of mountains, their heights eclipsed by the soaring and snow-capped cone of the Lanín Volcano. Junín (pronounced *hu–nin*) nestled in the shadows of the volcano, flanked by a maze of protected mountain parklands. The cone rises skyward at the confluence of several major ecosystems, where the vast, windy, brush-filled eastern steppes meet the grassy Andean foothills to the west.

The Patagonian region straddles Chile and Argentina, but the two countries could not be more different. Unlike the alpine crest of Chilean Patagonia, the Argentinian region is dominated by windy and arid steppe habitat all the way to the coastline. It really reminded me of the sage brush prairies of eastern Montana, a land dissected by cold, clear, clean rivers that today are filled with popular but non-native trout. The grasses give way to bamboo thickets and then stately beech forests as you climb into higher elevations toward the alpine rock and ice.

The higher you go in the Andes, the wetter it gets, with moisture spilling over the Andean Divide from Chile in the form of rain and snow, and feeding lush bamboo forests. Draped in lichen, lenga trees (southern beech) create a mountain canopy that that eventually become rocky alpine ledges near the summit ridges. And at this height, in every direction, shining snowfields and glaciers cloak the summits. Patagonia is more than wild and beautiful, it inspires.

Junín de los Andes is something of a hotbed of wildlife biologists, and soon Martín and Graciela were introducing me to the town's active and youthful scientific community. The center of that community is Andrés Navarro, a fit forty-something who manages the Wildlife Conservation Society's Andean Steppe program and serves as a lead Wildlife Research Scientist for the Argentine National Research Council. He earned his PhD from the University of Florida in 1997 before returning home to study Patagonia's culpeo fox ecology. Martín, Andrés, and others have a built an innovative team of fiercely passionate local scientists that is shaping the future of wildlife conservation in Argentina.

Some people, when you meet them for the first time, leave an immediate and powerful impression. With Andrés, it took all of about an hour to realize I was in the company of one of Argentina's premier wildlife researchers, a quiet but confident statesman proud of both his country and his colleagues.

He was the perfect guide to introduce me to the fascinating wildlife work being done in Junín de Los Andes. Already, I was beginning to understand that with the vastness of the South American landscape came an equally vast set of challenges for scientists working to understand the impact of humans on this far-flung land. Miles were long, roads were few and rough, and dollars were scarce. Puma habitats were diverse, but so were the myriad threats to the big cats—ranchers, gauchos, and, especially, energy developers; habitat loss, fragmentation, and degradation; guns and poisons; and most of all, a profound lack of human tolerance.

In some ways, it was as if I'd never left home—except that down here, every threat was magnified. We had work to do.

CHAPTER 11

AUSTRAL WILD

In conclusion, it appears that nothing can be more improving to a young naturalist, than a journey in distant countries.

— Charles Darwin, *The Voyage of the Beagle*

I come from a wild mountain landscape so rugged and beautiful that it is known as the Crown of the Continent. Here in South America, I had arrived in the throne room itself—a place so sweeping and immense that it made the wild Crown and Montana feel cramped.

The Crown is a tremendously large landscape—a full four degrees of latitude north to south, mountains ranging across 18 million acres. Patagonia dwarfs even that tremendous scale, sprawling across 250 million acres. That's the size of the entire Eastern Seaboard—more than Maine, New York, Pennsylvania, Virginia, North Carolina, South Carolina, Georgia, and Florida combined.

Both are home to prairie and to mountain, to snow and rain-drenched forests and thirsty desert savannas, to pumas and their prey. And, perhaps most importantly, both the Crown and Patagonia are sparsely inhabited by humans—both have approximately the same population density, about one person for every 120 acres of land. Of course, most of those people are gathered into the larger towns, leaving an immense big empty where wild nature rules. That means freedom to roam, and a powerful potential for more wildlife habitat conservation.

Just as the Crown's high peaks capture Pacific rain and snow before sending cold, dry air racing eastward onto the prairie, so do the southern

Patagonia pumas are a bit larger and a bit lighter in color than their North American relatives. Chile. LAURA CRAWFORD WILLIAMS

Andes Mountains catch moisture before it can reach the arid steppes and remote Argentine coast. Cold air is dense and heavy and it runs downslope in atmospheric rivers from the mountain ice caps—fierce, icy winds that wail across those unbroken flatlands. The topography literally shapes the life here, and the immense ice caps that shroud the Andes hold a significant portion of our planet's fresh water. And here, at the end of the world, rises a summit immediately recognizable by people who populate the mountaineering world—Cerro Fitz Roy. This wind-battered granite spire takes its name from Robert FitzRoy, an adventurous sea captain who in 1831 shuttled a young Charles Darwin from his home in Great Britain to the wilds of Patagonia. Darwin's voyage on the HMS *Beagle* helped open the naturalist's eyes to the inner workings of nature, strengthening his theory of evolution by natural selection.

It was a powerfully insightful scientific concept. "Descent with modification with natural selection acting as the operating mechanism," was Darwin's way of declaring that species changed through time, adapting to their local conditions and passing on their genes to the next generation. The road to that revolutionary insight led straight through wild Patagonia, with its rich web of bizarre species each influencing the other and the place itself reshaping them all. FitzRoy and Darwin first explored Argentine Patagonia, recording many wildlife and marine life observations before rounding treacherous Cape Horn near the island of Tierra del Fuego. From there, they sailed north to explore Chilean Patagonia on the other side of the Andes Mountains.

When it comes to big predators and prey—Patagonian charismatic megafauna—it's all camels and cats. The region is home to two wild camel species, guanacos and vicuñas, which have been bred into domestic llamas and alpacas. Guanacos are larger and more robust (a male can reach 300 pounds), but both are about the size of a deer—which is to say, the size of puma prey. Pumas are the largest carnivore in Patagonia, and Darwin was a firsthand witness to the ancient interplay between camel and cat. His journal, dated April 22, 1834, chronicles the scene near the Santa Cruz River south of Buenos Aires:

> Ostriches (Darwin's Rheas) are not uncommon, but wild in the extreme. The guanaco, however, is in his proper district, the country swarms with them; there were many herds of 50 to 100, and I saw one, with, I should think 500. The puma and the condor (Andean) follow and prey upon these animals. The footsteps of the former might almost everywhere be seen on the banks of the river. The remains of several guanaco with their necks dislocated and bones broken and gnawed, showed how they met their death.

A mature Patagonia puma feeds on a fresh guanaco kill. Guanacos represent an important prey species for pumas in Chile and Argentina. Torres del Paine National Park, Chile. PABLO CERSOSIMO

Darwin marveled at the playful and gregarious guanacos, which are among my favorite Patagonia wildlife species. He writes of how they communicate in shrill whistles and squeals, often shy but always questioning and inquisitive. "That they are curious is for certain," Darwin noted, "for if a person lies on the ground and plays strange antics such as throwing up his feet in the air, they will almost always approach."

Guanacos remind me of pronghorn antelope in Montana. Pronghorn are also very vigilant and curious and will approach anything they see as different, often coming quite close. In fact, many pronghorn antelope hunters will simply wave a white flag, or some other strange object, to coax a nosey pronghorn into investigating at close range. Pronghorns and guanacos both have excellent vision and can detect movement from a long way off, an adaptation to life on open grasslands. Both species also require large, unfenced blocks of land to survive, and undertake seasonal migrations to stay warm and find food. And both are endemic, which is to say they exist only in one region of their respective continent. Selective evolutionary pressures have created unique animals at opposite ends of

Late afternoon sunshine lingers on the towering Mount Fitz Roy. In the shadows far below a guanaco stands alert. Chile. REX BRYNGELSON

the world, and yet these species are surprisingly quite similar and occupy similar niches.

The Quechua peoples have a long and intimate history with these South American camels, and gave them their modern name from the traditional *wanaku*. Guanacos have been hunted for meat, wool, and skins for centuries. And they've been hunted by pumas for far longer than that. Since the last Ice Age, guanacos have been the only large herbivore to spread throughout the Patagonian region. They occupy the grassland steppe and a long-legged gait to outrun predators. Guanaco, in fact, have been clocked at thirty-five miles per hour on the prairie flats—they are adapted to outrun cats. But these same guanacos also range across dryland and alpine country.

Earning their living on grass and shrubs, guanacos are highly adapted to arid environments and can squeeze a remarkable amount of energy from low-nutrition foods. In other words, guanacos get better gas mileage, and can go days without water. They've even been known to track the Atacama Desert, portions of which haven't seen rain in fifty years. There, a cool-water ocean meets a hot-sand coast, creating a foggy mist that feeds cacti and lichen—which in turn feed guanacos. And with an alpine agility to amble steep slopes with ease, guanaco also have carved a high-mountain niche. Like North American mountain goats, guanacos have large and flexible sole pads that work like climbing shoes; and their blood—with 68 million red cells to a teaspoon—can make the most of the thinly oxygenated Andes air. An odd blend of prairie speedster and desert mountaineer, the guanaco makes a wild, wooly, and fitting prey for Patagonia's pumas.

Despite their astounding ability to survive in extremes, today's guanaco range has diminished dramatically in the face of human development, with the largest herds in Argentina persisting at ancestral levels in just three protected regions: the La Payunia steppe, north of Junín de los Andes; the San Guillermo Biosphere Reserve, near Mount Aconcagua; and the Torres del Paine, in the southern reaches of Chile. That these regions are protected is tremendously important because they cover what scientists believe are historic guanaco migration routes dating back thousands of years.

When left undisturbed in these and other protected areas, guanacos often gather into tremendous herds, packing the landscape and making meals for pumas. Guanacos and pumas have evolved together in Patagonia, just as deer and mountain lions have developed side by side in North America. To stay safe from the predators, guanacos have taken to living in large herds composed of a dominant and protective male with numerous females and juveniles. It's not unlike the way big bull elk protect harems of females back in Montana. The male guanaco, or *relincho*, defends his herd by either stand-ing guard himself or ensuring that another guanaco is posted as a sentinel. An approaching puma or human elicits a loud and high-pitched horse-like whinny from the sharp-eyed lookout, giving the herd a heads-up and a head start. Guanacos also have evolved the rather messy survival tactic of spitting on aggressors, whether puma or human—and though we know a well-placed gob will put off a human at close range (I have some personal experience with this), the effectiveness of expectorating on a hungry cat remains unclear.

Pumas are the primary hunters of guanacos, but they're not the only predator. Culpeo fox, colorful wild canids similar to a coyote or a small wolf, also prey on guanacos. The striking orange and gray culpeo is quite attrac-tive, but can also be quite deadly to newborns and young. The real threat to guanacos, however, is the human threat. Just as cattle have replaced bison on the North American prairie, so have domestic sheep replaced guanacos in South America. Gone are the tremendous herds of South American camels

The arid and windy grasslands of Patagonia are home to a unique ostrich-like bird called a Darwin's rhea. In Chile, they are referred to as *ñandú* and in Argentina they are called *choique*. Patagonia National Park, Chile.
JUSTIN LOTAK

Darwin observed and then recorded in his journals. European ranchers wiped out those wild herds to make room for sheep—for wool and meat—across Patagonia's native grasslands and foothills. Poachers kill guanacos, for meat and sport, just as poachers kill deer and elk up in the Crown. And landscape development—oil, gas, hydropower, urban sprawl—erodes guanaco habitat and fragments the critical seasonal migration routes that are only now being documented by biologists.

But the fundamental problem is this: Wild guanacos eat grass. And sheep eat grass. So sheep ranchers kill guanacos. Today, the guanaco population has dropped to around 500,000—from perhaps 50 million prior to the arrival of Europeans—with 90 percent of remaining guanacos living in the steppes of Argentina. And when the guanacos are gone, the natural system collapses and the pumas eat sheep. So ranchers kill pumas. Just like back home, puma survival ultimately comes down to tolerance and habitat. It's up to local communities to determine whether there's room for guanacos and pumas in Patagonia. And here's where Montana and Argentina diverge in a profound way: Unlike the Crown, where healthy herds of deer and elk still feed native predators, the Patagonian wild has been unraveled by non-native livestock. To achieve the kind of tolerance we've won up north, we'll first need to face a *gaucho* culture that makes the Buckhorn Bar back in Augusta look downright progressive.

Gauchos are the weathered cowboys of Patagonia's Pampas and mountains. Typically of native South American or mixed European-Mapuche descent, these hardy men are the horse-borne labor force for this region's large ranch operations. There are no bears and wolves down here for them to worry about, so they chase pumas. Darwin saw them in action while traveling the region in 1832:

> *The Captain had bought from the Gaucho soldiers a large puma or South American lion, and this morning it was killed for its skin. These animals are common in the Pampas and I have frequently seen their footsteps in my walks: It is said they will not attack a man; though they evidently are quite strong enough. The Gauchos secured this one by first throwing balls (boleadoras or bola) and entangling its front legs, then they lassoed or noosed him, when by riding round a bush and throwing other lasso's, he was soon lashed firm and secure.*

The gauchos of Chile and Argentina are legendary, skilled animal handlers, and they have been romanticized much in the way of our Western cowboy myths. Once, perhaps, they embodied freedom and independence;

today, they labor for wealthy ranch owners and are experts in animal husbandry. My first encounter with Argentine gauchos was in Junín de los Andes, with Martín and Graciela. It was a summer gaucho rodeo, and the cowboys had arrived in full gaucho dress, their long *facón* knives tucked neatly into their colorful belt sashes. They were stern and stoic, in the way of cowboys everywhere, and simply nodded when I tried to approach.

A Patagonian gaucho rodeo is a far cry from the familiar rodeos of the American West. Rather than straddling a bucking bronco or enraged bull, Patagonian gauchos actually ride their wild steeds with the horses' front legs reared up and pawing at the sky, as their mounts hop on powerful hind legs around a large pole anchored into the dusty ground. All the while, the rodeo announcer sings rousing songs describing the action. The entire audience sings along, joining the shifting and impromptu chorus. It's an interactive spectator sport, a whole story unfolding in the moment, and beer and wine help smooth the narrative.

The isolated and rural gaucho community is, not surprisingly, a close-knit group. Hard work and a remote lifestyle create strong community and family bonds. It is an insular world, not overly bothered by the conventions of urban culture; its relationship with the land is complicated. On the one hand, there are few who know wild Patagonia as well as the gauchos. On the other hand, their work has often been the downfall of wild Patagonia. Their livestock have unraveled the native food web, destroying the ancient dance between predator and prey. Their ranch culture killed off the guanaco to replace them with sheep, and then killed off the puma because the cats ate the sheep.

This is why I had traveled to Patagonia—to bring some lessons of tolerance from Montana so that the wildlife biologists, *estancia* owners, and the gauchos, together, could begin restoring Patagonia's wild puma heart. It is slow work, and will take time, but I am confident in Darwin's observation: given enough generations, we can adapt and change to better fit the world in which we live.

CHAPTER 12

ALTERED ANDEAN LANDSCAPES

The most important thing is to preserve the world we live in. Unless people learn and understand about our world, habitats, and animals, they won't understand that if we don't protect those habitats, we'll eventually destroy ourselves.

– Jack Hanna, TV show host

A ll is not well in the wilds of Patagonia.

I knew that even before I touched the ground there. At first, from 30,000 feet, Patagonia looks as natural and untamed as any wild country I've known. Flying south from Buenos Aires, the land unfolds against a scattering of small towns and hamlets, which soon give way to farms and orchards, then to the great Pampas grasslands that strain the horizons. The spiderweb of roads soon thins to single tracks dwindling into a great, distant open. Out beyond, farther south still, the tracks lead to the doorsteps of vast private ranches, remote estancias tucked into a maze of broken hills. Some of Argentina's ranches are the size of America's national parks.

And throughout the flight, the Argentine countryside near the mountains is hidden beneath a cloak of dark green, the scattered pine forests that were my first clue that all was not well.

Pine trees? In Argentina? I thought this ecosystem was defined by southern beech forests, by colorful deciduous lenga trees, and the spruce-like coihue. I expected majestic alerce to pierce the sky like so many towering redwoods. I imagined ancient araucaria, the iconic monkey puzzle trees that have grown here since the Mesozoic. Frame one of those living fossils up in front of an Argentine volcano and you would hardly be surprised to see a sauropod dinosaur amble by. Some paleoecologists, after all, reckon

Diving head first into the fierce Patagonia winds, a mature Andean condor navigates the alpine spine of Patagonia's spires. Aguja Guillaumet, Argentina. AUSTIN SIADAK

those long-necked dinos actually evolved specifically to nibble the araucaria canopy. But pine trees?

Turns out, European settlers wanted European houses, so they imported pine trees for timber and lumber. How were they to know that a pine evolved in the company of wildfire was dangerously out of place in an ecosystem where fire was a rare event? As any Montanan can attest, frequent wildfire is an essential part of a pine forest's life cycle. The trees are literally built to burn. Not so with an Argentine beech forest. Trouble is, once the pines were established, they provided the fuel that scorched tremendous swaths of native forest. All it took was a lightning strike—or, more often, a careless human—to ignite a whole ecosystem. Ancient forests can go up in smoke overnight, and recovery time is measured in generations, if at all.

Of course, complex networks of flora and fauna have grown up with those native beech forests, their lives and livelihoods an elegant tangle of co-evolved neighbors. Hummingbirds and insects fine-tuned to rely on brilliantly colored purple and pink fuchsia flowers. Small rodents making their living from southern sorrel. Lupine seeds, feeding people for at least 6,000 years. Underfoot, dwarf paramela and lady slippers and porcelain orchids. Overhead, green Patagonian parakeets, *chimangos*, caracaras. Black-chested buzzard eagles and the band-winged nightjar. And, of course, native huemul deer and pumas, locked in that old dance of hoof and tooth. Locals who know these old forests measure the quality of the air by the quantity of old man's beard hanging from the lenga trees—the purer the air, the longer the lichen. All of these intricate relationships and many more are destroyed and displaced when native habitat is overrun by invading pine or blackened by unnatural fire.

I wanted, badly, to find a wild and untrammeled Patagonia, up close and personal. But like all close-ups, this one revealed the scars and blemishes that have marked this landscape. Many of the species that inhabit Patagonia's native ecosystem are endemic. And unfortunately, the place that they have evolved in has been fundamentally altered. It wasn't a chemical pollutant like arsenic, or a physical disruption like an oil field. It was biological. And it didn't end with those invasive pines.

A century ago, the Patagonian landscape looked pretty desolate to arriving Europeans. Apart from the guanaco, there didn't seem to be much life out there—or at least, not much to eat. So in 1896, exactly thirty-six European hares were transplanted from Germany to a large ranch in Argentina's Sante Fe Province. Folks wanted food, and sport, and hares seemed just the ticket. Of course they bred like ... well ... like rabbits, and set off a chain of consequences that has affected every living creature in Patagonia, right up to the mighty puma.

The hares exploded across the countryside and by 1907, Argentina's government was forced to declare them an agricultural pest. They ran like wildfire, nibbling their way through native grasslands, gardens and farms, orchards and plantations. They completely remade the plant ecology in some areas. A century after their release, research showed European hares distributed across every corner of Argentina, with the lone exception of Mendoza Province's high, dry mountains. They had spread across South America at a rate of more than five miles per year, quick as a hare and steady as a tortoise.

All that bite-sized, high-density meat on the land provided whole new niches for native carnivores. Some endemic species—including the Pampas cat and culpeo fox—completely altered their natural hunting habits and now they prey almost exclusively on European hares. This has disrupted traditional predator-prey interactions, to the benefit of some and the detriment of others.

Unfortunately, the Europeans weren't content with their pine forests full of hares. They also brought European red deer—a species not unlike North American elk—which immediately filled niches long occupied by guanaco and vicuña further north. Those pine forests made great cover for red deer, and the big-game hunters loved it. Even today, European and American demand for big-game hunts on private Patagonian ranches is driving a lucrative business.

Like the hares, these new grazers and browsers profoundly trimmed back native vegetation. They also put a tremendous amount of protein—meat with feet—in places where it had never been. Things with teeth were sure to follow, as the entire ecosystem shifted to meet the new reality. The native grazers were further marginalized by these deer, making their populations susceptible to predators. It was not unlike what happened with the caribou up north—the fundamental injury is man-made, and the predator is just the insult on top of that injury—a final straw that can break a population already damaged by habitat change.

But the biggest change of all, perhaps, came in the wooly shape of sheep. The Patagonian region has long rivaled New Zealand for legendary wool production, and to this day Patagonia is synonymous for high-quality wool. Like the hares, sheep were introduced to Patagonia in the late 1800s, and expanded rapidly across their new range. Along the way, they made their owners a tidy sum of money, assuring sheep ranchers a position near the center of economic and political power.

Almost all of Patagonia's famed grasslands, nearly 400 million acres, are found in Argentina. It's a region of few predators and minimal competition from native grazers, making it attractive to both sheep and the ranchers who raise them. By 1950, those initial settlement herds had reached a high

Intense sheep grazing of the grasslands has resulted in increased desertification. Domestic sheep have become a common part of the puma's diet. Valle Chacabuco, Chile. TIM DAVIS

of nearly 22 million sheep in Argentina. Numbers have dropped since those boom times, but close to 9 million sheep still graze the (formerly) wildlands of Patagonia.

All those non-native grazers have remade Patagonia from the ground up, affecting the most fundamental elements of rangeland flora and soils. This is especially true on those ranches where the land is grazed year-round, with no cycle of rest and recovery. Over time, those hard-hit pastures wither into desert-like brushland, with little or nothing in the way of grasses and forbs. The fierce Patagonia winds then blow the soil to the Atlantic in a hurry.

This desertification, perhaps even more than the pine-driven wildfires, reduces or eliminates habitat for a whole host of South American songbird and mammal species. Of course, desertification is tough on sheep, too, and competition for good grass can be fierce—even on the traditional grassland steppes, which for millennia prior to being overgrazed by sheep, supported a proper sea of prairie grass. In the resulting fight for grass, wildlife, not surprisingly, have paid the price. Guanaco, the puma's favored meal, have long been persecuted and even eliminated from their historic habitats in order to save grass for sheep.

Again, the situation reminds me of the North American pronghorn, which competes with cattle for grass in the high, dry prairie of eastern Montana. For a time, ranchers there also went after wildlife with a taste for grass. Pronghorns, like guanaco, are extremely visible on the landscape; ranchers can watch them from the kitchen window. Best-case scenario, the rancher would call a wildlife biologist or local game warden to complain about the crop damage. Worst-case scenario, he'd fix it himself with a rifle.

But in Montana today, we're fortunate that antelope enjoy game-animal status—they are popular prey for hunters. That popularity has evolved into support and protection, even from the ranchers themselves. In fact, most ranchers and farmers are proud of the wildlife their lands produce, regardless of a little competition for grass. Modern farm and ranch methods—like rotating crops, resting pastures, and cycling livestock through different fields—help keep the grass growing, which reduces the competition, which reduces the friction between wildlife and livelihood.

Today, Patagonian landowners are learning some of these lessons about how to live with wild nature. In fact, they are finding it easier and cheaper and more productive to do so. But for now, guanaco continue to struggle. Of course, that means puma must find their meal elsewhere—and where better than in the sheep pasture? You can hardly blame them. After all, we've closed the traditional grocery store, and there are certainly enough sheep to support a thriving puma population.

Two young guanacos and an adult communicate below high Andean hillsides. Guanacos are inquisitive and make a variety of vocalizations. Perito Moreno National Park, Argentina. DARIÓ PODESTÁ

The culpeo fox is native to Chile and Argentina and is a bit larger than its North American counterpart. Argentina. DARIÓ PODESTÁ

But if there's one thing a rancher hates more than an herbivore eating his grass, it's a predator eating his livestock: a puma or a coyote-sized culpeo fox or even the smaller zorro fox, as small as a North American red fox but still big enough to take a young ewe or lamb. Never mind that compared to wily guanaco, these sheep are easy pickings. Never mind that we haven't given the puma or the fox any alternatives—except for sheep, or hares, or European red deer. Never mind that the species we introduced may well be the cause for what are, perhaps, unnaturally high cat numbers in some areas. Never mind, because an entire gaucho culture, generation after generation, has grown up around the idea that the only good predator is a dead predator.

All is not going to be well in Patagonia any time soon. Under normal conditions, puma and guanaco get along just fine—at least at the natural balance of population levels. But with guanaco numbers dramatically reduced, and cat populations fat on non-native species, it may well be that puma predation is limiting the potential recovery of guanaco, and even the highly endangered huemul deer. It's a complicated system, with each player affecting all other players in a complex ecological network of cause and effect. And the pine trees aren't going away any time soon, nor are the hares, deer, or sheep. That makes it a nightmare for my colleagues who are the local wildlife managers and who are accountable both to the ecological integrity of the system and to the demands of gauchos and ranchers.

Whether it's Indian tigers, Mexican jaguars, or African lions, the conflict between carnivores and livestock is the same worldwide. Even at home, in the Crown of the Continent, we haven't solved it. But we have established an uneasy truce, and I'm hopeful we can export those experiences to places such as Patagonia.

Already, my friends in Argentina and Chile are dreaming big. Passionate people like Andrés Navarro and Martín Funes are working with international organizations such as the Wildlife Conservation Society and The Nature Conservancy—as well as with regional outfits such as Conservación Patagónica and Fundación Patagónica Natural—to conserve and restore critical grassland habitats. They're teaching the gospel of rest-rotation grazing strategies, and they're removing sheep fences to allow nature to move through Patagonia naturally again.

They have one potent but unlikely ally in their struggle: the sheep ranches themselves. The wool market, like any other commodity, has fluctuated over time as prices climb and fall. Across the years, some ranches have failed while others have thrived—and the survivors have gobbled up neighboring outfits to consolidate into tremendous holdings that sprawl across millions of acres. And some, surprisingly, are becoming Patagonia's newest national parks.

CHAPTER 13

RANCHING
FOR WILDLIFE

*In the end it's the local community that is often the most
steadfast and resolute in protecting nature. After all, they
have the most to lose and most to gain. Without them as
allies, conservation is merely an arm's-length enterprise.*

– M. Sanjayan, conservationist

My friend Martin Monteverde has a tough job. Martin is just one
of several professional biologists and scientists who reside in the
small community of Junín de los Andes, located in west-central
Argentina. The town is downslope of the high Andean crest bordering
Chile, and sits surrounded by protected parklands in the shadow of ice-
capped Lanin Volcano. Its topography—where grasslands meet forests meet
mountains—makes it an incredibly rich place to study biodiversity and
ecosystem relationships. And its nearby protected designations make excellent "laboratories" for conservation biologists. That's why so many scientists
choose this tiny town for their base, and in this way it reminds me of home.
An inordinate number of my Montana neighbors are "ologists" of some
sort, drawn to my little community by the intersection of ecodiversity and
Glacier National Park's world-class "workshop." It's tricky to study wildlife
unless you live where the wildlife lives.

Martin is the lead wildlife biologist for the local branch of the Centro
de Ecología Aplicada de Neuquén (CEAN). CEAN is much like my state
wildlife agency, which makes Martin my South American counterpart.
That's how I know he has a tough job. Like me, he's on the front lines—the
guy sheep ranchers and farmers call to chew out when a wild carnivore,
usually a puma, has been dining on domesticated livestock.

Herds of native guanacos can be seen on the grassland steppes of Patagonia. They are often killed or driven
away by ranchers who worry that guanacos compete with sheep for available grass. Patagonia National Park,
Chile. CONSERVACIÓN PATAGÓNICA

Fences are often no protection from pumas hunting livestock. Torres del Paine National Park, Chile. PABLO CERSOSIMO

In fact, I recognized the office of a fellow wildlife biologist immediately—posters and pictures of native birds and mammals, science journals and books on natural history, jars of specimens, the clean, white polish of bones and teeth and skulls. The only difference was that in place of the coffee maker, Martin had an old steel tea kettle for brewing traditional *maté* (pronounced *maw-tay)*, a strong drink that tastes, at first, a bit like alfalfa hay. It grows on you. I have since learned that *maté* is the social glue that holds all of Patagonia together. I picked up a large cat skull from the shelf, a puma that could just as easily been found a world away in Montana. "It looks just like ours," I said.

"Yes," Martin replied, "but we have other wildcats, too."

Every wildlife biologist's office has a specimen freezer, and Martin's was full of wonders. He showed me a Pampas cat—about the size of a bobcat—light brown and black striped and native to the steppe. Then a güiña, a small and dark-colored felid, about the size of a house cat, that is rare and has proved remarkably elusive. Martin said he and his colleagues had long been surveying güiñas amid the bamboo and lenga forests, but so far have detected only a very few. Remote camera technology has helped the survey, but still the tiny black cats have remained—in the way of cats—mysterious and largely invisible. In Montana, I often give visiting wildlife biologists a tour of the specimen freezer, showing them lions, bears, lynx, and wolves. I smiled, holding that tiny güiña, and felt at home—despite the fact that I was drinking *mate* from a gourd while leaf-cutter ants marched by outside, in the shade of a volcano.

The next day, we left the windy steppe for the forest to check some wildlife track pads in nearby Lanin National Park. The pads are essentially little sand traps that biologists rake smooth to capture animal tracks, and Lanin Park—which, at about a million acres, is almost the same size as Glacier National Park—is the perfect place to look for wildcat prints.

Most of Argentine Patagonia is dry, wide, open, and windy. The two exceptions are the undeveloped coastlines to the east, and the cooler jungle of bamboo and lenga snuggled up next to the Andes in the west. Lanin National Park is what we call a moist temperate climate, with some parts of the reserve averaging more than 100 inches of precipitation per year. It's a little bit of Chile in Argentina. The closer you get to Chile, the wetter and greener it gets, and we drove all the way to the Chilean border guard station.

We passed steep canyons filled by sparkling blue lakes the color of azure. We flushed *carranchos* (a tropical falcon known as caracaras in the southwest United States), *chimangos* (a clever raptor known by researchers for its problem-solving skills), and other wonderful bird species on the gravel park roads. Looking all the while at a backdrop of glaciers hanging on the mountains above, we hiked through bamboo that towered over our heads as green-colored Patagonia parrots flew and chortled around us. At the track pads we found only common culpeo fox prints; the secretive güiña remained hidden in its mystery.

Later in the week, Martin ushered me into the epicenter of wildlife science in central Argentine Patagonia—the office of the Wildlife Conservation Society's Patagonian and Andean Steppe Program. We pulled into the driveway of a beautiful yet modest riverfront home. I could hear water flowing and birds singing as Andrés Navarro, the director of the program, approached from the house. Today, he wanted to share with me the work of his colleagues here in Junín. And one by one, the student researchers laid out the biological map for me.

They were studying guanaco in places eerily similar to Montana's sagebrush prairie and Missouri River Breaks country, where new roads for oil and gas operations were providing poachers access to remote herds. Fewer guanacos, of course, meant fewer native meals for puma. And the student researchers were studying Darwin's rheas, which the Argentines call *choique*

There is a long history of zero tolerance for pumas on Patagonian ranches. For generations *leoneros*—lion hunting gauchos—have killed any puma that they can. Argentina. LORENA MARTINEZ

and the Chileans call *ñandú*. These flightless birds—which take both their common and scientific name from the Greek goddess Rhea, daughter of earth and sky—look like mini ostriches and are native to the Patagonian steppe. Rhea gather in social flocks, and are an easy prey base for fox and puma despite the birds' sharply clawed toes.

But Rhea populations are strained by habitat loss and poaching, which again means fewer native meals for the predators. Throughout the day, the theme persisted: native ecologies disrupted by industry and non-native species, undermining the prey base which in turn distorted the predator behavior. No guanaco? No rhea? Eat a sheep. Dead sheep? Kill a puma. I knew this domino effect only too well from a long career in Montana, just as I knew that passions always run high when it comes to predators killing livestock. The traditional cowboy and gaucho response is the same world-wide: kill the cat.

There are other alternatives, however, and solutions that grow from other sets of values are certainly more ecologically justifiable. That's what Martin and Andrés and my team up north were trying to explore, and that's why

Martin Monteverde, foreground, works with local Argentinian ranchers to minimize puma-livestock conflicts. Junín de los Andes, Argentina. MARTIN MONTEVERDE COLLECTION

I was here—to share information north to south, and south to north, on behalf of wild pumas and whole ecosystems.

Patagonian pumas do differ from North American mountain lions, in terms of genetics and appearance and also in the natural niche they fill. Unlike cats in the north, which must contend with wolves and bears and other big predators, pumas are the largest carnivore in all of Patagonia. In fact, the males, in particular, are even a little bit larger than their North American cousins—weighing in at up to 180 pounds, compared to 130-pound average for a Montana lion. They're also a bit lighter in color, with slightly longer ears. Beyond those subtle differences, however, they're the same cat, roaming what are essentially the same habitats, among the same ranches, to the dismay of the same hired hands. So we went to meet the gauchos.

Martin and Andrés and I had meticulously planned the public meeting over endless gourds of *maté* at Monteverde's CEAN office. We'd all been in enough meeting rooms to know how quickly things could go sideways when the topic was livestock and predators. We even chose the venue—the local livestock cooperative's center—with an eye toward keeping the peace. Meet them on their own turf, we figured, and it might not seem so threatening.

Monteverde had been advertising for weeks that a wildlife biologist from Montana was in town to share puma-conflict information, and we didn't have to wait long before local students, agency personnel, and ranchers began to fill the room. At home in Montana, you can always pick out the ranchers by the proud way they carry themselves and the clothes they wear—jeans and flannel, big belt buckles and bigger hats. The Patagonian ranchers were similarly easy to identify—fine leather boots or lightweight blue gaucho shoes with roped soles, neck scarves, and leather vests, all capped off by beret-like *boinas*. They also had a certain facial expression I recognized. It said, "Who is this guy, and what's he going to tell me that I don't already know?"

With Monteverde translating, I began to run through my slides of puma-conflict management in Montana. When a cat kills a cow or a sheep, I explained, we don't immediately kill all the local pumas we can find. Instead, we target only the culprit. Yes, every now and again an individual puma figures out that livestock make an easy meal. So we deal with that. But the rest of the population is protected as game animals. This was a new concept to most of these Patagonian ranchers, and heads were shaking. But I kept on, and Monteverde kept translating, and soon the ranchers were getting engaged and interested in how other regions manage pumas and deal with conflicts.

Slowly, the awkwardness evaporated as they realized that I had some tangible knowledge they could take back to their estancias. By the end of the meeting, I was surrounded by smiling ranch owners inviting me to come check out their operations. The idea of public hunting was intriguing to them, but mostly they wanted to know more about Montana's wildlife-conflict specialist jobs—remember Erik Wenum and the cat under the deck? Turns out, there was widespread support among the Patagonian ranchers for a local CEAN government biologist who would deal exclusively with predator conflicts, and they thought such a model would work well in their communities.

In fact, they already had a similar expert on the ground—the gaucho *leonero*, who hunts cats year-round for the sheep interests. It was a remove-them-all operation. Perhaps we could adapt that admittedly deadly model to establish a conflict-specialist program? The value of hiring a professional conflict specialist is that you can begin to insert some real puma science into the discussion. Leaving a few big males around may actually reduce some predation impacts, for instance, but that is a tough pill for the traditional *leonero* to swallow.

Guard dogs for livestock have been used successfully by Dr. Paula Herrera—causing the number of sheep killed by pumas to drop from thirty a month to two—in Patagonia National Park in Chile. JIMMY VALDES

The stakes are tremendously high when it comes to establishing some small amount of predator tolerance among Patagonia's ranchers. Their spreads are mind-boggling huge, sprawling across millions of acres. So if you can convince just one single rancher to protect guanaco herds, or to tolerate wild pumas, then you have made a landscape-level effect on a place bigger than Yosemite National Park. The sheer size of these ranches make them critically important to wildland conservation, and the fact that they're controlled by a relatively small number of people makes it possible to work one-on-one toward fundamental ecosystem changes.

In Patagonia, one-on-one means *maté* and *asados*—the South American equivalent of coffee and burgers—and over many meals we shared generations of experience in living with cats. I was particularly intrigued by the work of Alejandro 'Nito' Gonzalez, who is experimenting with specialized guard dogs to defend livestock. Nito grew up in a family of climbing guides, and spend his youth exploring the snow-capped spires of Lanin Volcano. But his passion was protecting cats.

At the time I met him, Nito was trying to get puppies to nurse on sheep and goat nannies, to establish a protective bond between dog and livestock.

Eventually, he perfected this method and began raising guard dogs alongside livestock herds. By marking the ranch territory with urine and scat, the dogs send a clear signal to pumas that this is hostile turf.

We have done predator work with dogs in Montana for years, but nothing like this. Our efforts have focused largely on Karelian bear dogs, which we train to haze grizzly and black bears away from urban areas. The black-and-white dogs originally bred in Finland chase and corner bears by barking in a very high, fast pitch and running back and forth around the bruins. Spinning around and around the bear, they nip at its backside and just generally aggravate the heck out of it. Up north, we use them to shepherd problem bears, and to help us teach grizzlies that human spaces are bad news.

But Nito's work was exciting and different, and more like guard dog programs in other parts of North America that I've not had firsthand experience with. He was actually bonding individual dogs to individual herds, and letting them keep watch against pumas and other predators. In 2012, he published his research in the scientific journal *Human-Wildlife Interactions*, and launched a widespread study that expanded the use of inexpensive mixed-breed guard dogs to see if doing so would reduce retaliatory killings of predators. He recruited twenty-five goat herders to test the use of dogs, as well as a control group of nine herders who didn't use the dogs. The puppies were brought onto the ranches just before the birthing period for the goats, so they would imprint and integrate both socially and visually. The result was one big happy canine-goat family, which the dogs fiercely protected.

What was perhaps more surprising, though, was the effect on the ranchers. Not only did the dogs protect the herds and reduce predation, but in doing so they actually changed the ranchers' perceptions of predation losses and retaliatory killing. By being proactive, the ranchers felt more in control—and that made them less likely to want to kill all cats. It's a bit like having a mountain lion hunt in Montana: it builds social license and involves people so they have some hand, some personal power, in managing the populations. When people feel empowered and proactive, they can afford to be a little more generous.

More importantly, the experiment proved it was possible to build partnerships between conservation biologists and ranchers—exactly the sorts of relationships that will prove essential to protecting pumas and their Patagonia habitats.

Other ranchers and biologists are experimenting with similarly novel solutions, sometimes borrowed from our work in North America and sometimes borrowed from even farther afield. One particularly promising tactic I saw being employed in Patagonia has its roots all the way on the other side of the world, in the Great Rift Valley region of southern Kenya and northern Tanzania.

The Great Rift Valley is home to the Maasai people, who live near the many game parks of the African Great Lakes region. And when you live next to a wildlife park, you learn how to deal with wildlife. For the cattle-herding Maasai, that means hungry African lions and other powerful predators. To keep the lions out, many Maasai choose to live in *bomas*—clusters of homes grouped within a circular thorny fence, usually woven from acacia trees. Typically, the men build the fence while the women erect the homes within the protective ring. The *boma* becomes a safe haven at night, both for families and for their valuable livestock, which they herd inside the ring of thorns each evening.

In Argentina, estancia owners also are now using Patagonia-style *bomas* to protect newborn lambs. The gauchos are, like many Maasai, seminomadic, traveling seasonally with their livestock from pasture to pasture within the vast borders of the ranches. But when the ewes are lambing, the herd's ability to move is greatly reduced. During this time, it's especially important to protect the lambs from dusk to dawn, when pumas are on the prowl. And so the gauchos build *bomas*—fences of sticks and branches and stacks of stone. Unfortunately, pumas are built to leap over high barriers and rocky walls. And that's where the wildlife biologists come into play.

Martin Monteverde and his colleagues have been improving the design of puma *bomas* in northern Patagonia. These newfangled compounds are more permanent metal structures, buried about fifty centimeters (nineteen inches) into the earth and topped with barbed wire. They also come equipped with a black curtain that not only provides some shade but also blocks the view so pumas can't quite see what's inside. The big cats are extremely visual, and although they can likely smell the lambs, they don't get that visual stimulus which can trigger an attack.

Bomas are ancient technology, but we're bringing them into the modern age. In Montana we string electric fences—often powered by small solar cells in remote areas—to keep animals as large as grizzly bears out of the henhouse, the beehive, the orchard, and the livestock yard. Advanced, lightweight, and durable materials have revolutionized the *boma*, dramatically reducing livestock loss to predation. Of course, the availability of these high-tech solutions is limited in the Great Rift Valley and the wilds of Patagonia, but we're finding ways to make them obtainable. The fences are relatively expensive, of course, but far cheaper in the long run than waging a labor-intensive and losing battle against nature.

CHAPTER 14

PUMAS BELOW ACONCAGUA

It is not the strongest of the species that survives, nor the most intelligent, but the one that is most responsive to change.

– Charles Darwin

Pumas are sly, secretive, stealthy, and seldom-seen cats of mystery, ghosts that keep to the shadows of deep cover and darkness. Except when they aren't.

There is a place in South America, along the spine of the Andes in west-central Argentina, where pumas prowl in the open and you can watch them hunt in the middle of the day. Here, at the very rooftop of the Western Hemisphere, the wild edge of natural selection has carved a very different kind of cat.

The place that shaped this remarkably unguarded puma is as extreme and unlikely as the behavior it has produced. Aconcagua, the world's highest mountain outside of Asia, towers to 22,837 feet above sea level, thrust aloft in the colossal collision of continental plates that drove the Andes crest skyward. The mountain's severe eastern flanks give way to rugged foothills, descending into Argentina, and partway through that abrupt transition a broad valley hangs high above the steppe at 12,000 feet. This is the San Guillermo Biosphere Reserve, a place so remote, so untrammeled, so unknown that it wasn't given protections until 1998. Today, it is sanctuary for one of the largest populations of wild native camelids in Argentina. We're talking super-high-elevation South American mountain camels. This is where pumas prowl visible and open, exposed to the light of day.

An immense mature male Patagonian puma is lord of his domain, vigilantly scanning the landscape for potential food, female pumas, or trespassing males. Torres del Paine National Park, Chile. PABLO CERSOSIMO

Cats evolved stealth not only to ambush prey, but also to slink through the margins between other big predators—between wolves and bears and people. But in the awesome remoteness of San Guillermo, there are no wolves, no bears, and no people. The land, too, is stark and wide open, a sweep of wind-scoured rock and dust not lending itself to deep-cover hiding places. It is perhaps the only place in the world where biologists can observe the dance of puma and prey laid bare.

Andrés Navarro calls it the Puna, one of the most intact ecological systems in central Argentina. The Puna, characterized by high-altitude deserts, is not unlike the short-grass prairies that meet the Rockies in the western United States—but at a much higher elevation and with much less precipitation. Here, extensive open plains are dissected by rocky canyons and surrounded by high Andean peaks. While it is mostly dry and cool, patches of vegetated meadows, called *vegas*, crop up sporadically throughout the Puna. These moist habitats cover less than 5 percent of the landscape, but appear to be critical for wildlife. They are highly productive and are shrouded by at least 80 percent vegetation. Compare that to the surrounding plains and canyons, where vegetation covers less than 10 percent of the ground—the rest a gravely mix of pebbles, sand, and rock.

Because the land is so open, and the vegetation so sparse, and the grazing grounds so concentrated, Andrés and his fellow researchers have witnessed pumas that have adapted to open-country survival and hunting methods never seen elsewhere. Back in his Junín office, I sat transfixed by his photos: a vicuña kill covered in gravel, the only way for a puma to preserve and conceal its kill in this grassless desert; a cat sitting mid-day on the valley floor, watching Andrés pass in his research vehicle; a puma treading through a skiff of snow in broad daylight, in an empty landscape completely void of brushy cover. I've known lions in Montana to cover kills in snow, when grass and brush are too far buried beneath winter's weight. But rocks?

Ecologically speaking, San Guillermo is one of the most intact assemblages of native predators and prey in the southern cone of South America. It remains so for one simple reason: darn few people. And that makes it especially important—it represents a living, breathing, intact laboratory, and offers biologists a window into untouched wild Patagonia. Guanacos live here, as do the smaller vicuñas—in fact, vicuñas are about ten times more abundant in the Puna. At first glance, you might wonder if they eat pebbles and rocks to make a living. But look closer and you find the isolated green oases tucked into canyons where water collects. Of course where vicuñas meet for a meal, pumas also come to eat—and biologists, likewise, gather at the watering hole.

Pumas cover their kills with whatever is available, even rocks in the arid San Guillermo Biosphere Reserve in Argentina. EMILIANO DONADIO

I learned much of what I know about San Guillermo from Emiliano Donadio, a young biologist working with Andrés Navarro. For years, Emiliano conducted fieldwork on culpeo foxes, exploring predation on sheep. Then, one day, Andrés penned a letter to Emiliano, writing that he'd just returned from an amazing new park called San Guillermo.

"He described hundreds of wild vicuñas grazing in open meadows and plains, and wild pumas wandering around during daylight at 12,000 feet and up," Emiliano told me later. "Condors were soaring overhead looking for carcasses, and there were no humans around."

Within months, Emiliano was on a plane into the high Andes, launching an exploration into the interactions between pumas, camels, and grass. How did puma behavior affect prey behavior? And how did prey behavior affect the ecosystem beneath? The grasses? The soils? Scientists call this trickle down a trophic cascade—could puma affect butterfly or beetle populations? Those are the sorts of questions that can be answered only with data driven by direct field observation—which meant it could be done only here, where pumas were directly observable.

Puma researcher Emiliano Donadio prepares to release a newly marked vicuña calf that will be tracked to determine the habitat use of these smaller South American camels. San Guillermo National Park, Argentina.
EMILIANO DONADIO COLLECTION

"Pumas in San Guillermo are uniquely tolerant of humans," Emiliano said. "The cats live as if we were just part of the landscape. Once, I had a male puma hanging around my truck for thirty minutes; he just did not care. They have never known humans or other predators to be a threat, so they just ignore us."

Emiliano's team began by tracking the large vicuña herds that concentrated together in San Guillermo's high meadows and open plains. It was spectacular country for observation; they could watch upward of 200 vicuñas per day. Because the animals did not perceive people as a threat, the scientists could venture as close as fifty meters (165 feet) without causing any behavioral response. Throughout the summer birthing season, Emiliano's team attached ear-tag transmitters to about one hundred newborn vicuñas. It was, relatively speaking, easy work. They would watch for females with swollen bellies and wait for the babies to be born. Then, after waiting about ten minutes while mother and newborn bonded, the team would simply walk up and clip on an ear-tag transmitter. Their work done, the scientists would simply sit motionless while the family wandered off to continue grazing.

The more difficult work began later, as Emiliano's team tracked the herd to record the fates of these female and newborn vicuña. The goal was to document separate mortality rates and causes for adults and juveniles in order to understand how the predator-prey system worked. In San Guillermo, it turns out, the heavier the newborn at birth, the better chance it would survive its first year. Makes sense. Throughout nature, healthier mothers typically give birth to heavier newborns. The team also discovered—through months of tracking adventures and endless hours of sit-still observation—that a full half of all vicuña mortalities, newborns and adults alike, were death by puma. Again, not surprising in a place where the big cats were the top dogs.

The more difficult question was, could puma predation affect vicuña behavior in ways that alter grazing habits—in turn affecting the entire system down to grasses and soils? Pumas everywhere, from Patagonia to the Canadian Yukon, ambush prey by relying on landscape features such as tall grass, heavy cover, and rocky outcrops. It followed, then, that even here in the wild open of the Puna the prey would be more vulnerable in canyons and breaks and other risky habitats where terrain and vegetation provide cover to conceal the stalk. Vicuña would know where they were susceptible and where they were safe, and Emiliano hypothesized they would adjust their grazing style in these different habitats—perhaps affecting the quantity and quality of vegetation from place to place. The vicuñas can't simply avoid the danger zones; the best food is in the moist meadows and the canyon bottoms where water collects—exactly the places with more cat cover.

The team measured the vegetation: How much? What kind? In which locations? They measured the topography: Grassy and open? Rocky and steep? Wet? Dry? They measured the vicuña: How many? Grazing? Heads-up vigilant? Just passing through? And they measured the pumas: Preferred routes? Successful kills? How often? Which prey?

Some of the findings were not surprising: vicuñas are nearly five times more abundant in the open plains (where they can see predators coming from a distance) than they are in the riskier canyons, regardless of how green the grass is. Other findings were more unexpected: vicuñas were four times more abundant in the nutritious wet meadows than in the dry wide open, despite the fact that pumas patrolled the high grass. In both the canyons and the meadows—the riskiest but lushest habitat—the vicuñas and guanacos were hypervigilant, always on the lookout for cats.

As for the pumas, making a living had more to do with finding cover for ambush than it did with prey herd size. For the cats, staking a prime piece of real estate to hunt, defend, and live was critical.

A newborn vicuña calf, its mother standing watch for pumas and other dangers on the horizon. San Guillermo National Park, Argentina. JOE RIIS

But the best of Emiliano's findings emerged when he correlated habitat risk with puma kills, vicuña behavior, and grass productivity, and actually measured the impact of pumas on vegetation. It's the kind of study possible only in this remarkably open landscape where the interactions are clearly visible. Turns out, when vicuña graze risky areas where pumas prowl, the camels do so warily, with their heads up, on the lookout. By contrast, when they graze low-risk areas safe from predation, they focus in on the meal and really go through the grass. The result: more and better grass in high-risk areas; and shorter, less productive fodder in low-risk areas.

Another surprise came literally out of the blue. Emiliano determined that in places with lots of vicuña, there were lots of pumas. And in places with lots of pumas, there were lots of Andean condors. The huge birds were scavenging puma kills, and making a living off the protein left by the cats. It was an important discovery, but it also revealed a problem with San Guillermo. The park, despite its remote and protected nature, is small—and surrounded by estancias. The neighboring gauchos were putting out poison-laced carcasses to kill pumas, and the condors were eating the carcasses and dying off. It's a sort of toxic trophic cascade in reverse, and one very good reason that protected parks need buffers around their borders, so that they do not become biological islands unconnected from the larger landscape.

Still, Emiliano's profound insight into the vicuña-puma-condor system was an important step toward understanding nature's interconnectedness and untangling the web of relationships we call an ecosystem. No puma, no condor. Who knew?

And it makes me wonder what sort of trophic cascades are flowing through my Montana mountain lion habitat, or through other parts of Patagonia further south. What surprising and complex and essential relationships are built on the backs of these top predators? Just how important are apex species to the health of entire ecosystems? Some of my colleagues have studied similar ecosystem connections among the wolves of Yellowstone and Glacier National Parks, and it makes sense that our lions are likewise affecting whole systems. In fact, some early research does appear to confirm those relationships—but our lions, so far, have proved too invisible to allow for such a detailed view into how wild nature really works, and how species rely on one another in astonishing ways.

Of course, pumas and vicuña aren't the only critters making their living in San Guillermo's high-mountain grasslands. Foxes, songbirds, butterflies, and insects share the Puna, as do microscopic soil biota. Where the green hasn't been browsed to the bare—in the high-risk areas where cats hunt—more species thrive and interact, from condors above to beetles beneath. Pumas appear to drive this system from the top-down, by altering vicuña grazing patterns and allowing green nature to take root.

In fact, Emiliano's next phase of research intends to tease out these relationships between the big cats of the Andes and the tiniest invertebrates, between pumas and butterflies and the dirt underfoot. "Pumas saving beetles," he wrote in a recent e-mail, and I'm sure he was smiling when he hit the send button.

CHAPTER 15

PUMAS AND PENGUINS

Pumas opportunistically take advantage of the most abundant and vulnerable prey.

– Ken Logan, author

There is a place in Patagonia where the ocean meets the shore, where flamingos fly through gales, and where pumas prey on penguins. It is an ecosystem unique in all the world—an unlikely tangle of camels and ostriches and killer whales. And I stepped into it wholly unaware, thinking I was just going to have a day at the beach.

Martin Monteverde had steered me toward the coast, arranging for local biologist Sandra Rivera to show me a marine park. I had no idea what to expect. All I knew is that we were headed to the coast, to a little point of land called Punto Tombo.

Ever since my California childhood, I get a thrill when I hear breaking surf and smell the tang of salt water and sand. But that thrill rose, crested, and broke into real joy when I stepped onto a shoreline dune and saw two Magellanic penguins. I'd never before seen penguins in the wild, and was scrambling for my camera. The penguins just watched quizzically, looking me over, while Sandra laughed and signaled me to be patient. Yeah. Right. These were penguins! I was beside myself.

Pulling me along, Sandra walked slowly to the top of the next dune where, stretching all along the shoreline horizon, were hundreds of thousands of penguins. A sea of black and white, as far as I could see. And there, in the seaside

Striking Magellanic penguins live in large colonies on the fragile coastline habitats of Argentina and extreme southern Chile. Monte León National Park, Argentina. MIKEY SCHAEFER

217

Argentina is home to many species that are quite unique; the Patagonia mara is a jackrabbit like rodent that looks similar to a small deer or antelope when running. Puerto Madryn, Chubut, Argentina. DARÍO PODESTÁ

scrub, overlooking the penguin colony, a small herd of guanaco grazed in the morning sun. Sandra just smiled.

Sandra Rivera at the time was the director of wildlife for the remote Chubut Province in Argentinian Patagonia. She'd brought me here, through endless miles of arid steppes, to see what is perhaps the most outlandish puma habitat I've ever looked at. Pumas live in the Canadian Rocky Mountains, in the icy grips of a Montana winter, on sweeping grassland prairies. They live in the swamps of Florida, in the high deserts of Argentina, even in the thick humidity of equatorial jungles. And now, it seems, they live in the dunes, among the penguins.

Which raises a question in my mind: where else might they live, if we gave them the chance? They are fairly specialized carnivores—as opposed to omnivore generalists like the opportunistic grizzly bear—and yet they rule the Western Hemisphere from top to bottom, through some of the most diverse habitat types imaginable. Clearly, the potential is tremendous for these big cats, if we can protect wild places and find room in our world for a fellow meat eater.

The Punto Tombo Reserve was created by the Chubut Province government in 1979, a protective reaction to a proposal by Japanese entrepreneurs that would have mined the colony for penguin oils. Since then, Dr. Dee Boersma from the Wildlife Conservation Society has been studying these little birds in their smart tuxedos. Today, she's known as the Jane Goodall of penguins. The flightless birds aren't always so thick on the coast; for up to five months at a time, in fact, they live on the high seas, and in a full year they might migrate more than 4,000 miles between summer and winter range. But unfailingly they return not only to the same nesting colony, but to the same nest.

These aren't the penguins of icy Antarctica. They are a more northern breed, and their nests remind me of a North American prairie dog town—a field of tiny burrows dug into the ground. Except here, in Patagonia, in each hole there is a penguin. The males dig these holes while the females are off in far-flung Brazilian waters. When the ladies return, the boys howl like wolves, and somehow amid the cacophonous commotion each female locates her life partner. Egg in the hole, dad stands guard, chick grows big, and everyone sets off again for Brazilian seafood.

As we watched a flock of perhaps sixty large pink flamingos glide in the updraft above the surf, Sandra wondered out loud about the local pumas. She has long wanted to know if those pumas had penguin on the menu—after all, cats like to chase birds, and here were hundreds of thousands packed into one big protein patch, flightless and easy pickings. She strongly suspected penguin predation, especially given the news arriving from points south.

Argentina's Monte León National Park is at the end of the world, way down close to the tip of South America. The name means "mountain lion," but it is home to a remarkable assemblage of coastal and upland wildlife species, jumbled together where the sea meets wild Patagonia. Before it was a park, it was a sheep ranch—the sprawling 165,000-acre Estancia Monte León. And like most sheep ranches, it wasn't exactly wildlife-friendly. Monte León had been grazed and tamed into submission.

But in 2002, a pair of visionary philanthropists and conservationists saw an opportunity. The ranch, for all its history of environmental devastation, still had twenty-five miles of undeveloped coastline habitat. It still had native steppe grasslands. It still had remote canyons threading through the interior. And so they bought it.

This is what I mean when I said that the ranches that have always posed a threat to wild Patagonia also present a solution. They are so tremendously huge that, with the right owner, they can serve as landscape-level protected parks. The consolidation of many smaller ranches into these enormous estancias has broken down entire ecosystems. But that same consolidation affords opportunities for real conservation. Convince just one rancher to change his ways for wildlife—or in this case, convince two philanthropists to buy the ranch—and you can make a profound benefit for wildlife. Back in Montana, we might have to work with hundreds of landowners to protect a place the size of Monte León. It would be quite improbable. But here, a single transaction could convert Estancia Monte León to Monte León National Park.

Kris and Doug Tompkins understood this better than anyone. These founders of the Conservación Patagónica land trust acquired the property in 2002, with the explicit intent of establishing Argentina's first coastal marine park and then giving it back to the Argentinian government. It's a foreign concept to those of us who inherited America's treasured public lands. In Montana, nearly one-third of the state—more than 30 million acres—is owned by the public, and managed by either the state or federal government on behalf of all Americans. Many western states have similar expanses of public land. You can hike, ski, fish, hunt, float, and camp on these lands. They belong to everyone, and they are a fundamental reason that mountain lions and wild nature still persist.

It is a birthright unique in the world, a legacy handed down from the first moments of our democracy. The kings and lords and men of means would not rule nature. The people would own it, and it would be their heritage. In Patagonia, however, there is no such tradition. Public lands are, for the most part, few and far between. The very idea of land owned by the people, for the people, is alien, a non-native import that was met, not surprisingly, with more than a little suspicion and skepticism. Why were these gringos really buying so much land? What did they really want?

Turns out, they just wanted to conserve this beautiful, undeveloped, deeply incised coastal habitat, along with its array of marine life and wildlife and human life. They wanted strong communities, tied to the land, and a land healthy enough to support everyone. The Tompkins hired biologists Pablo Rosso and Lorena Martinez to survey and monitor wildlife populations, and to begin the work of rewilding this remote Patagonian outpost. Lorena has been to my home in Montana on a Partners of the Americas science exchange, learning about our northern puma conflicts. Not all the neighbors were thrilled, of course, but the Monte León crew was persistent—meeting in kitchens, and in horse paddocks, and in the field. They built relationships, one by one and day by day—working at politics rather than biology.

Along the way, unnoticed initially, the wildlife quietly returned. First, the guanacos came back. Then, the native mara, a deer-like species that looks a bit like a cross between a giant guinea pig and an oversized jackrabbit. The mara occupies an ecological niche similar to that of the antelope back home. Then the culpeo fox arrived. And finally, the pumas. These are the southernmost pumas in the Americas, and they're still a hard sell for some of the neighboring ranchers. The gauchos had spent generations clearing the land of predators. Now, the pumas were padding through the new park, and often outside of the park as well. It's fortunate that pumas, given the choice, will select guanaco over sheep. But until guanaco numbers are again robust, a serious tension remains, despite the trust that the Monte León team has created among their community.

A puma kitten clings to the branches of a southern beech tree. Patagonia National Park, Chile.
CHANTAL HENDERSON

In addition to building bridges between people, Rosso and Martinez also catalogued a fantastic collection of data. As wildlife rediscovered this unique and complex ecosystem, the biologists discovered surprising and unexpected relationships. It was like watching nature build herself from scratch. And one of the most startling discoveries happened on that long and empty stretch of coastline.

The researchers clearly understood the possible implications of returning the puma to the top of the ecosystem, the potential trophic cascades that could affect the entire web of life, and so they explored the food habits of the big cats. Placing remote cameras on guanaco carcasses, it didn't take long to identify puma predation. Later, closer to water's edge, they found puncture wounds on dead penguins. So they put cameras there, too. And what do you know? Pumas eating penguins. It seems Sandra Rivera was right to suspect this extraordinary and unprecedented cat-and-bird relationship, completely new to the scientific record.

We still don't know the end of this story. The penguin colony on Monte León is not nearly as large as the population farther north, and may not even be stable and sustaining. If that's the case, and the cats are back, then these penguins may be in for a rough ride. Nature is complex. Take a piece out, add another back in, restore the pathways she needs to move, and you can almost guarantee a cascade of unintended consequences. The sheep ranches proved that, and local biodiversity collapsed. A more biologically diverse parkland will certainly prove more resilient and robust, and will shelter far more species, but there will be some species that fare better than others. That's how nature works. I can afford to be philosophical. I'm not a penguin.

With its powerful tail, an austral orca sends a southern sea lion—a favorite food—sailing into the air. Valdes Peninsula, Argentina. PABLO CERSOSIMO

Not far (as a penguin swims) from Punto Tombo and Monte León is hope. Estancia La Esperanza—Hope Ranch—was purchased in 2000 by the World Land Trust, which has since partnered with Fundación Patagónica Natural to turn it into a 16,000-acre wildlife reserve. Ricardo Delfini, a marine biologist working with Fundación Patagónica Natural, took me there on a road that drove off the end of the planet. At least, that's what it felt like. There is solace in empty spaces, and the road to Hope was at the same time lonely, haunting, and invigorating—miles and miles and miles of arid native steppe pierced by a narrow gravel road that unrolled to the horizon. A person could get lost out here.

But drive that road long enough and you come to an old wooden fence with a locked gate, and when you get out to swing it open, you catch a whiff of salt water on the breeze. A herd of guanacos raised their long necks in unison, watching as we drove by. The old ranch compound, complete with a windmill, is headquarters to the La Esperanza conservation field station. From the outside, it looked like a Clint Eastwood movie set: gauchos in full garb, vulture on the roof. Inside, it was clearly a science station: bone specimens carefully labeled, Darwin's rhea eggs on the shelves.

The expansive La Esperanza Reserve is located on the Gulf of San Matías, near the Valdes Peninsula Natural Heritage Site. Though still privately owned by the conservation groups, it has been designated a provincial wildlife refuge by the province of Chubut. The goal here is to study and conserve coastal steppe habitats, including the ancient guanaco-puma ecosystems that have been allowed to recover here. Thanks to a combination of philanthropy and government designations, guanacos are now retracing historic migration patterns throughout the coastal regions of Argentine Patagonia, and pumas are following.

It's not unlike the remarkable spread of mountain lions across North America, pulled by deer populations into an ever-expanding range. Yes, there are portions of Central and South America where pumas struggle in the face of human population growth, habitat loss, poaching, and a lack of effective wildlife laws. The path of the puma is, in many places, a dangerous trail. But throughout the Crown and across Patagonia, these most-widespread of all mammals in the Western Hemisphere are expanding, and at a time when wild nature in general and large predatory mammals in particular are diminishing planetwide. Hope indeed.

Traveling deep into La Esperanza, the route winds into a steep canyon. When the rutted road got bad, we slowed. When it got worse, we walked. Eventually, the track spilled us out onto what I can only describe as a spectacular, undeveloped marine coastline. Prime ocean-front real estate, empty from horizon to horizon. It was like stepping back in time, to a seaside California before realtors and hotel chains.

This, finally, was wild Patagonia. You can watch pumas stalk and ambush guanacos here, and you can watch killer whales stalk and ambush sea lions. Endangered southern right whales, weighing in at sixty tons and feeding on tiny copepods and krill. Southern elephant seals, sounding irritable and topping out at more than 1,000 pounds. Seabirds, foxes, pumas, and, yes, more Magellanic penguins.

Slowly, surely, and with the help of good people, nature is reclaiming her own. Patagonia does not have the extensive public lands we take for granted in the United States, and for many years that meant the land itself was held hostage by a very few for profit. But today, thanks to enlightened ranchers, philanthropists, and conservation-minded governments, a new network of protected places is emerging that, if successful, could outshine even North America's famed national park system. Punto Tombo was designated by the government. Monte León was purchased and given to the government for protection, and to the people of Argentina for enjoyment. And La Esperanza remains owned by private conservation, but is managed in cooperation with the government. It is a new era for wild Patagonia, and it is made possible by the very ranches that unraveled these ecosystems for more than a century.

CHAPTER 16

KODKODS AND OTHER SOUTH AMERICAN CATS

Indeed, the appeal of domestic cats may be that they are just a whisker away from their wild relatives.

– Mel and Fiona Sunquist, *Wild Cats of the World*

"Let me tell you about kodkods."

That's not a line you often hear in a South American bar. But Fernando Vidal is the sort of guy you warm to quickly, so I joined his table at the microbrewery in Coyhaique, an outpost town in southern Chile.

Vidal is a broad-shouldered former commercial pilot who gave up his wings to found a new conservation organization, Fauna Andina; today he also works at the Huilo Huilo Biological Reserve in the heart of Chile's Patagonian rain forest. But his real passion is kodkods, or güiñas, the smallest wildcats in the Americas. In fact, Vidal has become one of the world's foremost experts on the captive rearing of these rare and tiny cats.

At just four or five pounds—less than many well-fed house cats, these pint-sized wild felids are generally brown with black spots, though some appear almost entirely black. Found only in the wet southern Andean forests, they have one of the most restricted ranges of any wild carnivore in the world. And within their small territory, kodkods are helpless against deforestation and direct persecution (trapping, shooting, poisoning, etc.) by encroaching humans. It's not surprising, then, that they are (along with the Andean mountain cat) one of the two most threatened wildcats of South America.

Kodkods spend their lives padding through the wet, green understory beneath a cool rain forest canopy, eating small mammals and the occasional

South America is home to an incredible ten native cat species—only the Asian continent has more. This Geoffroy's cat was photographed at Cabo dos Bahias, Chubut, Argentina. DARÍO PODESTÁ

bird and reptile. Like all cats, they are agile hunters—little stalk-and-ambush experts—though beyond these basics not much is known about the species. Vidal, for years, had tried to unlock their mystery and save their populations by attempting to breed captive kodkods, but to no avail.

One day, he noticed that their water dish kept getting dirty. The cats, it seems, had taken to splashing around in the bowl. A few weeks later, he was holding a kodkod in his arms while drawing a bath for his young daughter. The cat strained to jump into the tub—so in they went, cat and kid together in the bath.

Ah-ha, thought Vidal. *These little cats are swimmers!* He immediately built a whole new enclosure for the kodkods, complete with water features, and within a year he had a kitten. Science had no idea, until that day in the bathroom, what was required for kodkod love. It made sense, of course, that these rain forest cats would be water-adapted, but science didn't know how that relationship would play out. Science also had thought that the tiny cats birthed up to five offspring at a time, but Vidal proved that it was a one-at-a-time kitten system. These sorts of tiny breakthroughs may not seem like much, but it's critical to understand habitat needs and reproductive rates if we are to save the species.

You may have actually seen a kodkod, if you were among the millions who watched BBC's excellent *Planet Earth* series. It features a beautiful moment with a kodkod in the moonlight, hunting moths. That scene was shot at Vidal's home; while the film crew lined up the camera, Vidal himself dangled a lure on some fishing line to get the tiny wildcat's attention.

South America is the cradle of felid evolution, which makes it a land of wildcats even today. Whereas North America's cats were hit hard by a mass extinction at the end of the last Ice Age, South America's lineages remained intact and flourished into a rich family tree. The most ancestral lineages branched to include big and charismatic *Felidae* such as pumas and jaguars, and also smaller species such as the kodkod, Andean mountain cat, Geoffery's cat, jaguarundi, and colocolo.

These less widely known cats are just as secretive as their larger cousins, and are perhaps even more mysterious because science has not focused on them yet. In fact, we are still discovering basic life history, distribution, and ecological information for many of these cat species, even as some of them struggle to survive. Patagonia is a wild felid research frontier, but time is rarely on the side of wildlife conservation. Despite modern conservation, which has pulled species such as bison and great whales back from the brink,

The pampas cat or colocolo roams the rocky canyons and windy steppe habitats of Patagonia. Like an African Lion, these cats have mane-like hairs around their neck and on their back. Patagonia National Park, Chile.
CRISTIÁN SAUCEDO

we are living in an age of extinction. We must learn quickly if we are to protect these wildcats.

The colocolo, or Pampas cat, enjoys one of the broadest felid distributions in Argentina, roaming the Andean foothills for almost the entire length of the continent. They are listed as near threatened by the International Union for Conservation of Nature (IUCN), though they still persist all the way north into the Gran Chaco forests of Paraguay. It's hard to describe a colocolo—their coloring varies tremendously, some red, some brown, some gray, some with stripes, and some with spots. All are small and heavy-set, like a bobcat, perhaps a couple feet long, and weighing maybe six pounds. Some say they hunt during the day; others say at night. They eat birds, according to some sources; guinea pigs, according to others. In mountain habitats, the cats prey on the viscacha, a furry, mountain-dwelling, rabbit-like chinchilla—a case of the cute stalking the cuter. What is known is that the colocolo has been part of native Andean culture for centuries, and the Aymara and Quechua people still use the pelts during ceremonies intended to protect their llama and alpaca herds. What is also known is that colocolos are losing habitat to the expansion of agriculture and energy development, and they are being killed in retaliation for their occasional attacks on chicken coops.

That struggle for survival is a common story throughout Patagonia's cat kingdom, from the colocolo foothills to the alpine haunts of the Andean mountain cat. These stunning animals look like mini-snow leopards with their hair-covered paws that silence their steps. They are unbelievably shy. Rarely seen and little understood, the Andean mountain cat is listed as endangered by the IUCN, with fewer than 2,500 thought to persist in the wild. Even the researchers who look for them rarely spot one.

It was only recently that the Wildlife Conservation Society biologists at Junín de los Andes made a startling discovery: a whole new subpopulation living in lowland canyons far south of the species' known range. Turns out, we may not yet even know where they live, let alone how they live. It's actually a local hunter who should be credited with the discovery. He killed an Andean mountain cat in this newly discovered habitat with a primitive *boleadora*—which immobilizes the cat by wrapping around its legs. A local park ranger spotted the pelt tacked to a shed wall and contacted the Junín de los Andes biologists.

The team immediately set up remote cameras, and before long verified Andean mountain cats in the lowland canyons. Seems they are making a living there on viscachas that are also favored by colocolos. Do these two cats share a range, and if so, how do they interact? There is so much still to learn about this complex cat family in South America. Scientists have begun teasing answers, not by studying the elusive mountain cats but rather by monitoring the more conspicuous viscachas. Map the rocky habitat of the prey, and perhaps you also map the potential distribution of these mostly invisible predators.

Viscachas also provide a glimpse into another, less threatened, Patagonian felid. The Geoffroy's cat prowls the backcountry throughout the southern cone of South America, preying on European hares, small mammals, and birds, along with viscachas. Listed as a species of least concern by IUCN, they are by far the most common of Patagonia's smaller felids—though their actual status remains unknown, and they are considered endangered in Chile, where commercial pelt hunters have devastated native populations.

The Geoffroy's cat is about the size of a large domestic house cat—they look like mini-leopards with their soft gray fur, black stripes, and spots. Creatures of the night, these striking little cats also follow the viscachas' range, and likely overlap with other South American felids. How they get along remains unclear. Perhaps they exist in separate ecological niches.

TOP: Occasionally seen on boulders, the diminutive kodkod prefers the seclusion of the dark forest understory. EDUARDO MINTE

BOTTOM: A secretive Geoffroy's cat moves silently through the winter landscape just above Lake Cochrane in Patagonia National Park. Chile. CRISTIÁN SAUCEDO

Perhaps they hunt at different times of the day and night. Perhaps they compete directly. Perhaps they even share the path with the occasional jaguar, or at least its smaller cousin—the jaguarundi.

The fact that the jaguarundi has so many names in so many languages—gato Colorado, gato moro, león brenero, onza, tigrillo, leoncillo, gato-mourisco, eirá, gato-preto, maracajá-preto—speaks to its broad distribution. From northern Patagonia to the southern United States, jaguarundis roam alongside pumas.

Short on leg and long on body, jaguarundis are uniformly light-gray to foxy-red—no spots, no stripes, no rings on tails. They look a bit like miniature pumas, actually, which is no accident; they share the same scientific genus. We used to think there were a whole lot of them, but now we're not so sure—and the IUCN lists them as near-threatened in Argentina. Trouble is, they live in the lowlands, near people, and so their habitat is being eroded as humans spread into cat country. Still, they stalk the hostile deserts and thorny scrub steppes, and move as gracefully through trees as they do swiftly across the ground.

From the highlands to the lowlands, these various wildcats define Patagonia's wild systems, intersecting and overlapping and, perhaps, meeting nose to nose now and again in the twilight hours. We don't know nearly enough about them, or about how they fit into these ecosystems, but we know enough about cats generally to make some educated guesses.

I can imagine how the relentless winds must feel, their fingers lifting the spots and stripes of an Andean mountain cat, driving dust and grit into her face as she prowls the flanks of Lanin Volcano. She steps silent through broken terrain. Maybe she is home, ranging for an evening meal. Maybe she's a traveler, heading down from northern Argentina. Young, on the move, eight pounds of pounce dropping through deep lenga forests and then into the dry and treeless canyons. She can smell other cats here, not mountain cats like her but cats just the same, and she stops to sniff the news at scrapes sites and urine markers along the way, tapping into the wild felid telegraph system.

The scent is strange here, the dialect difficult to understand—this is not her language. Geoffroy's cats and Pampas cats and big rangy pumas have their own chemistry, but it's close enough that she understands the basic message: someone already lives in this territory. Patagonia's upper steppe is where wildcats converge, mingle, mix, and blend.

She moves out of the strong wind, into a leeward canyon where she can more easily catch the scent of dinner. Here, the sun warms red desert stone and she can feel the heat beneath her furry paws. It's hot in her thick mountain coat. Ears up, eyes sharp, sitting still so still like an Egyptian cat statue, blending invisibly into the brushy outcrop, she waits for viscachas. She hunts them up high, at 10,000 feet in the Andes, back in her northern home range, and she knows their scent, knows how to ambush the long-eared little meals.

Then movement from above, over her right shoulder, and she swivels her head toward her prey. But it's not viscachas. It's another cat, slightly larger, darker. A colocolo going about its life, jumping from bush to bush down the slope. Below, the viscachas scurry between patches of green, packing their cheeks with seeds and grasses. The Andean mountain cat leaps through the rocks—she knows she can outpace any cat in these rocky steeps—and the colocolo freezes, then hunkers in a curious crouch. The mountain cat peers over the outcrop, takes aim at the prey below, twitches her tail, and then startles as an unseen Geoffery's cat pounces on her dinner, a leopard streak of spots and claws.

At least, that's how I imagine it, in this land possessed by cats. Unfortunately, I can also imagine that the young Andean mountain cat can read other smells in the canyon—the smell of domestic sheep and gaucho leather, the tang of metal snares and the sweet oil of well-kept guns. The overlap of food and home ranges has been sorted out between them since the Pleistocene. But the overlap between wild felids and people is still being sorted out. And time is not on our side when it comes to understanding and protecting these southern cats.

We know so little of these rare and disappearing Patagonian felids, and even less of their relationships—how they overlap, how they interact, how they share space and share prey, how they combine to drive entire ecosystems. How they shaped Patagonia, and how Patagonia shaped them. Amid this lack of data, we are left to imagine. What is clear, however, is that in the absence of wolves and grizzlies, these cats rule in South America. The fact that they range as widely and as broadly as they do—jaguars crunching caimans in thick Amazonian jungle, pumas stalking guanaco amid deserts at 12,000 feet, colocolos hunting guinea pigs across the forest floor, jaguarundis ranging throughout the Americas—is testament to their potential.

Almost everywhere you go in Patagonia, a cat is watching you. Yes, the threats remain the same: humans and our habits. But the diversity of South American felids, and the spread of pumas across the full diversity of the Western Hemisphere, suggest that with just a little bit of connected habitat and a healthy dose of tolerance, the potential for cats is tremendous.

REWILDING PATAGONIA

Wilderness without animals is mere scenery.

– Lois Crisler, *Arctic Wild*

When many people think of Patagonia, mountains come to mind. Big, rough, treacherous, picturesque mountains. The craggy and spectacular peaks of Torres del Paine; the massive and dangerous Cerro San Lorenzo; the colossal and iconic Fitz Roy range. Patagonia is defined in the collective imagination of many of us as a soaring jumble of alpine summits—what my climbing friends call "a target-rich environment."

And when it comes to conservation and protection, Patagonia's mountains have it pretty good—they're remote, undeveloped, sparsely populated, and still wild. It's the rest of Patagonia that I worry about. Protecting high-elevation rock and ice is important, but the critical—and complicated—work lies in conserving the rich wildlife habitats below the peaks.

A notion has taken hold in parts of Patagonia: an ambitious effort to protect and maintain entire ecosystems for the benefit of both people and wildlife. Some call it the "rewilding" of this region, and it begins far closer to sea level than to Patagonia's peaks. The vast, brushy, wind-scoured grassland steppe; the wet, often impenetrable coastal forests and valleys of Chile; the lower reaches of the Andes; the region's majestic and wide-open coastline—these represent Patagonia's true conservation potential. Of course, these living lowlands are also where the people reside, generations of families in vast

Pumas, like this adult female and young kitten, require wild landscapes and a healthy dose of tolerance from humans to thrive and raise their young. Chile. LAURA CRAWFORD WILLIAMS

ranches and local communities. Question is, can they make room for pumas, and for refinding the wild?

Landscape rewilding is a seductive proposition. It's also controversial and political. Rewilding efforts often pit the development crowd against the conservation community, and as a result the politicians usually aren't far behind. It's complicated work. But rewilding doesn't have to be controversial. There are direct environmental and economic benefits for everyone when you combine wildlife habitat with human livelihood.

Rewilding has been defined by some as the three C's; core habitat, connections between habitats, and carnivores playing their natural role in the system. Core habitat is a simple idea—wildlife need a place to live. Connectivity is somewhat more complex, but basically boils down to the need for species to move from core to core as the seasons turn—from winter range to calving range to summer range. The trickiest of the three C's, not surprisingly, is carnivores. Science has proven that these apex predators play a critical role in maintaining ecosystem integrity. Pumas change guanaco browsing habits, which changes vegetation patterns, which change entire habitats, which change even the soil composition. The structure, resilience, and biodiversity of many ecosystems are sustained by these complex interactions. But that can be a tough sell to a cowboy or gaucho, no matter what the science says.

Still, we have shown that we're capable of healing landscapes and re-creating wild conditions in special places—and that people will cherish and even pay to visit those places. We've also shown that it's possible to re-create a connected and natural landscape while at the same time maintaining—and often enhancing—existing ranching operations and traditional ways of life. The two are not at odds. In fact, they are ultimately inseparable.

The concept of rewilding means returning, restoring, and protecting a bit of nature's most fundamental processes to places where those processes have broken down. For city dwellers, temporary rewilding might consist of a simple bird feeder or flower box on the patio. The feeder and flowers attracts native birds that eat the insects that chew the plants that anchor the soil. The birds and flowers can be viewed up-close, inspiring us with their beauty and evoking our natural curiosity about how the world works. Predators and prey, right there on the patio! It's simple but profound, and returns a small part of the wild back into our concrete jungle, where it had previously been banished.

Farther afield, a rancher might choose to rest a pasture that's been grazed heavily by livestock, as part of a cyclic grazing system that enhances pasture grass, feeds more livestock, promotes soil productivity, and creates better wildlife habitat. Or perhaps the rancher installs a wildlife-friendly fence, or plants a shelterbelt of trees to block wind and reduce soil erosion—which in turn provides passage, cover, and even core habitat for wildlife along the way.

Rewilding efforts can also be landscape-scale and permanent. Think national parks. Think wildlife management areas. Think wilderness designations. These protected areas, scattered across our planet, often create safe havens for species that are not typically tolerated by private landowners—tigers, lions, grizzly bears, bison, herds of hungry elk, and, of course, pumas.

Even in Patagonia, where so much of nature has been unraveled by non-native species and habitat loss, newly protected areas are now sheltering large herds of guanacos, predators such as pumas and native foxes, and immense scavenging Andean condors—all thriving together in a complex and ancient dance of eat-and-be-eaten.

These large, protected areas have real value to communities, beyond their inherent value to wildlife. They provide what economists call "ecosystem services": the necessities for human survival that nature supplies, free of charge. Pollinators and photosynthesis and nutrient cycling. Soil creation and decomposition and the evapotranspiration cycle. Erosion and flood control. Air and water purification. These aren't new concepts. Plato, back around 400 BCE, noted that deforestation was causing soil erosion, which was in turn drying up local drinking-water springs. He called for protecting what we now call ecosystem services.

Consider a wetland: it retains seasonal water; controls floods; provides habitat for waterfowl and bird hunters, fish and fishermen; serves as a natural water filter; affords recreation; stores carbon—all for free. My Montana community recently spent several million dollars to purchase a conservation easement on corporate timberland, allowing loggers to continue a sustainable harvest but prohibiting subdivision of the land for residential homes. Why? Because that forest provides the town's drinking water, and filters it for free. Protecting the ecosystem service was, in the long run, far cheaper than building, maintaining, and operating a new water treatment plant.

In Patagonia, we've undone the system to the point where it threatens to now undo us. Without quality pasture land and clean water, even the sheep ranchers can't make a living. Fortunately for Patagonia, committed people are dreaming big—Andrés Navarro and his colleagues at Junín de los Andes; Martin Monteverde and Martín Funes at Wildlife Conservation Society (WCS); Kris (and, previously, Doug) Tompkins at Conservación

Cristián Saucedo, director of wildlife conservation for Conservación Patagónica, herds a couple of captive Darwin's rhea in a captive rearing facility. Patagonia National Park, Chile. CONSERVACIÓN PATAGÓNICA

Patagónica. They understand the value, to all of us, of protecting, connecting, and restoring Patagonia's wild heritage and way of life.

Andrés Navarro imagines a world full of guanacos, vicuñas, rheas, and pumas, but he knows that's not possible without the habitat to support them. So he and his team at the WCS Andean Steppe Program have partnered with the Argentina's National Park Service and local communities to restore habitat, enhance ecosystem integrity, and protect large landscapes. They are mapping core habitats and migratory pathways, monitoring wildlife movement, exploring life cycles, discovering interactions, and designing a vision for new protected parks. Their work begins, as always, with community education—building the relationships and the social license necessary for translating science into public policy. Because without the willing support of the ranchers, gauchos, and locals, the science doesn't stand a chance.

And over on Patagonia's eastern coast, Guillermo 'Graham' Harris and his WCS team are doing much the same, on behalf of the penguins, pumas, and marine-system wildlife. There, millions of breeding penguins share space with elephant seals, southern right whales, and a whole host of seabirds. Harris has his eye on rewilding and protecting enormous coastal steppe habitats all the way to the seashore. Some of those lands are historic estancias, and protection requires working closely with traditional ranching families to preserve not just wild nature but also a way of life. Other parts of that landscape are under government jurisdiction, and Harris works daily with official Argentine state biologists.

Of course, one of the easiest ways to get almost everybody's attention is to talk dollars. Parks, it turns out, aren't just good for wildlife. They're also good for business. The outdoor recreation industry in the United States is worth about $887 billion per year, in terms of consumer spending. That's 7.6 million jobs. The industry is especially important in places with lots of protected land, such as Montana, where outdoor recreation generates $7.1 billion each year—and an additional $286 million in annual tax revenue for state and local government coffers. Hard to argue with cold cash.

National parks offer particularly good examples of the benefits that come with protection and rewilding (beyond the ecosystem services we get for free). In 2015, visitors to America's national parks spent $17 billion in local communities. That trade sparked another $11 billion in labor income. Total economic value related to US national parks is more than $90 billion—a mighty good deal for an agency that costs taxpayers about $3 billion, or just one-seventeenth of one percent of the federal budget. My own backyard, Glacier National Park, played host to nearly three million cash-carrying visitors in just the past year. It's a heck of a return on investment, and serves as a strong counterpoint to the economic might of the ranching, logging, mining, and other traditional interests.

Additionally, in my experience the ranchers love their remote and rural lifestyles, and want to protect their landscapes as much or more than anyone else. They are proud to reside in untamed places, and they are essential partners in the effort to live more closely with wild nature. And so Andrés and Graham share a rewilding vision that necessarily includes people. The rewilding of Patagonia is a vision for bringing wildlife back, not pushing people out. We need protected public lands and private lands, both.

Imagine, for example, a severe winter that forces guanacos to leave a park in search of food and refuge. They'll need protected travel corridors, and they'll need lots of habitat choices along the way, and they'll need a sanctuary at the end of the journey. The guanaco will need the private ranches that, managed properly, have the potential to provide immense safe havens between the government parks.

The people of Patagonia—like the people of the Crown of the Continent—advertise their parks and wild nature to a worldwide audience. The peaks and snowfields of the high Andes, the free-flowing rivers, and shining glaciers. This is as wild as it gets. But the advertisements don't mention the vast countryside beneath the peaks. It's no wonder. Look at the native fauna and flora. The sad truth is, the plants and animals and natural systems are in trouble. Without some element of rewilding, Patagonia may be a biological dead-end for native wildlife in many areas.

The Patagonia scientists I work with refer to this collective vision as "Tehuelche Landscapes," a name that evokes a time when the native people and species of this region thrived together. That's the vision. It's as simple and as complicated as that. Nothing more and nothing less than healthy lands, healthy wildlife, healthy people, and healthy communities coexisting, codependent, and cooperating into a far-off future.

CHAPTER 18

THE CARRETERA AUSTRAL

I believe it's a moral imperative that all creatures on this planet have an intrinsic value.

– Kristine McDivitt Tompkins, conservationist

There is a road in my backyard that hangs precariously from rocky cliffs, curls along shorelines of bright blue lakes, and runs beneath white shining peaks and over spectacular mountain passes. It's called the Going-to-the-Sun Road, and it slices through the wild and scenic heart of Glacier National Park.

It's snowbound from October until June, sometimes July, but at the height of summer the Sun Road is fifty miles of the most stunning alpine panoramas you can imagine. For decades, this road has been my favorite route into mountain country. At least it was until I made my way to Chilean Patagonia where the journey itself is both high adventure and rewarding destination.

A long series of flights out from Montana and you touch down in Santiago, Andean peaks rambling in every direction. Stop here for a while and try some *calafate* berries—the tart and juicy flavor of wild Patagonia. Legend has it that anyone who tastes these berries is destined to return to Patagonia. So far, it seems to be working.

Head south then, where warm orchards give way to lush green foothills, and great winding river systems drain the Andes into the Pacific. Next come towering volcanoes casting conical shadows all around—Cerro Tronador, whose eight glaciers straddle the Chilean border with Argentina; Osorno,

One of the most scenic byways in the Americas, the long and winding Carretera Austral is the access route to the new national parks in Chilean Patagonia. LINDE WAIDHOFER

which Darwin watched erupt in 1835; and finally colossal Cerro Corcovado, its prehistoric lava flows now draped in a thick cover of green.

There's a feeling I get, an insistent rush in my brain and butterflies in my belly, every time I set out on new and unknown adventures—especially in Patagonia. But there's another feeling, a warm sense of homecoming, when I'm met by old friends at the start of those adventures. Dr. Cristián Saucedo is just such a friend and he met me in his mountain town of Coyhaique, on the doorstep of the finest mountain road I've ever traveled.

Saucedo is tall, long-haired, often unshaven, always gracious. I met him first a world away from here, in Montana, where he was traveling with my team as a visiting biologist on a science exchange. We've been fast friends ever since. Educated as a veterinarian, Saucedo caught the wildlife biology bug while volunteering on a project to capture and study the iconic Andean condor—a remarkable bird with a seventy-year lifespan and a ten-foot wing-span. Darwin noted that he watched these condors soar for thirty minutes and more without a single flap of the wings.

For several years after the condor project, Saucedo worked for the Chile's National Forest Corporation, conserving the highly endangered huemul deer (a favorite of pumas but, like the woodland caribou up north, struggling to survive in the age of man). And since 2005, Saucedo has served as conservation director of Conservación Patagónica, monitoring and protecting huemul, rhea, condors, and, of course, pumas.

But for now, Cristián was simply my guide. The Carretera Austral, or Great Southern Road, tracks puma routes through the Andes, running from Puerto Montt in the north to the tiny settlement of Villa O'Higgins in Patagonia's remote south.

Not far out of Coyhaique the road winds over a nest of high peaks clustered around Cerro Castillo—Castle Mountain. It is a fine and handsome summit, well named with its turrets of stone rising above sparkling glaciers, and will perhaps be soon named as a new national park. It's lonely country. The only others on the road were colorfully dressed gauchos heading for work, standing shoulder to shoulder in the back of an old paneled stock truck. The morning commute, Patagonia style.

A midsummer snow squall blew over us at the pass, but skies cleared as we dropped elevation to cross the deep Ibáñez River gorge on a narrow bridge. Following the river deeper still, we drove along the chocolate-colored Murta River out of the cool Andean foothills and into the damp of temperate rain forest. Biologists call this a wet Valdivian forest type, a green and lush contrast to the arid summit country. Bamboo, beech, lenga, towering evergreen coihues, and giant Chilean rhubarb leaves the size of elephant ears dominate the foliage.

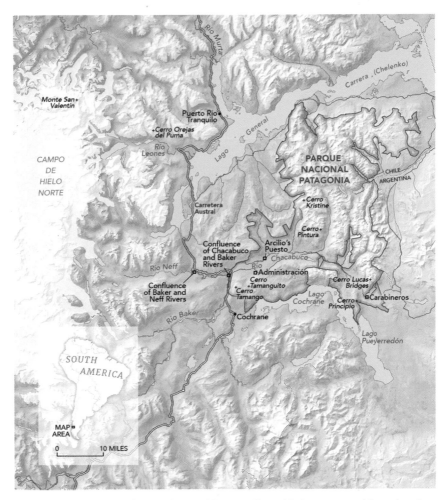

PATAGONIA NATIONAL PARK The newly designated Patagonia National Park sits just east of the northern Ice Cap in southern Chile. The unique east-west Chacabuco River valley and it's dry steppe habitats down low give way to older beech forests up higher and glacially carved Andean peaks above. SOURCES: CONSERVACIÓN PATAGÓNICA, NASA, IGM CHILE, IGM ARGENTINA

The Carretera Austral highway tracks these forests wet with Pacific moisture to Lago Chelenko, a lake so impossibly turquoise that it seems like a dream, a ragged line of snowcapped peaks reflected on its mirror surface. Big cats patrol here, too, and it wasn't long until we crossed the Rio Leona—the Puma River. Towering above its banks is the summit of Cerro Orejas del Puma—Ears of the Puma—which takes its name from a remarkable resemblance to the head of a puma, complete with two geologic ears (rock spires with a glaciated ridge between). I will be back one day to

TOP: Doug Tompkins radio name was *Aguila*—the eagle—and every day, weather allowing, he was in the air. Much of what has been done comes from his keen sense of landscape learned through flying. SCOTT SOENS

BOTTOM: This is the location of the Doug Tompkins Hut that looks out onto the lake and his favorite peak in the world—Cerro San Lorenzo. Chile. RICK RIDGEWAY

climb this puma peak. It seems far more accessible than the nearby Cerro San Valentín—Patagonia's highest summit—which even from a distance looks Himalayan, like a mountain on top of mountains. Not everyone who ventures there returns.

The road rolls on, to the confluence of two great rivers where glacial melt roars over waterfalls into dangerous and icy pools, swirling, churning, and mixing before thundering off toward the Pacific. This is where we bade goodbye to the Carretera Austral. We had arrived, finally, in the Chacabuco Valley, at a vast and former sheep ranch, on the doorstep of Patagonia National Park.

One day, I expect this road will deliver countless visitors to a wild, protected area. It will bring a new generation of guardians, it will bring investment, it will bring conservation, it will bring economic stability, and it will bring global attention. And most importantly, it will bring inspiration.

But for now, the Carretera Austral brought only me, a gringo biologist, to the sweeping grasslands of the Chacabuco Valley. Male guanacos, standing sentinel, whistled our arrival with warning cries to the herd. If the *calafate* berry is Patagonia's flavor, guanacos are the sound of wild Patagonia.

The Chacabuco Valley is an ecological hub, with nature's spokes ranging into a wild diversity of habitats in every direction. Head north, and you climb into the rugged vertical of the Jeinimeni mountains, sprinkled with glistening glaciers. Head east, and you spill out onto the open steppes of Argentina. West, the northern Patagonia ice cap. South, the deep snow-pack of Mount San Lorenzo. All of these habitats flow together into the Chacabuco Valley—a little bit of dry, windy Argentine Patagonia leaking into wet, forested Chilean Patagonia. It is a mixing zone, biologically speaking, with tremendous species diversity.

We have a similar valley back home—the Lamar Valley in the northeastern corner of Yellowstone National Park—where I've often watched wolves, grizzlies, elk, and bison play out their ancient dramas. In the Chacabuco, the players are pumas and guanacos, but the storyline is much the same. Rooted in volcanic soil, Chacabuco climbs through grass and shrub to colorful lenga forests, eventually reaching into rarefied alpine habitats—and pumas stalk the whole of it. Scoured by storms, Antarctic storms that blow off the northern ice cap, the valley can feel like an icy wind tunnel. But when the blasts subside, it is as sublime a place as I've known on this planet.

Doug and Kris Tompkins knew immediately that this rich assemblage of wildlands and wildlife held incalculable potential as a protected sanctuary. And they had the talent, the know-how, and the assets to make it happen. In fact, together Kris and Doug have achieved some of the most successful efforts to rewild Patagonia.

Kris Tompkins is the high-energy former CEO of Patagonia, Inc. Doug Tompkins was the founder of both The North Face and Esprit companies. (Doug died in a kayaking accident in 2015.) Together, they founded

Conservación Patagónica to protect their beloved Patagonia through large-landscape conservation and park creation. To date, their efforts have permanently protected some two million acres of priceless wildlife habitat in Argentina and Chile. That's the equivalent of two Glacier National Parks.

Doug first saw Chile in 1961 as a ski racer. Not long after, in 1968, he returned alongside Patagonia, Inc. founder Yvon Chouinard for a famous surf-and-climb pilgrimage that featured an old Ford van, a successful climb to the formidable summit of Mount Fitz Roy, and an adventure film called *Mountain of Storms*. Doug told me he and Yvon had longboarded the same Southern California breaks of my youth, and we clicked immediately over stories of surfing, climbing, mountains, wilderness, and wild nature.

Kris—a California ranch girl, turned ski racer, turned successful CEO— moved to Chile to marry Doug in 1993, and ever since this dynamic duo has been building powerful philanthropic teams to buy large ranches such as Estancia Valle Chacabuco—centerpiece of the new Patagonia National Park. Often, they add to existing protected areas by purchasing adjacent lands and slowly and carefully rewilding the old sheep pastures. They then put in the park infrastructure—trails, campgrounds, and so forth—before throwing the gates open to the public.

It's a unique approach, and works extremely well in these countries where accessible public lands are hard to come by. It's a model that Doug began experimenting with more than a quarter century ago, ever since 1991 when he and some partners began buying Patagonian land, restoring its native habitats, and then handing it over to local governments to manage both for wildlife and for local people. The key word there is local. He actually. was giving the land back to the people. It is an incredibly generous act, and I never cease to be amazed by his understanding of long-term philanthropy. Imagine, handing over a ready-made national park, a permanent sanctuary for pumas and predators and prey as well as a source of solace and pride for an entire nation.

That's where the staggeringly beautiful Carretera Austral route leads, this small gravel road and a wooden Conservación Patagónica sign, a scattering of park headquarters buildings, and a hundred wild guanacos grazing lazily in the sun. I dropped my bags in the lodge-like Butler Guest House and sat down with Kris and Doug to talk about their vision for this new park, and how they came to be in the business of large-landscape conservation. Kris knew I'd worked with private ranchers back in Montana, and wanted to talk about the park's pumas and how best to protect them.

Hours later, the sun long set and the southern stars shining, we still sat drinking tea at the kitchen table. Doug was explaining how all this got started, in a prehistoric forest on the flanks of a volcano. He, Chouinard, and

With Lito Tejada-Flores, left, and Doug Tompkins, right, in the Patagonia National Park headquarters, Chile.
KRIS TOMPKINS

some Chilean friends were concerned about development plans that threatened an ecosystem of monkey puzzle trees, some of which were more than 1,000 years old. So they bought it, protected it, gave it back to the people, and today it is Santuario El Cañi—El Cañi Sanctuary.

"It's a small park," Doug said, "but special."

It was also a harbinger of things to come. Kris and Doug have since founded several partnerships and organizations to help with the rewilding of Patagonia. They've established Pumalín Park, paying absentee landowners for 715,000 acres of rare and critical habitats that stretch from high along the Andean Divide to the Chilean coastal fjords. These are the tremendous rain forest ecosystems that remind visitors so much of America's Olympic Peninsula, with giant alerce groves towering like redwoods over the land.

Similar ecologies persist in 726,000-acre Corcovado National Park, where, in 1994, Tompkins and his partners bought and donated more than 200,000 acres with the understanding that the Chilean government would join those properties with public lands to establish Corcovado as Chile's fourth-largest park. Corcovado is a mind-boggling wilderness park, its nearly one hundred lakes ringed by ancient forests full of pumas. Its

A flock of pink flamingoes flies below the mountains and glaciers in Patagonia National Park, Chile.
LINDE WAIDHOFER

In 2004 it was hard to find even small herds of guanacos in the hills, by 2014 their numbers had rebounded in the grasslands, and they had found the grasses around the buildings especially to their liking. Patagonia National Park, Chile. LINDE WAIDEHOFER

many terrestrial and avian species track the Corcovado and Tic Toc Rivers to the bay of Corcovado, where they meet immense colonies of shorebirds mingling with penguins, seals, sea lions, and, just offshore, Earth's largest animal—the blue whale. The bay is under consideration to become Chile's first marine sanctuary, assuring a corridor of protection from the top of the world to the bottom of the sea.

After long but inspiring days exploring the new park, my guide on the Carretera Austral Cristián and I spent evenings listening to tales of Patagonian adventure. Doug flipped through photo after photo on his computer, sharing stories about every mountain, river, and valley. He knew them all because he had climbed them, hiked them, explored them, or flown over them. He'd snapped the images while hanging out the window of his plane, holding the steering yoke between his knees.

"Look at this," he said, pointing to a string of wilderness waters strung out on the screen like a line of sapphires. It was remote country, steep and rugged. "If livestock can't get in there," he said, "then it's likely that humans have never penetrated those thick forests or scaled the granite to get to these lakes. Never." A place without people. It fired our imaginations. What new geologic wonders might be discovered there? What new species? Perhaps, we imagined, there's a native cat out there we don't know about yet.

Exploring unknown places is sustenance to folks like Kris and Doug, and every year they journeyed further south into Patagonia, traveling by foot, boat, and horseback. And the more Kris saw of the ravages wrought by a century of overgrazing in extreme southern Chile, the more she wanted to restore the ecology of the region. In 2000, she founded Conservación Patagónica to do just that. The organization's first big park project was Parque Nacional Monte León—Mountain Lion National Park—which the Tompkins established alongside a team of conservationists from both Chile and Argentina.

With that success under her belt, Kris turned her attention to a most ambitious project: protection of the Chacabuco Valley's rich habitats. Chacabuco was not only a confluence of diverse ecosystems, it was also everything that stirred Kris Tompkins and her drive to protect the wild. The park would restore damaged grasslands, protect the surrounding 650,000-acre region, link private protections with public protections, develop public access, and spark local economies with conservation-based tourism in a wild, intact ecosystem. It was, in many ways, a clean slate, as there remain unnamed and unexplored lakes, rivers, and peaks throughout this rugged region.

In 2004, Conservación Patagónica purchased the 178,000-acre Estancia Valle Chacabuco—one of Chile's larger domestic sheep ranches—and set about eliminating livestock, removing fences, restoring grasslands and forests, developing wildlife restoration and monitoring programs, re-establishing free-roaming guanaco herds, and of course, protecting the resident pumas. Then they filled the gaps, purchasing smaller parcels to connect Chacabuco with the adjacent Jeinimeni and Tamango National Reserves—which protect approximately 460,000 acres of public-land wilderness.

The Tompkins knew that with a project of this scale, they would need a respected and capable Chilean scientist to spearhead their vision for Patagonia National Park. They needed a leader with the right education, the right temperament, and the right imagination. Someone like my friend and guide down the Great Southern Road, Dr. Cristián Saucedo.

As conservation director for the project, Saucedo's first order of business was to hire a team of rangers who could also serve as wildlife technicians. He needed people who could live independently and survive in the wilds, knew wildlife and how to track it, knew the flora and fauna, and who didn't mind hard work. And so he hired the local gauchos from the former sheep ranch. It was a brilliant move. Hiring the gauchos got him a staff that already knew the country, and how to live in it, but perhaps more importantly it got him a staff that had credibility with the nearby communities.

It got him trust, that rarest of commodities between conservationists, ranchers, and locals.

And it worked. The gauchos who once hunted cats to kill them now tracked pumas to study them. Today, thanks to a professional staff, a steady stream of volunteers, and some generous donors, Conservación Patagónica has achieved the unthinkable. A landscape-scale park built by the private sector for the public's pleasure. And it's chock-full of pumas.

When I stayed with Doug and Kris in Chacabuco, I stayed in what they call the Butler Guest House. Reaching from floor to ceiling are fantastic black-and-white photographs of big cats in the Patagonian wild. I spent my evenings there swapping stories about climbing and surfing, and later of protecting and rewilding. And when the conversation turned as it always did, to wild places and predators and prey, we invariably talked cats and camels.

From a biological perspective, most of Patagonia is no longer wild. But it is getting wilder. And here, just as in North America, big cats are expanding their range and finding their way into old haunts. The pumas of Patagonia have survived the destruction of the frontier years, the predator purges, and the unraveling of ecosystems. And they are spreading out, slowly but surely, from their scattered mountain strongholds into their former homeland.

We are privileged to be witness to one of the rarest events in the modern era: a clear wildlife success story. And not just for a major carnivore—though that is remarkable enough—but for a big felid, one that is rewilding the Americas at both ends of the world, against all odds.

In North America, they are expanding across our vast network of public lands, an inheritance from the very roots of our democracy. In South America, the cats are tracking private lands that are being converted into public parks. I appreciate, perhaps better than most, the challenges of living with carnivores and predators. But I see these cats on the move, and so I also cannot help but be hopeful—willingly, eagerly, enthusiastically, and wholeheartedly hopeful.

RIGHT: Kris Tompkins explores new areas of the park that no one has seen on foot before. Patagonia National Park, Chile. JIMMY CHIN

NEXT SPREAD: Two pumas closely watch their home range below from their protective day bed under a rocky ledge. Chile. LAURA CRAWFORD WILLIAMS

LEFT: These two South American grey fox pups watch from the mouth of their den. Patagonia National Park, Chile. HERNAN POVEDANO

TOP: The chinchilla-like vizcacha lives in the rocky terrain at lower elevations in South America. Patagonia National Park, Chile. HERNAN POVEDANO

BOTTOM: The Patagonia hairy armadillo tentatively explores the grasslands along a river on the Peninsula Valdes, Chubut, Argentina. DARÍO PODESTÁ

257

THIS SPREAD: This dominant male, who researchers call Principio, ruled over half of the Chacubuco River Valley wildlands until he was shot by a rancher. Patagonia National Park, Chile. CONSERVACIÓN PATAGÓNICA

NEXT SPREAD: Mature male Andean condors can soar at heights up to 16,000 feet. El Condor Estancia, Santa Cruz, Argentina. PABLO CERSOSIMO

PREVIOUS SPREAD: The puma is also an important keystone predator in the high Andes desert ecosystem—called the Puna. San Guillermo Nation Park, Argentina. EMILIANO DONADIO

ABOVE: The curious gaze of a *ñandú* or Darwin's rhea in Patagonia National Park, Chile. CHANTAL HENDERSON

TOP: Tiny Patagonian pygmy owls also call the park home. Patagonia National Park, Chile. CONSERVACIÓN PATAGÓNICA

BOTTOM: A caracara lands next to a black chested buzzard eagle to feed on a puma killed guanaco carcass. The kills made by pumas feed many species. Patagonia National Park, Chile. HERNAN POVEDANO

NEXT SPREAD: Patagonia is a landscape of dreams. Chile Chico, Chile. RENAN OZTURK

265

ARCILIO
THE PUMA TRACKER

*We need freedom to roam across land owned by no one but
protected by all, whose unchanging horizon is the same that
bounded the world of our millennial ancestors.*

– E. O. Wilson, Harvard University

W hen you chase pumas in Patagonia, Cristián Saucedo explained,
you need to weld crampons onto your horseshoes. *Crampons*,
I thought. *On horseshoes. That doesn't bode well.*

The main road through the Chacabuco Valley runs east to west, fifty
miles of gravel tracking the meanders of the free-flowing river as it winds
around mountain foothills. It's dry steppe country but shadowed by snowy
summits and by the vast northern ice cap.

We'd left the road after a bumpy hour, turning down a narrow track that led
to river's edge. There, in some trees near a gravel bar, three horses were teth-
ered and waiting. I noticed the saddles, resting on white sheepskins—a rough
cross between western and English style, with no saddlehorns. I don't mind
horses, but I prefer hiking boots.

Cristián had roped me in for some science and adventure; we needed to
change out the radio collar on one of Patagonia National Park's female pumas.
But before we came to this gravel bar, we'd stopped in a large meadow with a small
riverside cabin, home to Don Arcilio Arias Sepúlveda and his puma hounds.

Arcilio is short, tan, and remarkably fit, with dashes of gray dusting his
black hair. His face, always set in a serious expression, has the weathered
look of a man who's made his living outdoors. He is a puma hunter. Arcilio
spent a lifetime working as a *leonero*, as did his father, paid by estancia

This puma, located with hounds above the Chacabuco River, will add information to the scientific knowledge
being collected by the wildlife team in the park. Patagonia National Park, Chile. CRISTIÁN SAUCEDO

owners to kill pumas. He went on his first hunt when he was just fourteen, he explained over gourds of *maté* warmed on a wood stove, joining his father to track a cat across the massive eastern face of Cerro San Lorenzo. It's a dangerous peak, where ice falls tumble from crumbling séracs. They caught up to the puma and did their job, but as soon as the cat was dead, large snowflakes began to swirl in the wind. And it howled. Arcilio and his father made camp and weathered out the storm—for two weeks. Two weeks, trapped by a blizzard in the high mountain wilds, with nothing to eat but puma. Welcome to the family business.

After Conservación Patagónica bought the ranch, Arcilio stayed on to maintain a small herd of sheep, pull weeds, and build trails. That's when Saucedo found him, and realized the value of this *leonero*'s puma lore. Arcilio taught the scientists where the big cats hunted, where they crossed between the mountain ranges, where they reared their kittens. Before long, Arcilio was lead puma tracker and wildlife ranger—still hunting cats, but now on behalf of science and conservation. Today, he would help us find an older female whose radio-collar battery was about drained.

At first, the gaucho-style saddle actually felt pretty good. I had one hand on the reins, the other on my camera, as my sure-footed pony ascended through blooming yellow nineo bushes. Steppe country is made for horse travel. We crested a bench and were surrounded suddenly by the whinnying and whistling of wild guanacos. We'd ridden right into the middle of a herd of females with young, 300 or more, and they parted nervously to let us pass in the thin morning light.

Accompanied by Arcilio and his rangy canine companions, we started the climb into steep mountain country. Now I understood why the Conservación Patagónica puma team needed horses to travel this park. I couldn't imagine how difficult their job must be in winter, with barbs welded onto horseshoes to pierce the ice underfoot. Higher still, we passed through a small patch of lenga trees and a large red-headed Magellanic woodpecker flew right over our heads. I took it to be a good omen; reminding me of the pileated woodpeckers back home. But when we flushed a flock of chortling green Patagonia parakeets, I knew I wasn't in Montana anymore.

Climbing higher still, through wet meadows and rocky breaks, we crested a high mountain divide with views in every direction. The summit of Cerro San Lorenzo—where a young Arcilio had waited out that storm with his father—was shining icebound under the warmth of a summer sun. The big male puma that claims this territory as his is called, appropriately, Lorenzo, and he dominates the land just as the peak dominates the horizon.

Assembling the radio receiver antennae, we couldn't pick up Lorenzo's signal today—but we did catch the telltale beep of Flaca's fading collar. She was

Don Arcilio Sepulveda tracks pumas in the Patagonia National Park using horses and hounds to navigate steep roadless areas. Chile. CRISTIÁN SAUCEDO

traveling to our west, and we followed her onto the steep forested slopes of Cerro Tamanguito. Descending swiftly through old growth forests and open hillsides, I kept sliding to the front of my saddle and wishing I had a saddlehorn to cling to. The journey was starting to feel long, and my backside worn.

I must admit to feeling not a little relief when they announced our day was too far gone to continue. When you turn loose the puma hounds, the chase might last ten minutes or it might last ten hours. We just didn't have enough daylight to make a capture attempt. Better to sleep on it.

Come morning, I winced back into the saddle and we headed west. The steady *beep, beep, beep* of Flaca's signal was strong, still coming from the same direction as the day before. Stop, take a listen, ride. Stop, take a listen, ride. The day fell into a rhythm as we rode through a wet tangle of thorny nirre trees and *calafate* shrubs. Arcilio, watching the ground as he rode, finally shook us from the morning's steady tempo with a sudden cry of "Puma!"

271

Without pumas there would be a tangible void in wild Patagonia. You may rarely see them but they are often closely watching you. Chile. KONSTA PUNKKA

He swung his horse around and dismounted. *No way*, I thought. *I don't care how grizzled and leathery this old gaucho is. There's no way he can spot a track on dry ground from atop a horse.*

We squatted in the dust, shoulder to shoulder. I was wrong. Apparently, even a ghost leaves a bit of a track. The dogs were getting fired up now, whining to be loosed. We assembled the antennae and took another bearing—seems we'd overshot the mark. The female puma was below us, in that wet tangle of green. She probably made a guanaco kill last evening, and was dining in the cover of shade.

Circling the dense and swampy bottomland, we contained the signal. She was in there. Arcilio turned the dogs loose and it wasn't long until we heard the baying of pursuit. I leaned back a bit in my saddle, thinking of how cat hounds sound the same everywhere in the world, and as I looked up I was rattled to see a puma sprinting above us. She darted across an open slope, stopped to look back toward the charging dogs, and then leapt into the cliffs above.

"*Mira la puma!*" I cried. "*Mira la puma!*" I was pointing excitedly. "Look at the puma!" The gauchos and Cristián kicked their mounts into gear and took off over the steep and broken terrain. I followed, galloping up the mountain behind the dogs, chasing pumas Patagonia-style. I was literally hanging on for dear life—fingers wrapped under the front lip of the saddle as we crossed grassland foothills into the high condor cliffs. By the time I caught up, all I found was their horses panting in the sun. I tied my steed and began hiking the cliff bands toward the sound of hounds.

Rounding a vertical rim of rocks, I reached the team, all of them peering high into a long, towering crack in the cliffs. The dogs were baying at the foot of this dark cleft, necks craned skyward. No cat. Only condors soaring above. Where was the cat? Suddenly, with an audible spit and growl, the puma shot out of the rocky chimney and took a swipe at Arcilio's oldest hound. The dog tumbled backward, then got up and raced back into the fray. The hounds had the female puma cornered in the shadows of the crevice.

Cristián was busy below us, loading a tranquilizer dart. It was an awkward shot—all he could see was her front shoulder—but at least it was close range. Arcilio quickly leashed the dogs and Cristián swung the gun up, aimed, and fired. The dart hit true and the puma wheeled back into the cleft, scrambling and leaping to scratch her way higher. She had almost reached the top when she fell backward, twisting to land on her feet. Turning, she raced straight down the fissure toward our surprised group. Hitting the bottom on all fours, she slammed into Cristián, sending him sprawling. The puma veered away, straight at the rest of us. I was pumped full of adrenaline by now, waving one arm and calling, "Hey girl! Hey girl!" The big cat veered back up to the base of the cliff, rounded a rocky ledge, and went down blearily as the tranquilizer took effect.

Cristián got to his feet, brushed off his pants, and shook the stars out of his head. He was shaken, but fine. Just another day at the office: It can be tough on the cat, tough on the hounds, tough on the biologists. But without a fully charged battery in that radio collar, we don't know where the pumas are ranging, hunting, denning, and rearing their kittens. We don't know how far they're traveling, or by what routes. We don't know which habitats to protect, which corridors to safeguard. Without objective data, all we have to go on are the ranchers' stories: pumas are everywhere and they're eating everything. Gathering the scientific data serves not only to target our conservation efforts but also to ease minds.

All wild animals need freedom to roam. Literally. They cannot survive without open, undeveloped natural habitats. Arcilio knows that, deep in his bones, from years of hunting. Cristián Saucedo knows that, too, in a biologist's way, from years of tracking collars and the animals that wear them. And together they are opening small windows into some of Patagonia's most spectacular puma migrations. These cats don't stick to the park. They don't honor property lines. They don't need passports to cross the Andean Divide between Chile and Argentina. Pumas simply move to where there is good food and ample cover. And, as more lands are rewilded and more guanacos graze those newly protected lands, the number of cats is increasing—which in turn causes young male pumas to disperse into yet more untracked cat country.

Cristián and Arcilio have proven that Patagonian cats, both females and males, scatter out from the territory where they were born and raised. Males generally travel the farthest; females with kittens generally stay closest to home. Generally. Cristián tracked one mama puma that covered thirty-three miles in a single day. Perhaps she was avoiding the territory of a dangerous and unfamiliar male? Perhaps she was looking for a good location to teach her young to hunt? Perhaps she was just restless, or curious, or on the scent of something we don't understand? Nobody knows. What we do know is that she is evidence that if we protect, connect, and restore wild country, then pumas will range far more widely than we imagine.

Within the Valle Chacabuco study area, male and female resident pumas move about the same distance—about eight and a half miles each day. The females have smaller home ranges, and those ranges overlap somewhat. The males mark their larger ranges and sometimes fight to defend their turf. It is surprisingly like the mountain lion dynamic I have studied in Montana—in both places, we find about three pumas per hundred square kilometers (forty square miles). Despite the ranchers' stories, pumas are not everywhere, eating everything. They are actually living at very low densities in very big landscapes and, given a choice, they'll eat a guanaco over a sheep most every time.

Using state-of-the-art satellite radio tracking technology, the Conservación Patagónica research team is revealing some surprising secrets about this region's pumas—both as a population and as individuals. Bagual, a resident eight-year-old male who weighs in at more than 155 pounds, has a tremendous territory

An adult female puma is bayed up into cliffs that are so rugged and high that they are also used by Andean condors to roost. Patagonia National Park, Chile. JIM WILLIAMS

in the southern half of the park. His kingdom sprawls across about 150 square miles, which is about what we'd expect from a mature and dominant male. But the real surprise from that satellite-collar data was the scope of his daily rounds. Bagual literally owns the entire southern half of the park, stalking the mountain slopes to the west, patrolling the Chacabuco Valley around park headquarters, haunting the extensive north shore of Lake Cochrane. In the past, the movements of South America's pumas were unknowable; now, with modern satellite collars, we can learn their habits, understand their needs, and watch their every step. Bagual is constantly on the move, sticking his nose into every corner in the southern end of the park—except the far-eastern corner, on the border with Argentina.

That's because someone else lives there. His name is Principio, and he also wears a satellite collar. A big cat, Principio sports a silvery cream-colored coat and he rules the region around his namesake Principio Mountain. This dramatic peak leaps straight from the Chacabuco Valley, running up and over the border into Argentina. There, the ridgelines give way to the Argentine steppe and its vast sheep ranches.

The collar signal showed Principio routinely touring his large home range, doing what cats do and slipping unseen from habitat to habitat. Unfortunately, that range overlapped with the nearby Argentine sheep ranches, where native predators and prey has long been killed off in the war over grass. When Cristián and Arcilio finally tracked down his body, it was in an estancia barn that had twelve more puma skins hanging on the wall—along with twenty Pampas cat skins, several Darwin's rhea, a handful of Andean condor carcasses, and numerous dead guanacos. It's an old and sad lesson—without tolerance, even a protected area the size of Patagonia National Park just isn't big enough.

That's an especially important lesson when considering the young males that are dispersing across the Western Hemisphere. Even more than Bagual and Principio—who, after all, have established home ranges—these sub-adult males travel incredible distances to claim a territory of their own. As mentioned earlier, this is how *Puma concolor* spreads its genes, distributes its impact on prey, and avoids the pitfalls of genetic inbreeding. It's a dangerous journey, though, avoiding the territorial males, finding food, crossing swollen rivers and soaring ridges, the heat, the dry, the cold, the wet—and then, at the end of the road, a bullet or a snare or a poison bait.

One of those strong young males from the Chacabuco Valley was named Arcilio, in honor of the team's finest tracker. The puma Arcilio was born in the shadow of Patagonia's northern ice cap, and when he was two years old, biologists fitted him with a satellite collar. He spent the next fifty days in the protected confines of Patagonia National Park before striking out.

It was a grand walkabout, even for Patagonia. Early in the autumn, Arcilio headed east, moving about seven miles per day, every day—which is quite a feat considering the rough mountain country and the need to stay fed along the way. After Arcilio passed the Argentine border station, with the wind at his back, he prowled the nineo shrublands and grassy steppe before heading south. And south. And more south, for 500 long miles, paralleling the Chilean-Argentine border before padding silently onto a large sheep estancia near the town of Tuco Tuco. It's a curious name for a farm town, given that the gopher-like tuco tuco is being killed off as an agricultural pest.

And there, in the far southland of Patagonia, at the very end of the world, where there are far fewer guanaco grazing the estancia's grass, Arcilio ate a sheep and was found out by a skilled *leonero*. All those miles, hundreds upon hundreds, through a wilderness of difficulty, looking for a territory to call home—from the tremendous northern ice cap to the tip of the southern cone. The puma Arcilio almost made it to the wild heights of Mount Fitz Roy. Almost.

CHAPTER 20

A TROPHIC CASCADE
IN PATAGONIA

It is that range of biodiversity that we must care for—the whole thing—rather than just one or two stars.

– David Attenborough, conservationist

We picked our way carefully up the mountainside through a thorny tangle of *calafate* and *nirre* shrubs, beneath a dense beech canopy where the air was cooler. Skirting an open meadow I caught a glimpse of fur upslope, then the entire animal—a Chilean huemul deer. She was rich brown—like a mule deer in Montana, but a bit shorter and stockier. It's a sturdy build evolved for scrambling this difficult mountain terrain. Her muzzle was rounder than a mule deer's, almost bulbous, and a splash of white marked her throat.

She saw me too, lifted her head, but was unconcerned. Her lack of fear reminded me of the caribou up north, and I worried for a second about how she and her trusting kind might survive this modern age. Then I stopped fretting and just lost myself in the moment, watching one of Chile's most endangered animals graze quietly on a patch of bright red flowers.

Huemul (pronounced *way-mool*) deer live at the heart of wild Chile, and their primary habitat is this nation's collective imagination. A huemul buck, crowned in gold and rearing, emblazons the national flag. But as with many cultural symbols—think America's bald eagle, which nearly vanished before finally winning better protection in the 1970s—the huemul is in trouble, highly endangered, with perhaps fewer than 1,500 left in the wild. And all

Deep in the park's secure lichen draped forests of lenga, or southern beech, an endangered huemul deer finds solitude. Chile. BETH WALD

Former gaucho turned deer tracker Don Daniel Velazquez listens intently for the tell tale beep of a nearby collared huemul deer. Patagonia National Park, Chile. JIM WILLIAMS

of those remaining live in Patagonia, a full third of them in and around the new Patagonia National Park.

Huemul are secretive deer, and inhabit the remotest southern regions of Patagonia. Most live in Chile, but a few spill over the Andean Divide into Argentina. In fact, they are sometimes called Andean mountain deer because they inhabit that high crest where lenga forests meet ice-cap glaciers. Huemul are endangered today because we've let them become so.

For centuries, huemul and pumas shared these wilds with guanaco and culpeo fox, and all was well. But then came the ranches and the sheep and the habitat changes: the impacts of year-round grazing, including the subsequent drop in forage quality, which can open new opportunities for disease introductions; the fences, fields, and barriers to seasonal migrations; the dogs and roads and poachers. Add these new challenges to a low-density species with naturally low reproductive rates and poor fawn survival, and we've set the stage for disaster. Of course, it's easier just to blame the puma.

The huemul story has more than a few unfortunate parallels to the plight of my transboundary caribou herd. Both species are naturally sparse on the landscape, living in small family groups in dense mountain habitat. Because their home is so remote, and so thick, and because they are so few and far between, they don't bump into predators with any great frequency. This has evolved in both huemul and caribou a temperament that can appear, to us humans, as a sort of trusting innocence—exactly the disposition that gets you killed when the dense habitat is opened with logging roads and livestock. And as we North Americans did with the caribou, the first thing South Americans did after endangering the huemul was to blame the predators for eating them all. Certainly, pumas do eat huemul—but they are only the insult on the injury. The real culprit is us.

Cristián Saucedo and his team at Patagonia National Park have spent years studying the interactions between pumas and prey. In particular, they've embarked on an exhaustive exploration of huemul-puma interactions. It all started with a former sheep-ranch gaucho who'd spent so much time watching his flocks that he could recognize individual animals on sight.

Daniel Velasquez stands five-feet eight-inches tall, is barrel-chested and strong, with a permanent smile beneath his dark mustache. He is one of the most cheerful and welcoming gauchos I've ever met. And when Cristián heard of his remarkable gift for identifying specific sheep, he quickly assigned Daniel to the park's huemul-monitoring program. In the seven years since, Daniel has applied his unique talent and learned to identify individual deer by their facial structures, their coloring, and their habits. The deer, in turn, have come to know Daniel. They watch as he quietly moves through their forest on foot and on horseback, tracking huemul movements. He lives, day in and day out, with these peaceful, rare, and iconic animals, and keeps a tiny cabin deep in deer country where he grows his own vegetables, makes his own saddles, carves his own tools, and lives largely off the land. He is happy, he says, because he is near his herd, where he can watch and observe.

To know his huemul neighbors more fully, he also traps, collars, and follows these deer with radio telemetry, identifying which habitats they use and when so that key areas can be properly protected. The collars also send out a mortality signal when no movement is detected for a prolonged time, allowing Daniel to visit carcass sites. What happened here? Was it a puma kill? A culpeo fox? A domestic or feral dog? Or perhaps a natural death: a hard winter, a deadly fall, or an unfortunate disease? It's Daniel's job—as an estancia gaucho turned wildlife research technician—to sort it all out. So I asked him if the pumas are eating all of the huemul. He took me into the field to answer my question.

"Is that a signal from a huemul?" I asked as Daniel waved the H-shaped radio-tracking antenna up and down while pointing toward the slope of the mountain behind his remote cabin.

"Yes," Daniel nodded, and up we went. It was a steep, dense, and thorny route, better suited for huemul than for me. My coat and sweater were soon covered in thorns, but Daniel's, somehow, were not. When we finally spotted the doe, grazing calmly amid the red blossoms, my heart was thumping hard from exertion and excitement. Daniel just crouched and watched, still smiling. I could see the female's radio collar as she browsed her way upslope, into the thicket of shadows.

The first step, after removing sheep from Patagonia National Park, was to bring back guanacos. It was a smart move, not only because visitors love to watch these long-legged camelids but also because the pumas would need something predictable, native, and natural to eat. Without guanacos on the ground, the cats may well have wiped out these last struggling huemul.

Instead, Cristián and Daniel's research shows that 73 percent of all puma kills were guanacos. Makes sense, considering their long-evolved relationship and the fact that more than 3,000 guanacos now graze the park. Given a choice, pumas choose guanacos. Next on the menu were those non-native European hares, which made up about 16 percent of puma kills, especially out on the grassland steppes. Then came domestic sheep, primarily from neighboring ranches but also from a small park flock, kept to feed the staff. These sheep totaled about 9 percent of puma predation. And finally, the huemul, which were the targets of 1.5 percent of puma attacks.

Of course, with deer numbers already dangerously low. any predation is cause for concern. When park managers are able to identify a cat with a specific taste for huemul they could, in theory, target that puma to protect the future for both species. And in the meantime, managers can remove the real threats to deer—the roads, poachers, dogs, and assaults on habitat. They can also emphasize programs that promote huemul fawn survival—like removing packs of feral dogs—which pay far bigger dividends than predator control.

Back home in Montana, survival rates for adult female deer are quite high, approaching 70 percent. My guess is that, regardless of puma predation, survival rates for female huemul are also typically high. Yes, if you put more pumas in the system you increase the probability of a cat-deer encounter. But for huemul to persist into the future, their numbers must be robust enough to withstand the puma predation they've evolved with for millennia. We simply need to give them the space to do that.

Giving huemul room—giving guanacos room and giving pumas room— also results in giving the rest of wild Patagonia room. In fact, while the huemul graces one side of the Chilean flag, a condor soars on the other. Of course, it's all connected. Find a huemul killed by a puma, and you'll find a condor. Andean condors are fantastically huge; with their huge wingspans, it's easy to spot them working a carcass. In fact, Cristián and his team have discovered condors scavenging an amazing 43 percent of puma kills. The condors of Chacabuco, it seems, rely heavily on pumas for their groceries—just as they do in San Guillermo. National efforts to protect the Andean condor, then, may well hinge on protecting pumas.

On a clear day, with an icy wind thundering down off the northern ice cap, condors appear wholly removed from the ways of the world, jet-black wraiths against a backdrop of high lenticular clouds. Circling. Circling. Riding the wild winds and mountain thermals, they can climb to more than 16,000 feet, soaring for nearly an hour without a single flap of the wings. Cristián and I watched from the Chacabuco's tawny grassland steppe as the scarcity of condors—that's what you call a flock of these birds—dropped out of the sky toward a hillside enclosure.

"It's working," Cristián said with a smile. He and his team were trying to return some young condors to the wild, three orphans that had been brought to the park by wildlife biologists working for the Chilean government. The plan was to do a soft release, meaning the three youngsters would be kept for several weeks in the mountainside enclosure. Carcasses would be placed nearby, attracting wild condors that would interact with the orphans through the wire mesh. Slowly but surely, the birds would come to know and accept one another. At least, that was the plan. I moved quietly toward the enclosure, and could see the identification tags on these youngsters' wings. Before their release, they'd be fitted with satellite tracking devices to monitor their movement and their fate.

Importantly, the team had partnered with the local community in this project, and was involving the neighborhood school. The children there were learning the wild firsthand, on the wings of condors. Tolerance and passion for native wildlife nearly always begins with the wonder and excitement of children. And condors are a safer bet, from a cultural perspective, than are predators such as pumas. Chileans identify with the free, high- soaring spirit of the condor. Protect the rocky cliff haunts of the condor, and you protect the puma. Protect a puma, and you feed a condor.

About a month after I looked in on that enclosure of orphans, the pen was opened and three young condors stepped out into the park. They tested their wings, and Kris Tompkins joined the biologists and the school kids to watch from below. One condor hopped onto a boulder and spread his wings wide. Then they lifted, one by one, into the sky, where a wild family circled high against the Patagonian blue.

The satellite signals showed them gliding over the park, beyond its boundaries, over mountains and valleys full of guanacos, huemul, and pumas. One landed for a moment atop Cerro Tamanguito. I'd climbed that mountain not long after visiting the enclosure, on a day of cold wind and sunshine.

The rocks near the summit are covered in long, filamentous lichens, and all around me, in every direction, was the wonder of Patagonia National Park. I understand, perhaps, some small part of why that young condor paused atop Tamanguito. The feeling of wind under the wing, the sound of the gale. The smell of stone and the taste of snow. And the views of the kingdom he commands.

Condors symbolize the freedom of Patagonia, and they have woven themselves deeply into local culture, a totem for the fiercely independent people who call this land home. But the image of condors is also complicated, in large part because they are routinely targeted by ranchers. Because the colorful bald-headed birds are often found scavenging a sheep carcass, lore has grown that these vultures kill livestock. They do not. They are simply the clean-up crew, working the long-since dead.

Often, they are cleaning up after a puma, and all the flapping, hopping, and pecking of a scarcity of condors can harass a cat right off its meal. Research shows that pumas eat about seven kilograms (fifteen pounds) of meat in the first twenty-four hours after a kill, then only about four kilograms (nine pounds) per day after that—because scavengers pester them off the meal. That means the puma must find another meal, killing more often than it might otherwise—and that puts more meat on the ground for the rest of the wild to feast on. Patagonia's pumas feed a multitude. The research by Cristián's team has shown a wildly varied clientele tucking in at the 'puma café': condors, of course, and black vultures, too. Culpeo fox, Patagonian skunks, caracaras, *chimangos*, shrikes, austral blackbirds, and black-chested buzzard eagles. Even a lizard. As a the species at the top of this food chain, pumas pump nutrients throughout the natural system.

But there is beauty in the messy violence of a shared carcass. Birds, small mammals, insects, microbes—all benefit by the precious nutrients that flow through this arid ecosystem like water into soil. Pumas are structuring this natural community simply by doing what cats do—killing prey. They are keystone species in this interconnected world, driving biodiversity and making sure that everyone eats. In Patagonia National Park, the researchers have found that each puma kills about six animals per month, and abandons about six kilograms (thirteen pounds) of meat per day—that's 172 kilograms (379 pounds) of meat every month, left by each puma for other species such as condors. That's a lot of fresh, valuable protein on the landscape.

It's also a lot of biodiversity—an interconnected system of soils, plants, birds, mammals, insects, fish, and amphibians, eating and being eaten. This is what people come to see. In Glacier National Park, and in Yellowstone National Park, and on the Serengeti, and, one day, at Patagonia National Park, here at the end of the Carretera Austral. They'll come from around the

A young Andean condor spreads it wings just outside a captive rearing facility in the park. The team has tracked condors back and forth between Chile and Argentina. Patagonia National Park, Chile. LINDE WAIDHOFER

world to watch a puma track a guanaco through open steppe country, and to see the enormous condors gather in their abundant scarcity.

They'll come for the whistle of the guanaco, the sharp bark of the culpeo fox, the lonely prints of the huemul. Patagonia, at its wild best, rivals the finest wildlife regions of the planet with its colorful and eccentric cast of characters. Pumas and kodkods and long- eared viscachas. Wildlife tourism in Patagonia has tremendous potential, as people discover the richness of a world where pumas stalk alongside penguins and even ostriches.

Generally, when folks think of ostriches they recall the grasslands of Africa or the stark emu habitats of Australia. But Darwin's rhea—called the *ñandú* in Chile, the *choique* in Argentina—runs in the improbable shadow of Patagonia's high summits. These large and flightless birds jog the grassland flats, where the Argentine steppe spills over into Chile's Chacabuco Valley. Co-evolved with guanaco, these sixty-five-pound birds should do well in the park's grassland, which they ran (as fast as thirty-five miles per hour) for millennia before being wiped out by poachers and egg hunters.

One of Cristián's duties as conservation director for Patagonia National Park is to recover and nurture native species that have been extirpated—

animals like the *ñandú*. I went on my first search for the *ñandú* on a predictably windy day, but found only a zorrillo skunk, and a wetland full of pink flamingos. Catch it in the right light, at the right time of day, and watch flocks of pink paint their way across a backdrop of ice and snow. The Chacabuco Valley is a migratory rest stop for Chilean flamingos, which are bit smaller and a lighter shade of pink than their Caribbean cousins. They linger in the shallow and brackish lakes of the steppe, on their way to Argentina's shrimp-filled wetlands. The journey has transported shrimp DNA over the high mountain divides and among different wetlands, proving again the connectedness of nature the nomad.

A few years back, in 2014, the Chilean border police found two orphaned *ñandú* chicks struggling in the wild. They brought them to Cristián, laying the foundation for a new captive breeding program in the park. (Augmented with ten more *ñandú* chicks from another breeding facility flown in by none other than former commercial pilot turned kodkod breeder Fernando Vidal.) Those two chicks are surviving as the basis of a long-term recovery program. Someday, it seems, the flightless flocks of *ñandú* may once again trot the length of Chacabuco—where for too long they have been absent.

Ostriches. Flamingos. Pumas. Camels. Huemul. Viscachas. Patagonia is animated by a remarkable array of forms, a patchwork of species that don't seem to fit together. And yet they do, and they have for ages before we arrived to remake nature. The era of the vast sheep ranches is coming to a close—broken not by conservation but by changing global markets and new technologies. It's often that way, though conservation—like pumas—often takes the blame.

The new threat to Patagonia, here in the waning days of the sheep empire, is energy production—both fossil fuel and hydro. Chilean Patagonia is home to some of the largest, cleanest, and most spectacular rivers that remain free-flowing on the planet. They are the veins and arteries that pump lifeblood through the country, quenching the thirst of countless animals (humans included) at a time when worldwide fresh-water supplies are dwindling. And yet there are those who think these rivers could be improved by dams. Under a previous government, the rights to all this water were sold to European companies, which intended to block them with huge hydroelectric facilities.

What the government and the international companies did not bank on was how deeply embedded these waters are within the Patagonian psyche. People from all walks of life—villagers, teachers, gauchos, business owners, and soccer moms—stirred a groundswell of opposition. "*¡Patagonia Sin Represas!*" Patagonia Without Dams! I saw this slogan again and again, spray painted on walls, billboards, business windows, and even houses. A new government was elected and has chosen clear, clean water at home over the export of profits to a few faraway shareholders. And that's an important decision, if you happen to be a puma.

In terms of habitat barriers, puma home ranges often are defined by large bodies of water—rivers or lakes that serve as hard boundaries difficult to cross. Cats can swim—I've watched Montana lions cross lakes and reservoirs, just as Cristián has seen his Patagonia pumas swim 1,500-foot-deep Lake Cochrane—but it's not something they do regularly. So these dam proposals, with their vast man-made reservoirs, would fragment wild habitat on a scale not before experienced in Patagonia. They would rearrange the fundamentals of the physical world, severing ancient migration routes. And perhaps most importantly of all, they would bring roads, development, and people into otherwise wild country. Wildlife would lose.

Silencio is a huemul deer, named by park deer tracker Daniel Velasquez. Some years back, Daniel was assigned to survey the remote Baker River country for a possible huemul population rumored to live there. The Baker River was being eyed for damming by a company called HidroAysén, and wildlife biologists wanted to know what lived in the steep canyon habitats of the river drainage. There, Daniel found Silencio, a huemul deer he'd come to know and name in the far-off southern reaches of Patagonia National Park. Silencio had dispersed from his birth range, crossed the forested flank of Cerro Tamango, heading west and then north across the Baker River canyon. Here, on the banks of the Baker, Silencio had beaten the odds—he'd found a female huemul. By the time Daniel caught up to him, Silencio was part of a four-deer herd, many miles from his birth home.

It's just one animal's journey, and not an overly long one at that. But at ten miles, Silencio's travels represent the longest huemul migration known to science. Not that science knows that much about huemul. We nearly wiped them out long before we asked any questions. But in Patagonia National Park, the inquiries have begun. How do huemul survive? What do pumas eat? How far do condors range? Where can flamingos still share space with ostriches? How do shrimp cross mountaintops? And how many species can a puma feed with a single guanaco kill?

How does this system work? And how can we keep it whole, intact, unbroken, undivided, robust, rehabilitated, and restored? The answers begin with protections, and parks, and bold rewilding programs that enlist *leoneros* as science assistants and gauchos as wildlife technicians. Because when the biologists, the businessmen, the estancia owners, and the schoolchildren all speak with one Patagonian voice, even the international corporations don't stand a chance against the wild biodiversity at this wonderful end of the world.

SILENCIO'S STORY

As told by Gaucho Park Ranger Daniel Velasquez

It was November of 2006, and we had spent several days following a pregnant female huemul named Puntilla. As part of our huemul-monitoring program, we use radio collars and telemetry to follow pregnant mothers so that we can find and monitor their offspring soon after birth. Newborn fawns suffer high rates of mortality, so ensuring a future for the species depends on identifying the major threats to fawns.

Puntilla gave birth on November 21, tucked away in the rocky terraces on the northern shore of the Cochrane River. She had hidden herself and her fawn well, making it challenging to locate them. As we observed the pair together and placed an ear tag in the young fawn, he made not one sound. Silencio, we decided, would be a fitting name for this quiet animal.

For the next year, I saw Silencio often during my days tracking huemuls, taking many photographs of his development. Always near his mother, he moved along the shores of the Cochrane River, gradually moving closer to its confluence with the Baker River. When Silencio reached one year of age, his mother left the area; when female huemuls are ready to give birth to a new fawn, they will often leave behind their year-old young to devote their energy to the newborn.

Puntilla gave birth to her new fawn, but Silencio seemed to have disappeared. His radio transmitter had stopped working. Although we searched for him carefully, we could not find any trace and never saw him in the park again. Since we found no evidence he had died, we classified him as missing in our study.

For five years I followed Puntilla, who still lives in the headwaters of the Cochrane River. Through tracking and monitoring, I have recorded all her pregnancies and tagged all her young. Yet of all her offspring, only Silencio made it to adulthood.

Neighbors told rumors of a small huemul family group living along the Baker River, prompting us to survey this area that had never before considered territory of the huemul. On the day we first saw huemuls in this area, we also rediscovered Silencio after four and a half years. Although his transmitter no longer functioned, we identified him by his ear tag.

To our surprise and delight, Silencio had survived and sought new lands to establish his own territory, clearly marked with his antler scrapings on trees. He had started a new family with various females and their offspring. Silencio appears well on his way to becoming the pioneer of a new population of huemuls in this area.

Silencio selected his territory wisely: on the steep banks of the Baker River, this area is forested and away from herds of livestock. But as he made a home and family here, he could not have known the human plans for the region. With the proposed construction of HidroAysen's Baker 1 megadam, Silencio's new home territory will be flooded. Heavy machinery and hundreds of construction workers will invade his silence, chopping their way through his home forests.

We returned to the park that evening inspired by these wild animals' ability to survive and thrive, yet worried that the fate of this area is in jeopardy. We share this story of the huemuls of the Baker River to tell the people of Chile how their totem animal, a proud presence on the national shield, is at stake in this decision.

TOP: Pumas on rare occasions will prey on a huemul deer but their diet consists almost entirely of readily available guanacos. Patagonia National Park, Chile. CONSERVACIÓN PATAGÓNICA

BOTTOM: A mother huemul deer and her new fawn are being tracked by park rangers to determine deer population trends. Patagonia National Park, Chile. HERNAN POVEDANO

CHAPTER 21

CONSERVING CATS IN BOTH HEMISPHERES

Wilderness is the breath and heartbeat of Nature herself.

– Doug Tompkins, conservationist

M anaging wildlife is a lot like climbing mountains: you almost never get it completely right the first time, and on many days it's the challenge you least expect that blocks the summit. But you're guaranteed to learn something new, especially from the failed summit attempts, and the journey is forever full of wonders. In the end, for most of us, it's really all about time in the wild with friends. Puzzling through the optimal route can be complicated, and the mix of variables complex and convoluted, but you can bet the cleanest line is usually the best.

I've been fortunate to stand atop Patagonian peaks, and to climb the Crown of the Continent, and to range across the mountains of the Americas. In all those places I've been on the track of cats. Mountain lions. Pumas. Cougars. Panthers. Pangi. *Skwtismyè. Naatāyō.* By whatever name, they're the same animal, the most widespread wild mammal in the Western Hemisphere, from top to bottom.

I recently took the boat across Waterton Lake, a wind-whipped waterway that straddles the border between Canada and the United States. It's the fastest way into the backcountry routes that lead to the summit of Mount Cleveland. That's the highest peak in Waterton-Glacier International Peace Park, and though the summit is located in Montana, the watery path in begins in Canada.

A mountain lion quietly and carefully stalks an unsuspecting bighorn sheep in steep alpine terrain. Glacier National Park, Montana. SUMIO HARADA/MINDEN PICTURES

Our heavily bearded captain was a climber, too, and said he'd made seven attempts before gaining Cleveland's 10,479-foot peak. That's not as high as other Rocky Mountain crests, but the long wilderness approach and the 6,000-foot vertical climb have turned many parties back before the summit. Snowslides. Rockslides. Thunderstorms. Wind. Whiteout. Grizzly bears. Any combination of the above, plus more.

I was climbing with Jerry Brown, a retired Montana wildlife biologist (and the man who'd invited me to the town of Libby to wrestle with lion-hunting regulations, so many years before). We'd tried to control the variables—weather, daylight, temperature, route—but so much wasn't really up to us. Nature can be inconvenient that way.

We camped our first night in a jumble of stone, and hung our food high on a meat pole to keep it above bear-level. Glacier National Park is home to more than 300 wild grizzly bears, and even more black bears. That's in addition to the mountain lions, wolves, wolverines, lynx, bobcat, coyote, fox, badger, otter, and marten. Not to mention the deer, elk, moose, bighorn sheep, and mountain goats. Keep a clean camp, though, and the critters don't give you much trouble.

We woke early and hit the mountain trail. Jerry and I agreed that we needed a drop-dead turnaround time—1:30 p.m. at the outside—because we didn't want to get stranded high on the mountain after dark. The early-mile work consisted of bushwhacking through dew-soaked alder and nettle—or at least, that was our chosen route—and by midmorning we were soaked, poked, scratched, and stung. That's when the climb begins. Up and up, over stone and rock, to a spire topping a narrow ridge. Then an old mountain goat trail through a string of steep, exposed, ice-scoured basins, and into the lower bowl on Cleveland's western face. It's dodgy business, with a whole lot of nothing underfoot.

We'd mapped the west-face approach, because the 6,000-foot north face is one of the highest vertical walls in the United States. Not everyone who attempts that route comes home. Cleveland has the potential to be a dangerous place. But the west face is safer, if not safe, and we'd chosen our route well. Bright white mountain goats perched above us on the rock wall, cooling beside a thundering waterfall. Our route went past the goats, which wasn't a problem.

But it also went past grizzlies, which was a decidedly sticky situation.

"Look there, mister," Jerry said, pointing to the snowfield we were about to ascend.

"Mama griz," I answered. "And a cub." Danger on top of danger. Can't go over. Can't go around. Got to go back. Some days are like that.

Most folks think of grizzly bears as formidable carnivores—and they can be lethal, certainly—but they are for the most part what I call 'opportunivores.' They graze flowers, roots, and grubs, and they scavenge the occasional carcass, and they'll run a mountain lion off a kill. Sometimes, if the timing is right, they'll nab some meat on the hoof. But here, amid the high summits, they climb for a seasonal feast of moths. The tiny army cutworm moths migrate into the alpine heights from the prairie grasslands—traveling hundreds or even thousands of miles to find cool summer temperatures and feast on the nectar of alpine wildflowers, pollinating them in the process. During the heat of day, they burrow into the rock crevices to find shade and protection from predators.

Bears roll the rocks and eat the moths—as many as 40,000 moths per day. It's a feast of fat and protein, and with a half-calorie in every moth, bears can pack in as much as 20,000 calories per day. That's hugely important to a big bear looking to fatten up for a long winter's sleep. But even in this remote wilderness, humans have unhinged the system. Prairieland farmers as far away as South Dakota hit the moths with pesticides, hoping to control crop damage, and the effects are felt by a grizzly 1,000 miles away on a Montana mountaintop.

We were watching mama and her cub when rocks started rolling down around us. Above, a third grizzly—probably a large male—was rolling rocks to look for moths. Every rock he rolled dislodged another, which displaced another, in a clattering geologic cascade, and the VW-sized boulder that whizzed by us made one heck of a noise as it passed. We were only a couple hundred vertical feet from the summit, but grizzlies guarded the ridge. Two more bears—yearlings or two-year-olds—worked the rocky slope below us and to our right. I looked at my watch. 1:45 p.m. Time to head home, on an exposed goat trail that now had grizzly tracks all over our bootprints.

That is what I call a 100 percent successful climb. No summit, but that was never really the point anyway. From the basin below the peak, we could see far into Alberta and British Columbia, into the Canadian Rockies, east across Montana's grassland prairie, south to the Bob Marshall Wilderness, far into the wild mountain heart of the Crown of the Continent. I felt like an Andean condor, spreading my wings atop a Patagonian peak. I felt like a mako shark, patrolling the waters off the California coast. I felt like a sleek Florida panther, silently padding through the Everglades. This was my turf. Except for the bit the bears had laid claim to today. The bears, along with the wolverines and mountain goats, have always owned the high reaches of Mount Cleveland. I hope they always do.

I have cats to thank for my life spent in wild country. It's been a windswept and wonderful career, big enough that it sprawled across an entire hemisphere, and small enough that I can sum it up in one word: Montanagonia.

It's not uncommon now to observe family groups of pumas behaving naturally in the protected areas of Patagonia. Laguna Amarga Estancia, Chile. PABLO CERSOSIMO

I have a ball cap with that word blazoned beneath the outline of mountain that could be Mount Fitz Roy, Mount Cleveland, or Cerro San Lorenzo. Montanagonia. That's where the big cats live.

I am fortunate indeed to live at a time when these amazing animals are, against all odds, spreading across entire continents. It is a rare and special happening, to see wildlife, but especially a predator, succeed in the Anthropocene—the Age of Humans. These cats have survived the assaults of the frontier, persisted through the predator purges, endured the domestication of their wild habitats. That a major carnivore can find freedom to roam in this modern world is nothing short of astounding.

I have also been fortunate to live at a time when the veil of mystery is lifting. For thousands of years, mankind has lived alongside mountain lions with no way to see them clearly. We spoke of their secrets, their mystery, their stealth, their inscrutable obscurity. We called them the ghosts of the forest, and we wove myths to fill in the story. Cats were defined, quite literally, by their lack of definition.

But in the short span of my career, we have invented radio collars that can pinpoint a lion's location and allow us to track the individual closely. We have built satellite collars that transmit a cat's path in real time. We have designed infrared lenses that allow us to see right through the forest canopy, to watch cats from airplanes and helicopters and even from drones. We have developed DNA analyses that enable us to determine relationships, untangle lineages, and even determine genetic connectivity between populations. For the first time ever in the relationship between humans and mountain lions, we can begin to see them for what they really are.

This new lens into the lives of cats offers tremendous opportunity—if we know how *Puma concolor* lives, and what the cats need, then we are in far better position to protect the species. But the window into their lives also comes with tremendous risk—if a primary reason this predator thrives among us is because it remains so invisible, then what will happen when it's not? That, I suppose, is up to us. Living with wild nature is a choice.

I, for one, choose a world in which I am not always at the top of the food chain. It's good, sometimes, to near the summit only to be turned back by a world that is bigger than your ambition. And there is nothing better than exploring places no one's been before. That, ultimately, is what the technology has done for us—it has allowed us to explore what was previously invisible. Recently, respected wild felid researchers around the Americas have been installing remote cameras in known mountain lion territory. The results have been astonishing: two males on one kill, females adopting kittens, family groups traveling together, mothers sharing parenting duties, even males joining the family for a meal. One image that was published captured seven mountain lions—male, female, young—all working the same carcass at the same time.

What happened to the solitary mountain lions I have known? Is this some new behavior, or have they always been social creatures? What other behaviors will they surprise us with? What new technology will help us see them—and all of nature—even more clearly?

I've spent a lifetime coming to know these cats and the people who fight for them, and just when I think I'm close to the summit, I am humbled by the unexpected. We still have much to learn, and for that I am forever grateful.

EPILOGUE
Keep it Wild

The careless rapture of my early studies has been replaced more and more by efforts to protect animals and their habitats, using argument and initiative that may have impact both locally and internationally: scientific, political, economic, aesthetic, ethical, and religious.

— George Schaller, *A Naturalist and Other Beasts*

Clint Muhlfeld is a rangy six-foot-three, which is an awfully tall frame to fold into a fish trap. But the big tom cat was in stalk mode, so Clint stayed put like a bird in a cage. Mostly, all he could see through the steel grate was the black tip of a long brown tail, twitching back and forth above the willows.

Muhlfeld, at the time, was working as a fisheries biologist for the Montana Department of Fish, Wildlife & Parks. His office was just across the hall from mine. It was 2006, and he was studying the interbreeding between native and non-native trout in the wild North Fork of the Flathead River, just beyond the western border of Glacier National Park.

A trout trap is about three feet by three feet, and four feet high, with a narrow slit at one end where the fish swim in. The top has a large hinged lid, for easy access to the trout. Muhlfeld, in wetsuit waders and neoprene boots, was deep in the gin-clear water removing debris from the trap when the hair went up on the back of his neck. He turned and saw that tail, twitching over the willow like a house cat stalking a mouse.

"Hey cat!" he yelled, standing tall and splashing around in the water. The tail just twitched. "Move on, cat!" Muhlfeld shouted, banging a pair of metal stakes together as he climbed to river's edge. Fight or flight, and flight

Rarely heard and almost never seen the mountain lion is perhaps the most mysterious of all large carnivores in the Americas. Bob Marshall Wilderness Area, Montana. STEVEN GNAM

was no option given this stalk-and-ambush predator and Muhlfeld's bulky rubber pants. The tail kept twitching.

So lifting the lid on a spare fish trap, Clint folded himself inside, wiring the door shut behind him. He continued to shout, to yell, to cajole, but the cat just prowled, pacing a ten-foot circle around the trap. It was thirty long minutes before Muhlfeld's fisheries team drove in and spooked the mountain lion into retreat.

Cats, as a rule, don't want much to do with people. When they do tangle with us, they almost always lose. But every now and again, nature has a surprise for us. Every now and again, a cat gets locked in stalk mode on the wrong prey image. It's been that way for a very, very long time between lions and people.

So consider how astonishing it is that these predators exist at all, how unlikely it is that they are increasing their range, how improbable it is that we would tolerate them and cede the predator its space. Muhlfeld gets it—that's why he was out there that morning, working to protect native trout in native waters. He understands that for nature to work, a cat needs to be a cat, and sometimes that means you lock yourself in the fish trap. Small price to pay for the survival of wild nature.

Fortunately, there are rivers like the North Fork of the Flathead left in the world, large swaths of protected land that anchor the wild from the Crown of the Continent to the southern tip of Patagonia. We would do well to remember that those places are not an accident. People with vision, courage, and passion fought and advocated and lobbied for creation of Waterton-Glacier International Peace Park, the Bob Marshall Wilderness complex, the Sun River and Beartooth Wildlife Management Areas. People built alliances and partnerships and entire organizations to protect Pumalín Park, Corcovado National Park, and the remarkable Patagonia National Park. Not one bit of this happened by accident. It was a choice.

These places have some things in common—they are rugged, distant, inhospitable, harsh, and mind-bogglingly beautiful. They're home to pumas and ranchers. They're pressed on all sides by loggers, miners, farmers, and realtors, by climate change and earth movers, and everywhere by humans. But what they have most in common, perhaps, is that they have impassioned champions—wildlife advocates, hikers and hunters, anglers and philanthropists, and of course biologists working the path of the puma from the Yukon to Tierra del Fuego.

They are like the core habitat—critically essential, but on their own still not enough. They need the rest of us to serve as the connective corridors of life. Wild nature needs each of us to make a choice. Choose to think about how to protect wildlife habitat. Choose to think about how to build human

Wild and scenic, the North Fork of the Flathead River is home to one big predator party of bears, wolves, lions, wolverine, lynx, and bobcats. Montana. DURAE BELCER

Three giants of conservation, Doug Tompkins, Rick Ridgeway, and Yvon Chouinard (l to r) rest on Cerro Kristine in what will eventually be the new Patagonia National Park. Chile. JEFF JOHNSON

tolerance. Think about nature the nomad, and what she needs to move freely on this planet we all share.

Think about carnivores, because they are charismatic, but most importantly think about their prey, and the grass the prey need, and the soil the grass needs. Conservation happens best from the ground up, when the whole system is intact. Were it not for deer and elk restoration in North America, we would not have mountain lions.

Write a letter. Go to a meeting. Make a phone call. Volunteer. Spend some time with people, over coffee or *maté*. Listen. Be heard. Give voice to the water and the air and the wild, because they have no representatives in the halls of power. Wildlife doesn't vote, but you do. Choose to act on their behalf, and to leave a wild legacy for those still to come. Support professional conservation organizations. Buy a state conservation license. Support hunters, whose license fees buy and protect habitat. Contribute to a local or national land trust, and urge them to focus on connectivity.

We have a saying up in my neck of the woods: If Glacier and The Bob leave you speechless, speak up!

These wild places aren't the 'other'—they are us. They define us. They feed us. Lions live at the intersection of our landscapes, our livelihoods, and our lifestyles. In the Crown of the Continent and in way-south Patagonia, wildlife thrives where conservation, community, and culture overlap. We're part of nature, and nature is part of us.

People want to live, work, play, and raise their families in spectacular landscapes, with clean waters and healthy environments and, yes, with whole systems that include native predators. Places with national parks and public lands in their backyards. Places with wildlife-rich private lands. And they want those parks and places open to the public—not the domain of a few wealthy individuals.

It's a powerful vision, and it takes many people to care deeply enough to make it a reality. We cannot afford to lose any of the champions along the way.

And yet, on December 8, 2015 news of Doug Tompkins' death reached me in Montana. Snow was falling then, and the world suddenly seemed colder. Doug died in a tragic kayaking accident down in Patagonia on a trip with friends including Yvon Chouinard and Rick Ridgeway. The writer and conservationist George Wuerthner, a longtime friend of Doug's, said it best in a brief note to me: "The Planet has lost a giant of a man."

Indeed. Doug and Kris Tompkins have made—and continue to make—one of the greatest conservation footprints on the planet. Monte León, Iberá, El Cañi, Pumalín, Corcovado, Yendegaia. Seashores and wetlands and steppes and foothills and rain forests and mountain heights. And, of course, Patagonia National Park. This isn't just a vision anymore, it's a two-million-acre reality. Doug and Kris believed these parks were more than habitat; the parks are also important social equalizers, open to everyone regardless of station or status. Access to nature, for them, is a human right.

And for mountain lions, it is survival itself. America's vast public lands, and Patagonia's newly conserved parks, are a bulwark against the crush of humanity. But the trajectory—despite the recent success and expansion of *Puma concolor*—is toward more people and less wild nature. Predators will continue to prey on livestock. Ungulates will continue to compete for grass. Mountain lions will continue to prey on pets. Subdivisions will continue to consume habitat. Hunters will continue to compete with carnivores. Game managers will continue to be pressured by hunters.

But some of us, at least, will continue to find a profound value in the wild, and to build tolerance for its most remarkable characters—even if they do corner us in a fish trap every now and again. People can live with large carnivores. My Montana home is proof of that. We're proud to live alongside the wolf, the bear, and the lion. Wolverine is our neighbor. Deer and elk feed our bodies and nurture our souls. In Montana, we make a choice to find the wild every day.

You, too, can make a choice. To learn more about the Path of the Puma and stay informed go to www.pathofthepuma.com.

WHAT YOU CAN DO

It doesn't matter who you are, where you come from, what you have in your pockets, the point is to get out of bed every single day of your life and do something that defends those things that you love.

– Kristine McDivitt Tompkins, conservationist

Go. Do. Join. Contribute. For Pumas. For Doug.

• Donate to **Tompkins Conservation** (www. tompkinsconservation.org), a group dedicated to restoring Patagonia's wild beauty and biodiversity by creating national parks, restoring wildlife, inspiring activism and ecological agriculture, and fostering economic vitality. Tompkins Conservation was the parent organization for Conservación Patagónica—which no longer exists now the parks have been given back to the people. To date, working with its partners, Tompkins Conservation has protected approximately thirteen million acres of parklands.

• Or join the **Wildlife Conservation Society**'s (www.wcs.org) Patagonia and Andean Steppe Program, which supports native Argentine students and professional biologists who are working to conserve Patagonia. WCS has a long history of employing some of the most respected wildlife scientists to conduct groundbreaking research, habitat protection, and wildlife-conflict resolution. The WCS North American Rockies program protects wildlands and wildlife throughout the western United States.

• On the coast, **Fundación Patagonia Natural** (www.patagonianatural. org) works to protect Patagonia's coastal and marine habitats; southern right whales, orcas, penguins, and guanacos are all better off, thanks to their work.

• If you can't get there yourself, travel virtually through the **Patagon Journal** (www. patagonjournal.com). Subscribe online or get them in the mail to keep up on what's happening at the end of the world.

• **Partners of the Americas**—with whom I made my first trip south all those years ago—remains active. Check out the Montana Patagonia Argentinian Chapter at www.partners.net.

• Farther north, **Montana's Outdoor Legacy Foundation** (www.mtoutdoorlegacy.org) helps with everything from climbing walls to mountain lion research and grizzly bear studies.

• And if you care about Glacier National Park—or all national parks—then join the **National Parks Conservation Association** (www.npca.org) now. These effective advocates safeguard all national parks, and work at both the local and national level to protect the wild.

• Here near my home, the **Glacier National Park Conservancy** (www.glacier. org) takes care of private philanthropy in Glacier National Park. They fund everything from wolverine research to visitor centers.

There is no question that having an idea doesn't mean you can realize it. Creating Patagonia National Park—and all the parks of the Tompkins Conservation—takes a first-rate team, partnerships with fellow conservationists, and the backing of friends and family. PABLO DURANA

- The **Montana Wilderness Association** (www.wildmontana.org) has a long and storied history in Montana. If you hunt, fish, hike, or find solace in wilderness, help them out.

- The **Montana Wildlife Federation** (www.montanawildlife.org) stands guard against threats to our treasured public recreational access. They work with rod and gun clubs throughout the Big Sky state.

- Or if pumas and other wild cats are your passion, join the **Wild Felid Research & Management Association** (www.wildfelid.org).

- Perhaps the largest and most effective wildcat conservation organization operating in the world today is **Panthera** (www.panthera.org), with an expert wildlife biology team working on everything from snow leopards to jaguars—and, of course, pumas.

- Donate to **The Craighead Institute** (www.craigheadresearch.org). Lance and April Craighead work hard to safeguard wilderness study areas and to protect grizzly bears, wolverines, pikas, and other rocky mountain wildlife species and the habitats they depend upon. The institute also helps local governments with land-use planning information that promotes wildlife movement and connectivity.

- In British Columbia, the guardians of caribou, grizzly bears, and wolverines are the professionals at **Wildsight** (www.wildsight.ca) and **Jumbo Wild** (www.keepitwild.ca). Both grassroots organizations are helping to protect spectacular wildlife and places just north of my home in Montana.

- Also, be sure to support the **Nature Conservancy Canada** (www.natureconservancy.ca) and **The Nature Conservancy United States** (www.nature.org). They buy and protect habitat for mountain caribou, grizzly bears, mountain lions, wolverine, elk, deer, bighorns, bull trout, and more.

- That model—protect habitat permanently by purchasing it outright or placing conservation easements on it—has been successfully adopted for years by American land trusts such as **Vital Ground** (www.vitalground.org), **The Montana Land Reliance** (www.mtlandreliance.org), the **Flathead Land Trust** (www.flatheadlandtrust.org), and **The Trust for Public Land** (www.tpl.org).

Now go outside. Find the wild.

WHEN PUMAS MEET PEOPLE

If anything can save the world, I'd put my money on beauty.

– Doug Tompkins, conservationist

Puma populations and their prey have been increasing since the mid-1960s. So has the human population and our trend toward urbanization. In many areas, this has meant more homes built in cat country, and more run-ins between people and lions.

Still, lion attacks on people are exceedingly rare. A scant 117 attacks in the United States and Canada between 1890 and 2005 resulted in just nineteen human fatalities. But the frequency of those attacks—almost half of them between 1989 and 2005—coincides with three things: the increasing number of homes in lion habitat, the increasing number of people recreating in lion habitat, and the recent recovery of mountain lions in North America.

Is there a lion behind every tree? No. Mountain lions are out there, but your chances of having an encounter remain extraordinarily slim. Most cat-human encounters involve habituated lions that associate people-places with food.

Mountain lions have a very narrow prey image—deer look like food to them, people do not. But if you're out jogging through deer country—especially at dawn and dusk when cats are hunting—it makes sense to stay alert. Also, you're always safer traveling with friends in the backcountry, as predators typically retreat from groups of people.

If you think you might have a lion on your property, take a close look at the tracks to make a positive ID. A lion track is basically round with four tear-drop-shaped toes, two lobes on the leading edge of the heel pad and three lobes at the rear. Because a lion's claws retract, you probably won't see their pinprick points in the track. Generally, the front track is about three inches long by three and a half inches wide; the hind track is about three by three.

To reduce the risk of problems with mountain lions on or near your property, follow this list of simple precautions. Prevention is always preferable to confrontation.

What To Do If You Live in Cat Country

To reduce the risk of problems with mountain lions on or near your property, follow this list of simple precautions. Prevention is always preferable to confrontation.

• If a lion has been recently spotted near your house, closely supervise your children when playing outdoors. Make sure that children are home before dusk and are not outside before dawn. Talk with your children about mountain lions and teach them what to do if they encounter one.

• Landscape or remove vegetation to eliminate hiding cover for lions; you should remove enough vegetation so that a cat cannot slink into your yard undetected.

• Do not attract wildlife, especially deer, into your yard by feeding them.

• Bring pets in at night. If you have outdoor pets, confine them in a kennel with a secured top. Do not feed pets outside. If lions have been sighted nearby, always place domestic livestock in an enclosed shed or barn at night.

• Encourage your neighbors to follow these simple precautions as well.

A sinewy puma cautiously prowls the vast high deserts of San Guillermo in search of vicuña or guanacos, not far north of lofty Cerro Aconcagua in central Argentina. JOE RIIS

If You Meet a Wild Lion

Most people live their entire lives without a glimpse of a mountain lion, much less have a confrontation with one. Those fortunate enough to see a wild cat generally describe them more as a fleeting shadow than an actual living and breathing mammal. Follow these recommendations to minimize the likelihood of attack.

• Walk in groups and make noise if you live in lion country. A sturdy walking stick can be used to ward off an aggressive lion. Make sure that children stay close and within sight at all times.

• Never approach a lion, and give them a route to escape the encounter. Pumas are unpredictable, but will normally avoid a confrontation.

• If you encounter a lion: stay calm. Talk to the cat in a confident yet calm voice. If it does not move away from you, yell and make louder noises. Let the puma know that you are not a deer.

• If you encounter a cat, pick up your children immediately. A scared child's rapid movement might provoke an attack.

• Do not run or turn your back on the lion; move slowly and back away in an upright position.

• Do all that you can do to make yourself bigger. Do not crouch down or attempt to hide.

• If a lion behaves aggressively, arm yourself with a large stick, throw rocks, and speak in a loud, firm voice. Convince the lion that you are not prey, but are in fact a dangerous animal!

• Fight back if a puma attacks. Many people have survived puma attacks by fighting back armed with rocks, sticks, dirt, snow, purses, bare fists, and even fishing poles.

ACKNOWLEDGMENTS

We are so fortunate that Montanans still care about wild things and wild places. From hikers and wildlife advocates to hunters and anglers, from elected officials to appointed Fish and Wildlife Commissioners, from livestock ranchers to timberland managers, and from Fish, Wildlife and Parks Director Martha Williams to Governor Steve Bullock, being able to enjoy and access fish and wildlife in Montana defines us. I am so fortunate to live in a state where everyone from all walks of life still fights to keep Montana the last best place and to keep it wild.

This book, and many of my recent adventures, would never have happened if it were not for Rick Ridgeway at Patagonia Inc. trusting me to jump in and get involved in the future Patagonia National Park. Rick asked me if I could host Dr. Cristián Saucedo from Chile at my home in Montana, a year later I got an email from Rick, while he was down at the new park with Kris and the late Doug Tompkins, asking if I would come down and see what they had created. My family's life has never been the same since. Rick then introduced me to Karla Olson, Director of Patagonia Books, to explore writing up some of my adventures. Karla is one of the most patient professionals I have ever worked with. She has graciously put up with my constant inquiries and questions for many years. She also knows the business of books and connected me with professional editors she knew would both tolerate me and enjoy the project. Karla and Patagonia Inc. have built one of the most unique and intriguing adventure and conservation portfolios in the country. Jane Sievert and Jennifer Ridgeway have brought the colorful Patagonia catalogues to life in photos for thirty years. I was so fortunate to have both of them as my photo editors for this book. John Dutton, Patagonia Book's chief editor, patiently worked with me and took the book across the finish line. He has a natural talent for the art of producing good books. Christina Speed was the creative director for the book. I owe everyone at Patagonia Inc., Rick, Karla, John, Jane, Jennifer Ridgeway, Jennifer Patrick, Rose Marcario, Yvon, and the entire Chouinard family as well as Kris Tompkins and her late husband Doug and their passionate team at Conservación Patagónica and Tompkins Conservation an enormous debt of gratitude for their trust in me and for their collective conservation ethos.

My dear wife Melora and our children, Jake and Mackenzie, were all part of these stories and supported me through thick and thin. Melora is my best friend and soul mate and has been part of or helped with many of the adventures in this book. We are so fortunate to have shared so many experiences together as a family. In many ways our South American friends have in part defined our family and these relationships will surely continue. My mother Joanne, my father Jerry and his wife Jettie have always pushed me to learn and made me realize that education and reading books was so important. I would not be where I am today without them. Thank you.

My Florida adventures were shared with my brother Dave and sister Rhonda. Many of the Montana stories and experiences were also shared with my wife's parents, Eddie and Norma Stubblefield, and my brother-in-law Ken Stubblefield and his family, and I am grateful to them for always being there for us. Bruce Steinberg and his family have always been supportive and now even enjoy summers in Montana. Thank you to all of my family.

My editor for the first half of the book, Joe Glickman, passed away far too young and midway through our project. Joe was an extraordinary writer. He was quick witted and had a great sense of humor. Joe and his wife Beth and daughter Willa were able to visit my family in Montana and Glacier Park before he passed. We all climbed to the summit of lofty Mount Oberlin on a sunny day, even despite Joe having recently gone through cancer treatments. Joe made the stories and my words leap of the pages and I will always be grateful and never forget him. I miss you Joe.

Will Carless was one of my editors for the second half of the book. Will conveniently lived in South America, loves surfing, spoke Spanish, and had actually experienced the future Patagonia National Park. I look forward to sharing more adventures with Will someday. Michael Jamison helped me bring the book across the finish line. He is a wizard at creating an entertaining narrative. Michael worked tirelessly with me on every word in the entire book to make sure it all came together in an engaging and entertaining manner. We spent many a day in Whitefish working together. Michael has a zeal for local conservation in the Crown of the Continent and working productively with all walks of life. Delivering conservation at a local level is not easy and Michael is one of the best. I respect him and consider him a friend. We celebrated the end of the book by skinning up the blustery white slopes of Big Mountain in Whitefish.

Marty Schnure and Ross Donihue at Maps for Good created the amazing maps for this book. Jeniffer and Chad Thompson and their San Diego team at Monkey C Media produced the attractive book cover and the engaging layout of the book.

One of the most inspiring natural history books ever written is *The Beast the Color of Winter* by Doug Chadwick. Doug also wrote *The Wolverine Way*. I first read the mountain goat book as a young grad student and it is now one of my prized first editions. Doug is now a good friend and neighbor in the Flathead Valley and has encouraged, coached, and taught me how to write a book over many cups of good coffee. Doug wrote the Foreword and helped us finish the project. When my kids were little, we were visiting Doug in his Whitefish, Montana office and my son looked at a bookshelf full of National Geographic magazines by his desk. My son Jake asked Doug, "Is that your collection?" Doug smiled and answered, "no, those are just the issues I have articles in." Doug has been one of the most prolific natural history writers on the planet. I have been fortunate to spend time and learn from him.

A heartfelt thanks goes to all who operate and protect Glacier National Park. Superintendent Jeff Mow is at the helm and is an inspiring leader. Wildlife Biologists John Waller and Mark Biel still keep track of all things wild in Glacier. John Waller's son Scott traveled with me to Chile and is studying to protect the wild. Retired park ranger and ski patroller Charlie Logan first welcomed me into his park when I was a grad student. Gary Moses, Scott Emmerich, Chuck Cameron, Kyle Johnson, Reggie Altop, and all the other seasonal and year-round park rangers have helped keep the park wild. Retired ranger Doug Follett continues to inspire me. Thanks to all of you.

My love of books came initially from my parents but was reinforced by two close friends. Craig Barfoot—a fisheries biologist and fellow MSU graduate student and bibliophile—has collected first editions of natural history related genres in which we both share a mutual interest. His zeal to collect good books is contagious. He is the most well-read person I know. Thanks buddy. John Fraley, biologist, historian, professor, and mentor, is the author of several northwest Montana books and we are coworkers at FWP. John has motivated me and coached me on what it takes to put a good story together. John is a master of the English language and never gives up. We shared many writing experiences while running on our lunch hour, while climbing peaks in Glacier Park, and hiking in the local wilderness areas. Thanks John. My dear friends Curtis DeBrau, Dr. Thomas Baumeister, Mark Walters RPh, and Dr. Roger Diegel all provided encouragement and field assistance with many of the adventures I have shared in this book.

I had always read and heard about Patagonia's landscapes, wildlife, and wonderful food but when I finally went down I ended up falling in love with the South American people and their cultures. I would like to recognize the Partners of the Americas program in Washington D.C. and the Montana Patagonia Chapter. Thanks to Rick and Kris Douglass, Arnie Dood, Mike Rotar, Wayne Hadley, Ryan Rauscher, Melissa Foster, Julie Cunningham, Kurt Alt, Germaine White, Matt Clausen, Dennis Shaw, Barbara Bloch, Abraham Cisne, Elizabeth Auciello Bush, Sol Rubio, Melissa Golladay, expert translator Grizzie Logan, and the Paraguay Kansas Chapter.

The Partners of the Americas Patagonia Argentina Chapter hosted me on my first trip down and they are now lifelong friends. I owe a debt of gratitude to my Argentine hosts and professional Wildlife Conservation Society colleagues Martin Monteverde, Martin Funes, Andres Navarro, and Susan Walker, Oscar Pailacura, Graciela Ema, Luciano Piudo, Natalia Radovani, Lorena Rivas, Alejandro Gonzalez, Sandra Rivera and Carlos, Emiliano Donadio, Omar Ohrens, Graham Harris, Ricardo Baldi, Silvana Montinelli and Ricardo Delfini, Jose Maria, Lorena Martinez, Nadia Guthman, Edgar Kopke, Renata Mueller, Flavia Mazzini, Claudio Chehebar, and Ramon Chiocanni. The Argentina Youth Ambassadors that have visited Montana are far too numerous to list but all of them have enriched my family's lives and continue to do so. Luciana Piudo, Martin Monteverde, Maria Aubone, Sol Rubio, Laura Demoy, Anahi Urgatar, and Flathead High School teacher Christy Peeples all bravely traveled with the Youth Ambassadors and hosted them in Montana homes and classrooms. Viva Argentina!

I also owe thanks to my Chilean Patagonia friends and colleagues. Of course, Kristine and Doug Tompkins were willing to allow me into their lives. I will always respect and support them. Dr. Cristián Suacedo and Dr. Paula Herrera hosted me in Coyhaique and in Patagonia Park and welcomed me into their family. Both have visited my family in Montana. Cristián and Paula are now respected leaders in international wildlife conservation. I look forward to many more adventures together. Author and filmmaker Lito Tejada-Flores who filmed the original 1968 Mt. Fitz Roy expedition, and his wife Linde Waidhofer, a professional photographer, became friends while I was with them in the Park and both helped me with stories, history, Macbook technical support, and beautiful photos. Retired Chilean pilot Fernando Vidal helped me translate at a government puma workshop in Chile and shared his huina stories and photos with me. Nadine Lehner, Maria Jesus May, Dagoberto Guzman, Esther Li, Alison Kelman, Vero Ves, and everyone else at Conservación Patagónica willing and proudly shared their Park with me. The former gauchos turned rangers, Don Aricilio Sepulveda, Don Delmiro Jara, Don Manuel Cabrera, and Don Dainel Velasquez all kept me alive on foot and horseback in the Patagonia backcountry and shared their magical austral wildlife with me.

Confederated Salish and Kootenai Tribal Fish and Wildlife Program team members Whisper Camel Means, Dale Becker, Germaine White, Terry Tanner, Stacy Courville, and Tom McDonald all provided information I have used in this manuscript. They have accomplished amazing feats of wildlife conservation and are always protecting the wild on the Flathead Indian Reservation, Mission Mountain Tribal Wilderness and beyond.

My Canadian friends and colleagues are still keeping watch on the northern Rockies wild things and wild places. Thanks to Leo DeGroot, John Krebs, Paul Rasmussen, Dave Lewis, Larry Ingham, Helen Scwhantje, Garth Mowat, Tara Szkorupa, Irene Teske, Patrick Stente, Darcy Peel, Ian Adams, Nancy Newhouse, Trevor Kinley, Richard Klafke, Jay Honeyman, Paul Frame, Jeremy Banfield, Ramona Maraj, Bill Jex, Grant Chapman, Brian Smart, Kyle and Aliah Knopff, and of course my good friend Michael Proctor.

Dr. Harold Picton, my graduate advisor, changed my life when he accepted me into graduate school. I will always thank him and my entire graduate school committee. Mammalogist Dr. Robert Moore reviewed the puma evolution chapter. We are so fortunate that Montana State University and the University of Montana have celebrated graduate Fish and Wildlife programs that produce so many professional wildlife biologists that continue to protect the wild. Dr. Maurice Hornocker has been a friend and mentor throughout my career and I can always count on him for advice on wild cats. I owe thanks to these other renowned wild felid researchers and mentors; Kerry Murphy, Scott Relyea, Greg Felzien, Toni Ruth, Jamie Jonkel, Rich Desimone, Jerry Brown, John McCarthy, Erik Wenum, Bob Wiesner, Shawn Riley, Keith Aune, Hugh Robinson, Lance Craighead, Terry Enk, Ken Logan and Linda Sweanor, Joel Berger, Melanie Culver, Howard Quigley, Alan Rabinowitz, Luke Hunter, Mark Elbroch, Jay Kolbe, Jesse Newby, Neil Anderson, Mark Lotz, Darrell Land, Sharon Negri, Rich Beausoleil, Kelly Proffitt and many more that are not listed here. I am also indebted to Rocky Heckman, Kelly Hirsch, Gary and Scott Langford, Don Clark, Terry Zink, Arlie Burk, Terry Comstock, Mort Hill, and too many other expert mountain lion hound handlers to recognize. They have always protected their cats with zeal and found the deepest wild. Big cats have taken them to places they would have never gone.

John and Nora McCarthy welcomed me into their family as a graduate student. FWP Wildlife Program Manager and mentor Graham Taylor took a chance and hired this "ex-California beach bum" into my first permanent and professional job in Great Falls, but virtually all of my professional Montana FWP peer biologists, partner agency, and tribal colleagues have inspired me and continue to do so to this day and they are too numerous to list. As trained wildlife and conservation professionals working as selfless public servants they are the most passionate bunch of people I have ever known. They often put their lives on the line for fish and wildlife conservation and answer to literally everybody who has an opinion or cares. That will never be easy. Just be glad that Montana's fish and wildlife is fiercely protected and in good hands. What we enjoy today, all species that still call Montana home, is in a large part due to their selfless dedication. They are a passionate bunch that will always find the wild.

MONTANA

Missouri
River Breaks

Little
Belt Mts.

Judith
Mts.

Snowy
Mts.

Theodore
Roosevelt
Nat. Park

Yellowstone R.

N. DAK.

ROCKY

Bighorn
Mts.

Black
Hills

S. DAK.

Missouri
River

WYOMING

MOUNTAINS

NEBR.

Platte R.

COLORADO

KANSAS

OKLA.

TEXAS